Edward Deering Mansfield

The political Manual

Being a complete View of the Theory and Practice of the General and State Governments of the United States

Edward Deering Mansfield

The political Manual
Being a complete View of the Theory and Practice of the General and State Governments of the United States

ISBN/EAN: 9783337071493

Printed in Europe, USA, Canada, Australia, Japan

Cover: Foto ©Suzi / pixelio.de

More available books at **www.hansebooks.com**

THE POLITICAL MANUAL:

BEING A COMPLETE VIEW OF THE

THEORY AND PRACTICE

OF THE

GENERAL AND STATE GOVERNMENTS

OF

THE UNITED STATES.

ADAPTED TO THE USE OF

COLLEGES, ACADEMIES, AND SCHOOLS.

BY

EDWARD D. MANSFIELD,

LATE PROFESSOR OF CONSTITUTIONAL LAW.

NEW YORK:

A. S. BARNES & BURR, 51 & 53 JOHN-STREET.

1861.

PREFACE.

The Political Grammar (now called the Political Manual) was originally written in 1834, to supply the want of a Text-Book on the constitutional elements (or rather science) of the American Government. It was received with decided favor; and notwithstanding at least a dozen other works of a similar nature—some of them prepared by able and distinguished men—have since appeared, this little book still maintains its ground as the clearest, simplest, and best adapted to the purposes for which it was intended. The author would have ventured no such opinion on his own judgment. But twenty-six years of trial before the public, with uniform success, authorize this assertion.

In the mean time the text has been several times revised. All the recent decisions of the Supreme Court on Constitutional Law, with the recent action of Congress and the Executive, are embodied in it. It is now the science of the American Government, as it exists in action, and is commended to all students of American Institutions.

CINCINNATI (Ohio), *November* 1, 1860.

INDEX.

D

E

F

G

L

M

N

O

P

INTRODUCTION.

POLITICAL DEFINITIONS.

1. Sovereignty,—is the highest power.[1]

Thus, for a *state*, or nation, to be sovereign, it must *govern itself, without any dependence upon another power.*[2] It must have *no superiors.*[3] But when a community, city, or state makes *part* of another community or state, and is represented with *foreign powers* by that community or state of which it is a part, then it is *not sovereign.*[4]

2. Government,—is the whole body of constituted authority.[5] Thus, from the very origin of society, one portion of the people have exercised authority over the rest. The authority thus exercised is called the *government*, and it derives its just powers from the consent of the governed.[6]

3. Law,—is a rule of action.[7] In this general sense, it signifies the *rules* of all action, and constitutes alike the rules by which the heavenly bodies move, nations

[1] Johnson.

[2] Vattel's Laws of Nations, p. 16; Martin's Laws of Nations, p. 23.

[3] Rutherforth's Institutes, p. 282. [4] Martin, p. 25. [5] Crabbe.

[6] Declaration of Independence.

[7] 1 Blackst. Commentaries, p. 38; Johnson.

are governed, and the plants grow. *Law*, in a political sense, however, signifies a *rule of human action.* In a particular state, "it is a rule prescribed by the supreme power in the state, commanding what is right, and forbidding what is wrong."

4. CONSTITUTION,—is the constituted form of government.[1] It is the *fundamental law;* the regulation which determines the manner in which the authority vested in government is to be executed.[2] It is delineated by the hand of the people.[3]

5. A DESPOTISM,—is that form of government[4] "in which a *single individual*, without any law, governs according to his own will and caprice." An example of this kind of government may be found in Turkey, where the sultan exercises all the powers of sovereignty, with respect to the general administration of public affairs, but, even there, he is limited by certain customs and rules, as it respects private justice.

6. A MONARCHY,—is that form of government in which a *single individual governs*, but according to *established* laws.[5] The governments of Austria, Prussia, France, and England, are examples of this form of government. The *limitations* placed upon the monarch are, however, very *different in degree:* thus, the power of the Prussian monarch is very great, while that of the king of England is so small as scarcely to be felt. The latter acts through his *ministers*, who are held

---

[1] Crabbe; Johnson. [2] Vattel, pp. 26, 27.

[3] Supreme Court; 2 Dallas, 304.

[4] Montesquieu, Spirit of Laws, book II., chap. 1. [5] Idem.

responsible to the *representatives of the people*, and can maintain their power only so long as they can satisfy public opinion.

7. A Republic,—is that form of government in which the *whole people*, or only a *part of the people*, hold *sovereign power*.[1] The people of Athens were formerly an example of the first kind of republic, and governed themselves by primary *assemblies of the people*, a mode which could only be adopted where the people were chiefly citizens, and inhabitants of one capital city. In modern times the United States are an example of the *same kind* of republic, with this difference, that the people do not govern themselves by their assemblies, but by *delegates*, or through the principle of *representation*. An example of the *second* kind of republics may be found in Venice, Genoa, and the Dutch States,[2] in all of which a *part* of the people, either absolutely or limitedly, exercised the authority. The difference between these kinds of republics will be understood from the following definitions.

8. A Democracy,—is when the sovereign power is in the hands of the *whole people*.[3] The term Democracy is derived directly from the Greek word *Demos*, signifying the *people*.

9. An Aristocracy,—is when the sovereign power is in the hands only of a *part of the people*.[4] This word is likewise of Greek derivation. It is compounded of

---

[1] Montesquieu, Spirit of Laws, book II., chap. 1.
[2] Martin, p. 39.
[3] Spirit of Laws, book II., chap. 2.
[4] Idem.

the adjective *Aristos*, signifying *best* or *wisest*, and *Kratos*, signifying power or strength; the whole word signifies that form of government in which a few of the wisest and best govern.[1] Both *Democracies* and *Aristocracies* are *Republics*.[2]

10. A Party,—is any number of persons confederated, by a similarity of objects and opinions, in opposition to others.[3] An illustration of this may be found anywhere. In England, the whigs and tories are two great parties, which have long divided the nation. In France, during the revolution, the jacobins and royalists were violently opposed. On the continent of Europe generally, there are the parties of the *liberals* and *absolutists*. In the United States, the federal and democratic parties divided the country till the termination of the last war.

11. A Faction,—is any number of persons, whether majority or minority, confederated by some common motive, in opposition to the rights of other persons, or to the interests of the community.[4] The *difference* between *party* and *faction* then is, that the former is a *difference of principle*, and is founded on a *general* or *public object*, the latter may have *any motive*, however personal or selfish, and be directed towards *any end*, however little connected with the public welfare. Thus, two divisions of the people, differing as to *how* the gov-

---

[1] This was the *original* meaning; but, like other terms, it is confounded in the using. Aristocracies are seldom either the best or the wisest.

[2] Both Athens and Genoa were republics—the first a democracy and the second an aristocracy. [3] Locke. [4] Federalist.

ernment shall be administered, are *parties;* but a section whose object is to keep one portion of the people from the enjoyment of power, or to aggrandize an individual, or *divide among themselves all the offices of state*, is a *faction.*

12. Legislature,—is the *law-making power.*[1] Thus, in a republic, it is that branch of the government in which the people have vested the power to make laws.

13. Congress,—is a meeting for the *settlement* of *national affairs*, whether relating to one or more nations.[2] In the United States, the *national legislature* is called the Congress; in Europe, a conference of different powers, by their ministers, is called a Congress; as the meeting of ambassadors at Laybach was called the Congress of Laybach.

14. Legislative,—that which relates to *law-making.*[3]

15. Executive,—that which relates to the *execution* of the laws.[4] Thus, the chief officer of the government, whether he be called King, President, or Governor, is denominated the *Executive*,—for on him, in most cases, the constitution devolves the duty of *executing the laws.*

16. Judicial,[5]—that which relates to the *administration of justice.* Thus, *judicial duties* are those which devolve upon the *judges*, who have to decide upon *what* is law, and to adjudicate between private rights.

17. Statute Law,—is the express written *will* of the *legislature*, rendered authentic by prescribed forms.[6]

---

[1] Johnson. [2] Idem. [3] Idem. [4] Idem.
[5] Idem. [6] 1 Kent's Comm., 319.

Thus, the statutes of Ohio are the laws enacted by the legislature of Ohio. It follows, from this definition in connection with those of *Constitution* and *Legislature*, that statutes can be *binding* only when, 1*st*, they are executed according to the *prescribed forms*; and 2*dly*, when they are *consistent with* the constitution; for, the constitution being the *fundamental law*, created by the people themselves, all other laws are *inferior to it*.

18. Common Law,—is that *body of principles*, *usages*, and *rules of action* which do not rest for their authority upon the positive will of the legislature.[1] In other words, it consists of those *customs* and *rules* to which time and usage have given the sanction of law. Of such, it is plain, must be the great body of the laws of every people; for the rules of business and the usages of society are so variable and complicated, as to be incapable of being made permanently the subject of statute law. The *will* of the legislature being, however, under the limitation of the constitution, that of the *people*, *statute law* is *superior* in force to common law; and wherever they are inconsistent with each other, the latter is abrogated by the former.[2]

19. A Corporation,—is defined to be a *body politic*, having a *common seal*.[3] It is an *artificial*, or *political person*, maintaining a *perpetual succession*,[4] by means of several individuals, united in one body through a common seal. They have a legal immortality, except so far as they are limited by the law of their creation.

[1] Kent's Comm., 439.

[2] 1 Blackst. Comm., 89.

[3] Johnson.

[4] 1 Blackst. Comm., 467.

These were originally created for purposes of charity, trade, and education; but are now used for all purposes in which it is wished to transmit a common property. Thus, all banks, turnpike companies, colleges, and chartered societies are examples of corporations.

20. CHARTER,—is the *act* creating the corporation, or separate government, or the privileges bestowed upon a community, or a society of individuals.[1] It is derived from the Latin term *charta*, signifying a writing.[2]

21. A COURT,—is defined to be a place wherein *justice* is judicially *administered*.[3] In our country, and in the New England States especially, Court has sometimes had another signification, that of the legislative body; thus, the General Court of Massachusetts is the legislature. The former, is, however, the correct meaning.

22. MUNICIPAL,—relating to a corporation. Municipal laws are *civil* or *internal*, in opposition to national or external laws.[4] Thus, the laws relative to the descent of property are municipal laws; but laws relative to war, the army, and navy, are external and national.

23. JURISDICTION,—is extent of legal power.[5] Thus, a court has jurisdiction over certain things, as all sums over a certain amount, when its legal authority extends over them. A government has jurisdiction over a certain territory, when its power extends over it.

---

[1] 1 Blackst. Comm., 109.
[2] Sullivan's Polit. Class-Book, 49.
[3] 3 Blackst. Comm., 23.
[4] Story's Comm., 159.
[5] Johnson.

24. Impeachment,—is a public accusation, by a body authorized to make it.[1] Such were the charges preferred by the British House of Commons against Warren Hastings, governor-general of India; and in this country by the House of Representatives, against Samuel Chase, one of the judges of the Supreme Court.

25. Verdict,—is the *true saying* of a jury.[2] It is the *answer* which a *jury* make to the court and parties, when the plaintiff and defendant have left the cause to their decision.

26. Judgment,—is the sentence of the law pronounced by the court.[3]

27. Crime,—a crime, or misdemeanor, is an act committed, or omitted, in violation of the *public laws*, either forbidding, or commanding it.[4] A crime is a violation of the duty to *society*, in its aggregate capacity; while a private wrong is a violation of the duty due to an *individual.* Crime is a *civil*, or legal term, signifying, not a moral wrong, but a legal wrong. Thus, a man may have committed a great moral wrong, without being a criminal; and so, he may be a *criminal*, without being a moral offender,—in the legal sense, *falsehood* on the one hand, and *killing game* at certain seasons on the other.

28. Treason.—Treason is defined by the United States Constitution to be,—*levying war against them, or in adhering to their enemies,—giving them aid and*

[1] Johnson; Crabbe.
[2] 3 Blackst. Comm., 377.
[3] 3 Idem, 395.
[4] 4 Idem, 5.

comfort.[1] The government of the United States is believed to be the only one which *defines precisely* the crime of *treason;* and, without that definition, the president Montesquieu said, liberty could not exist.

29. Felony,—is defined to be any species of *crime*, which occasions a *forfeiture of lands* and *goods.*[2] Felony, in common speech, however, signifies a *capital* offence. It may legally include others.

30. Reprieve.—A reprieve is the withdrawal of a judicial sentence, for a time, so that its execution is *suspended.*[3]

31. Diplomacy,—signifies the intercourse which is carried on between different nations by means of their ministers, or agents.[4]

32. Revolution,—is a radical change in the government of the country. It may be made in various ways —by force and blood, as in France, 1792; by the expulsion of one family and settlement of another, as in England, 1688, and in France, 1830; or by a separation of one part of a country from another, as in the United States, in 1776. Thus, also, all acts in opposition to the laws, and which are not legitimate under the constitution, are *revolutionary*, because their tendency is the overthrow of the *laws.*

33. Ex post facto.—An ex post facto law is *a retrospective criminal law.* A retrospective law is one which acts upon *things already done*, and not merely upon those which are to be done. An *ex post facto law*

---

[1] Constitution United States Court, 3 Sec., 31. [2] 4 Blackst., 94.
[3] 4 Idem, 394. [4] Sullivan's Polit. Class-Book, 225.

makes something *criminal* which was *not criminal when done.* Thus, if the legislature should pass an act, declaring that all persons who had not attended church last year should be imprisoned, that law would be *unconstitutional*, because *ex post facto.* But if the legislature should pass an act that those who attended militia duty last year should be excused from paying taxes, and those who had not should not be so excused, such a law would be *retrospective*, but not ex post facto, because not criminal. An *ex post facto law* makes *past acts criminal*, which were *not so before.*[1]

34. A Bill of Attainder,—is a special act of the legislature, inflicting capital punishments upon persons supposed to be guilty of high offences, such as treason and felony, without any conviction in the ordinary course of judicial proceedings.[2] If it inflict a milder punishment, it is called a bill of pains and penalties.

35. A Bill,—is a term used in legislation, and signifies the *written form* of a *legislative act* proposed to be passed.

36. Revenue,—is the *money* raised for the *uses of government.* It may be derived from various sources, but must be raised by the public consent, and converted to public uses.

37. A Treaty,—is an *agreement between independent nations*, and by the laws of nations can be made only by the *sovereign power*, and is binding on the whole community.[3]

---

[1] Story's Comm., 212, 213. [2] Idem, 211.

[3] 1 Blackst. Comm., 257; Puff. Laws of Nations, b. 8, ch. 9, sect. 6.

38. Naturalization,—is the *act*, by which *a foreigner* is made *a citizen.* The law by which this is permitted is called *a naturalization law;* and the acts by which a party avails himself of this law are *the naturalization.* America is believed to be the only country where a *general law* is enacted for this purpose. In England, and most other countries, it may be done as a matter of *special favor;* but, even then, the privilege never extends so far as to make a foreigner eligible to the higher offices of state.[1]

39. Bankruptcy,—is the *act* of becoming a *bankrupt. Bankrupt, bankruptcy,* and *bankrupt laws,* are legal terms, signifying a particular kind of insolvency, or failure to pay one's debts. In common speech, one who cannot pay his debts, is a bankrupt,—but it is not so in law. Thus, by the law of England, a bankrupt is *a trader,* who secretes himself, or does other acts tending to *defraud his creditors.*[2] In the United States, no general bankrupt law has been made; but, were there one, a bankrupt would be one defined and described by that law.[3]

40. Test Act,—*Religious test;* these are also legal terms, and refer to certain legal acts of past times. A *Test Act* is one which requires all public officers and persons becoming citizens, before they can enter upon

[1] 1 Blackst. Comm., 374.

[2] This is the definition; but the bankrupt is, now, one who *honestly*, as well as fraudulently fails, and gives up his property to his creditors.—2 Blackst. Comm., 471.

[3] Special bankrupt laws were passed in 1800 and 1841, each continuing but two years.

their duties, to subscribe to certain religious *opinions*, and perform certain *religious acts*. By the Constitution of the United States, this is expressly forbidden. But, under all other governments, something of this kind is required; thus, by the statutes of England, *all civil* and *military officers*, are required to make a declaration against *transubstantiation*, partake of the Sacrament of the Lord's Supper, and obtain certificates of the same, before they can enter upon any such office.[1]

41. THE BALLOT,—signifies the *ball*,[2] or ticket, by which persons vote at an election. *To ballot* signifies *voting* by *ballot*, i. e., by ball, or ticket. Formerly, voting was altogether *viva voce*, that is, by the *voice*,—the elector designating by name the person voted for; now, elections are generally made by *ballot*. The name of the person voted for is written on a ticket, and deposited in a box.

42. QUORUM,—is such a number of any body as is necessary to do business.[3] Thus, when it is said there shall be eleven directors of any institution, and *seven* shall constitute a quorum, seven is the number necessary to do business; and unless the contrary is expressed, a majority of a quorum only is necessary to a decision. Hence it often happens, that less than a majority of the whole decide important questions.

43. MAJORITY AND MINORITY.—A majority is *any number greater* than one *half*, and a minority is *any*

---

[1] 2 Blackst. Comm., 58.; Wat., 25, ch. 2. [2] Johnson. [3] Idem.

number less than one half. One half, then, neither constitutes a majority nor minority; and, if a public body were so constituted, as to have an even number, with equal division of opinion, and no chairman, there never could be a majority, and consequently, no *positive action.* This has been the case in some public bodies, and is always attended with difficulty.

44. A PLURALITY,—is to have *more than another* number, though not always to have a majority of all the given numbers. Thus, when there are several candidates at an election, one may have a *plurality*, though not a *majority;* for he may have more votes than any one, though not more than all put together.

45. INDICTMENT.—An indictment is a *written accusation* of one or more persons, of a crime or misdemeanor, *preferred to*, and presented upon oath, by a grand jury.[1]

46. A GRAND JURY,—is a number of men not less than twelve, nor more than twenty-three, selected from the people in the body of the *county*, to inquire into offences against the state.[2] They are instructed by the court in the matters pertaining to their inquiries, and then withdraw to receive indictments, which are *preferred to* them, in the *name of the state*, but at the *suit of a private prosecutor.*[3] After an examination, such of the bills as are found correct, are indorsed "A true Bill,"—signed by the foreman; and hence becomes an *official* accusation, to be rebutted only by proof at the trial.

---

[1] 4 Blackst. Comm., 302. [2] Idem. [3] Idem.

47. Taxes.—*All contributions* imposed by the government upon individuals, for the service of the state, are called *taxes*, by whatever name known.[1] Thus, the tithes imposed upon the people of England for the support of church government are a tax: so also imposts, duties, excises, &c., are taxes.

48. A Legal Tender,—is the *tender* of such an article as the *law requires* to be made, in *payment of a debt.* In the United States, *gold* and *silver coin* are the *legal tender;* and the states are forbid making any thing else a tender; but it is not so in many countries, nor has it always been so in this.

---

[1] 2 Story's Comm., 419.

CHAPTER I.

ORIGIN OF THE CONSTITUTION OF THE UNITED STATES.

§ 1. The continent of North America was chiefly settled by emigrants from Great Britain. The jurisdiction over the new region, as well as the title to its lands, was claimed by the mother country, under the color of *discovery* and *conquest*. Hence, to acquire the right of property, as well as to sustain themselves against opposition, the authority of Great Britain became necessary to the early colonists. This was given in the form of grants and charters, to companies and large proprietors. Such was the grant of the territory of Massachusetts to the Plymouth Company, and of Maryland to Lord Baltimore.[1]

§ 2. There were originally *three* different *forms* of government in the colonies, viz.: The Charter, the Proprietary, and Royal governments. The Charter governments were confined to New-England; the middle and southern colonies were divided between the Proprietary and Royal governments.

§ 3. The charter governments were[2] composed of a Governor, Deputy-governor, and Assistants, *elected by the people;* these, with the freemen, i. e., citizens of the colony, were to compose the "General Courts," which

[1] Pitkin's Civil History, p. 81. [2] Idem, p. 86.

were authorized to appoint such officers, and make such laws and ordinances for the welfare of the colony as to them might seem meet. These first forms of government in New England contained the same principles as, and were doubtless the origin of, our republican system.

§ 4. The proprietary[1] governments were those of Maryland, Pennsylvania, the Carolinas, and Jersey. Part of these soon became royal governments. In the proprietary governments, the power of appointing officers and making laws, rested in the proprietors, by the advice and assent, generally of the freemen. In some of them, as in the Carolinas, singular irregularities were found. In all, great confusion took place.

§ 5. In the royal[2] governments, which were New York, Virginia, Georgia, and Delaware, the Governor and Council were appointed by the *crown;* and the people elected *representatives* to the colonial legislature. The Governor had a *negative* in both houses of the legislature; and most of the officers were appointed by the king.

§ 6. These different governments, operating also upon a people of different habits and manners, as the Puritans of New England, the Cavaliers of Virginia, and the Quakers of Pennsylvania, produced many diversities of legislation and political character. Notwithstanding these, however, the necessities of a common danger from hostile tribes of Indians, and of a common interest from similarity of circumstances,

[1] Pitkin's Civil History, p. 55. [2] Idem, p. 71.

soon induced a union, or confederacy of the colonies. Those of Massachusetts, Plymouth, Connecticut, and New Haven, as early as 1643, formed a league, offensive and defensive, which they declared should be perpetual, and distinguished by the name of the United Colonies of New England. This confederacy subsisted for forty years, under a regular form of government, in which the principle of a delegated congress was the prominent feature.

§7. A congress of commissioners, representing New Hampshire, Massachusetts, Rhode Island, Connecticut, New York, Pennsylvania, and Maryland, was held at Albany, in 1754. This convention[1] unanimously resolved that a *union* of the colonies was absolutely necessary for their preservation. They proposed a general plan of federal government, which, however, was not adopted.

§8. In October, 1765, a congress[2] of delegates from nine states assembled at New York, and digested a bill of rights on the subject of taxation.

§9. In September, 1774, an association of twelve states was formed, and delegates authorized to meet and consult for *the common welfare.*

§10. In May, 1775, the first congress[3] of the thirteen states assembled at Philadelphia; and in July, 1776, issued the Declaration of Independence.

§11. In November, 1777, Congress agreed upon the celebrated Articles of Confederation, under which the United States successfully terminated the Revolution.

---

[1] Kent's Comm., 191, 192. [2] Idem, 193. [3] Idem, 195.

This was the first formation of a general government of all the states, and continued till the adoption of the Constitution in 1788. This, however, had inherent defects, which forced the states to the adoption of the present system. During the Revolution, the pressure of an instant and common danger kept the states in a close union, and incited them to make all possible efforts in the common defence. When that was over, however, mutual jealousies and separate interests, weakening the common bonds, soon proved the utter insufficiency of a mere confederacy for the purposes of national government. Then it was that the ablest heads and the purest hearts in the nation exercised their faculties in devising a new and better form of government. General Washington, in June, 1783, addressed a letter[1] to the governors of the several states, in which he says, "There are four things which I humbly conceive are *essential* to the *well-being*, I may even venture to say, to the *existence* of the United States as an *independent power*. 1. An *indissoluble union* of the states under *one federal head.* 2. A sacred regard to public justice. 3. The adoption of a proper peace establishment. 4. The prevalence of that pacific and friendly disposition among the people of the United States which will induce them to forget their local politics and prejudices."

§ 12. Under the first head he remarked that, "It is only in our united character that we are known as an empire, that our independence is acknowledged,

[1] Marshall's Life of Washington, vol. v., c. 1., p. 46.

that our power can be regarded, or our credit supported among foreign nations. The treaties of European powers with the United States of America will have no validity on a dissolution of the Union. We may find by our own unhappy experience, that there is a natural and necessary progression from the extreme of *anarchy* to the extreme of tyranny; and that arbitrary power is most easily established on the ruins of liberty abused to licentiousness." Such were the sentiments of Washington, and such were those then of the nation.

§13. In January, 1786, the legislature of Virginia recommended a meeting of commissioners from the several states, to review the powers of government. The delegates of five states met at Annapolis, but adjourned, proposing a general convention at Philadelphia.

§14. In 1787, the convention of delegates from twelve states was convened, and, after much deliberation, formed the present Constitution of the United States.

§15. By resolution[1] of the convention, it was directed to be carried into effect when ratified by the conventions of nine states, chosen by "the people thereof." That ratification, after much opposition, scrutinizing discussion, and the adoption of several amendments, it finally received; and all the states, eventually assenting to its provisions, became members of the Union. In 1789, it went into practical operation, and from that

[1] Marshall's Washington, vol. v., p. 129.

period to this, more than seventy years, has withstood unharmed the various violent influences of local feuds, opposing interests, domestic insurrection, and foreign violence.

§ 16. We have seen that, at several different periods, viz., 1643, 1754, 1765, 1774, 1777, and in 1787, the territories composing what is called the United States, formed associations for the purposes of a common government and general welfare. Let us now examine how these were originally constituted, and in what manner modified by time and experience.

§ 17. By the articles of *confederation* made in 1643, between the colonies of Massachusetts, Connecticut, and New Haven, it was expressly declared to be a *league*, under the name of the United Colonies of New England. The chief points in this confederation were, —1st. That each colony should have *peculiar jurisdiction and government within its own limits.* 2d. That the quotas of men and money were to be furnished in *proportion to the population*, for which purpose a *census* was to be taken from time to time of such as were able to bear arms. 3d. That to manage such matters as concerned the whole confederation, a congress of two commissioners from each colony should meet annually, with power to weigh and determine all affairs of *war and peace*, *leagues*, aids, charges, and whatever else were proper concomitants of a confederation offensive and defensive; and that to determine any question, three-fourths of these commissioners must agree, or the matter is to be referred to the general courts. 4th. That these commissioners may choose a president; but that such president has no power over the business or proceedings. 5th. That neither of the colonies should engage in any war without consent of the general commissioners. 6th. That if any of the confederates should *break* any of these articles, or otherwise injure any of the other confederates, then such breach should be *considered* and *ordered* by the commissioners of the *other colonies*.

§ 18. Now, it will be observed that this confederacy was, by agreement, a mere *league*, from motives of amity, for objects of general offence and defence. *As such*, it was as good a model as any which history presents us; but *as a government*, it was utterly inefficient: its principal defects in the last point of view were,—1. The want of an executive, without which it could never act *as a whole*. All the acts of the commissioners had to be enforced by each separate colony: they did not act upon individuals. 2. The want of a general judiciary, by which offences arising between the several members, or against the whole confederacy, might be taken cognizance of. 3. The want of any general power to obtain credit or emit money. In short, this league did not pretend to be a *government*, and was deficient in nearly all the attributes of *sovereignty*.

§ 19. Upon the last provision, that providing a remedy for breaches of the league by one of the confederacy, it is worthy of remark, that it never entered into the heads of people *then*, that it was possible for one party to a compact to make *itself judges of its own breaches of it:* on the contrary, it was provided that such breaches should be judged of by *the other members of the confederacy.* It was reserved for a much later period of history, and, it would seem, for far more ingenious men, to divine a mode by which a party to a contract can at once make itself a judge of its own violations of it, and invalidate at pleasure its provisions.

§ 20. The next plan of association was that formed by the commissioners who met at Albany in 1754. It was not accepted by the mother country, but may serve to show what progress in ideas of government had then been made by the colonists. It is remarkable that the scheme proposed did not purport, like the other, to be *a league*, or confederation, but *a plan for one general government.* Its principal provisions were,—1. That the general government should be *administered* by a president-general appointed by the crown, and a grand council chosen by the representatives of the people in their general assemblies. 2. That the council should be chosen every three years, and shall meet once each year. 3. That the assent of the president be necessary to all acts of the council, and that it is his duty to see them executed. 4. That the president and council may hold treaties, make peace, and declare war with the several Indian tribes. 5. That for these purposes they have power to levy and collect such duties, imposts, and taxes as to them shall seem just.

§ 21. It will be seen that this was a much nearer approach to an organized government than the confederacy of 1643. It provided for a strong *executive,* but was without the sanction of a general judiciary, and made no provision for regulating the currency.

§ 22. We come now to the *articles* of *confederation.* During the early part of the Revolution, the powers of a general nature were executed without question or hinderance by a congress[1] of deputies from the several states. Patriotism and a common danger absorbed all other principles, and made ordinary ties unnecessary. A universal opinion, however, prevailed in favor of union; and after much deliberation, Congress,[2] in November, 1777, agreed upon the articles of confederation. They were, after various delays, ratified by the different states; the principal objection being in respect to the wild lands, which were claimed by several of the states, but which others urged should go to bear the common burden. In the sequel, these lands were nobly ceded by the states who held them, to the common benefit of the Union.

§ 23. The Articles of Confederation provided,—

1st. That the style of the Confederacy should be the "United States of America."

2d. That each state should retain its sovereignty, independence, and such rights as were not delegated to the general Congress.

3d. That the object of the league was the general welfare, and the common defence against foreign aggression.

4th. That the citizens of one state shall have the privileges of citizens in another, and that full faith and

---

[1] Journal of Congress, vol. ii., p. 475. [2] 1 Kent's Comm., 197.

credit shall be given to the records, acts, and judicial proceedings in another state.

5th. That for the management of the general interests, delegates shall be annually appointed to meet in Congress, each state having not less than two nor more than seven;-and that in determining questions in Congress, *each state* shall have *one vote.*

6th. That no state shall, without the consent of Congress, enter into any treaty or alliance with any foreign power or nation, or with any other state, nor lay any imposts or duties interfering with any stipulations contained in any treaty made by Congress; nor keep any vessels of war or armed forces in time of peace, except such as Congress may deem necessary; nor engage in any war without the consent of Congress, unless the state be actually invaded, or the danger imminent; nor grant letters of marque, unless such state be infested with pirates.

7th. All charges for the general welfare shall be defrayed out of a common treasury, which shall be levied in proportion to the value of land within each state.

8th. The "United States in Congress assembled" shall have the exclusive right of making peace and war; entering into treaties and alliances; granting letters of marque, and establishing courts and rules for the trial of piracies and felonies, and determining questions in relation to captures; and that the Congress have the power to determine all questions and differences between two or more states, concerning any cause whatever; which authority shall be exercised by instituting a court in manner and form as provided, where judgment shall be final and decisive; and that they have power to fix the standard of weights, measures, and coin; establish post-offices and commission officers; that they shall have power to appoint a committee of the states, and such other civil officers as may be necessary to manage the general affairs of the United States, under their direction; to elect their president; to fix the sums of money to be raised; to borrow money and emit bills of credit; to agree on the number of forces to be raised, which are to be distributed among the states in proportion to their white inhabitants; that "the United States" shall not exercise these powers unless nine states assent to the same; nor shall any question except that of adjournment be determined unless by the votes of a majority of the states.

9th. It is further provided, that the committee of the states, or any nine of them, shall be authorized to execute, in the recess of Congress, such of the powers of Congress as the United States, or any nine of them, shall think proper to vest them with.

10th. All debts contracted under the authority of Congress, shall be deemed and considered as a charge against the United States, for which the public faith is pledged.

11th. That every state shall abide by the *determinations* of *Congress* upon the questions submitted to it, and the *union* shall be *perpetual*.

§ 24. Such is a synopsis of the articles of confederation, under which the United States terminated the war of the Revolution, and continued till the adoption of the Constitution. It will be remarked,—

1st, that the states still assume the style of a league or confederacy; and that, 2dly, they had notwithstanding granted away many attributes of sovereignty, even greater than those proposed to be vested in the President and Council by the plan of 1754.

§ 25. This confederacy had many obvious and palpable deficiencies, as a government, principally, however, in the *mode* and process of its administration.

1. There was still wanting an *executive* in form, though nearly all its powers were granted to Congress and the "committee of the states."

2. No general *judiciary* was provided; yet they had gone so far as to provide a Marine or Admiralty court, and a general tribunal to settle conflicts and disputes between the several states.

3. The great deficiency was, that the articles of confederation did not act upon *individuals*, but upon the *states;* and that to raise men and money, it was necessary to act through the medium of many distinct governments.

§ 26. By a comparison of the original association of 1643, the plan of 1754, and the articles of confederation, we find that the minds of the colonists had gradually tended from the notion of separate sovereignties to that of a general and united government. Each change, founded on experience, had given *additional strength* to the confederacy. Thus the association of 1643 was a simple league, existing by means of treaties, and exercised through commissioners; and though possessing many of the attributes of sovereignty, holding them only through an *alliance*. The plan of 1754, though not adopted, was that of a general government, and had a strong executive. The articles of confederation, though reverting back to the form of a confederacy, greatly increased, in *theory*, the powers of government: for example, it superadded to the powers of former congresses, those of emitting bills of credit, establishing Marine courts, and judging between the states. Under this confederation, the United States, by the peace of 1783, achieved their separate and independent existence as a nation. Yet, we have already seen, it was found insufficient for the purposes of a stable government, and how, in 1787, the present Constitution was formed and adopted.

§ 27. In this chapter we have established these propositions:—

1st. That the idea of a union of the colonies originated in the very earliest stage of their existence.

2d. That their idea was that of a government exercised for the *general welfare*, and founded upon a *representation* of the *people*.

3d. That for this purpose they from time to time formed *leagues* and *confederacies*.

4th. That these associations were made *closer* and *stronger*, as time and experience progressed.

5th. Lastly, that they were all merged in the "more perfect union" and general government formed by the Convention of 1787.

CHAPTER II.

CONSTITUTION OF THE UNITED STATES.

Preamble.

§ 28. We, *the People of the United States, in order to form a more perfect union, establish justice, insure domestic tranquillity, provide for the common defence, promote the general welfare, and secure the blessings of liberty to ourselves and our posterity, do ordain and establish this Constitution for the United States of America.*

§ 29. In this preamble are asserted,—1st, the *power* making the Constitution, "We the People," &c.; 2dly, the object for which it was formed, the *more perfect union, general welfare*, &c.; 3dly, the subject of it, the United States.

§ 30. The first position, that "We the People do ordain," &c., is the foundation of the most solemn inquiry which ever agitated the American people,—whether this phrase be a mere nullity, or whether the Constitution was indeed formed by the *whole people!*

§ 31. It is one of the rules[1] for *interpreting laws*, that they must be understood according to the context, i. e.,

---

[1] Blackstone's Comm., 59.

the whole must be *taken in connection*. This passage will, therefore, be better understood when we have reviewed the entire Constitution. The preamble throws light upon the instrument, and the instrument upon the preamble. It is sufficient to remark here, that the terms used are in perfect accordance with the mode by which the Constitution was ratified: this was by *conventions*[1] of the *people*, and not by the *legislatures* of the *states*. On the other hand, the convention[2] which formed the Constitution was composed of delegates chosen by the state legislatures. The necessary inference is, that the *states*, in their official capacity, proposed the Constitution, and the *people*, by ratifying it, gave it *authority*: it is therefore a *government founded by separate states*, but receiving its *sanction* and *validity* from the *whole people*. This point has received a judicial construction, in the case of Massachusetts *vs.* Rhode Island.[3] The Supreme Court then declared "the government of the Union is a government of the People. It emanates from them. Its powers are granted by them, and are to be exercised directly and for their benefit. The government of the Union is *supreme* within its sphere of action."

§ 32. 2d. The objects proposed are exactly consistent with this idea. A *perfect union*, and a *government* legislating for the *general welfare*, are incompatible with *separate* and *independent sovereignties*. The terms *independence* and *sovereignty*, used in relation to matters

---

[1] Pitkin's Civil Hist., ii., p. 264. [2] Pitkin's Civil Hist., p. 219.

[3] 12 Peters', 657.

of government and politics, must of course be understood in a *political sense*, and according to our definition. There are some common acceptations of these terms in which a much lower importance is attached to *sovereignty*. Thus, a man may be perfectly sovereign in his own house, and yet be subject to the laws of society. An animal may be utterly independent of another animal, and yet a member of, and subject to the laws of, the animal kingdom. In this sense *the states*, considered as composing a society, are sovereign and independent in their *domestic* and *municipal relations*. These terms, in their political sense, have a higher meaning: as applied to *nations*, independence does not admit of a *close union*, nor sovereignty of another government legislating for the *general welfare*.

The Constitution.

§ 33. The Constitution of the United States contains seven articles,—to which were added several miscellaneous amendments.

Article 1st. Relates to the legislative power.

Article 2d. To the executive power.

Article 3d. To the judicial power.

Article 4th. To the *validity of public acts* and *records*,—the rights of *citizenship*,—the admission of *new states*,—and the forms of *state governments*.

Article 5th. Relates to the mode of amending the Constitution.

Article 6th. To the national *faith* and the binding *force* of the Constitution.

Article 7th. To the mode of its ratification.

§ 34. That we may have an accurate view of the Constitution, not merely as it is written, but as it has been construed and acted upon by the various departments of the government, we shall take these Articles up by sections, and consider them in connection with judicial and other decisions upon them.

Article I.

§ 35. Section 1st. *All legislative powers herein granted shall be vested in a Congress of the United States, which shall consist of a Senate and House of Representatives.*

§ 36. Whenever power is vested in a representative body, it is usually divided between a body of direct representatives and one more remote and differently constituted. Thus, in Great Britain, the legislative power is vested in the Commons and the House of Peers; so also in France, the House of Deputies and the Peers; so also the legislative power of the several states is similarly vested in two houses. The provision is a wise one, in rendering measures less precipitate, and in removing one portion of the legislature from the immediate action of popular passion, while it retains it within the ultimate influence of the people.

§ 37. Section 2d. First clause. *The House of Representatives shall be composed of members chosen every second year by the people of the several states; and the electors in each state shall have the qualifications requi-*

site for electors of the most numerous branch of the state legislature.

§ 38. About the frequency of elections there has been much dispute. In England, the period for which a representative is chosen is seven years; in some of the states it is two, and in some only six months. In the Constitution it is fixed at two years, as being a period sufficiently long to give the people some time for reflection, and yet sufficiently short to secure the responsibility of the representative.

As the *electors* of the different state legislatures varied materially, it was thought proper that the representatives from each state should be chosen by the people, in the manner they had appointed for the choice of their own legislature.

§ 39. 2d clause. *No person shall be a representative who shall not have attained to the age of twenty-five years, and been seven years a citizen of the United States,* AND *who shall not, when elected, be an inhabitant of that state in which he shall be chosen.*

§ 40. The propriety of requiring a seven years' citizenship cannot be doubted; *aliens* cannot be regarded as a part of the nation; and length of time, as well as naturalization is required, to make them acquainted with the interests of the country.

§ 41. A representative must be an *inhabitant* of the state from which he is chosen. In respect to this provision, a question has arisen, whether a man residing at the *seat of government* in his *official capacity* ceases to be a *legal inhabitant* of the state of which he was a citizen? It was decided in the case of Mr. John Bailey,[1] a representative from Norfolk district, Massachusetts, who had for several years been a clerk in the Department of State, that an official residence in the District of Columbia did take away his qualifications as a citizen of the state whence he came. This decision will probably not be sustained. How can a man be deprived of his citizenship by a merely *official* residence elsewhere?

Mr. Bailey, however, returned to Massachusetts, and within five months was re-elected and admitted to his seat. The point is, therefore, undecided.

§ 42. 3d clause. *Representatives and direct taxes shall be apportioned among the several states which may be included within this Union, according to their respective numbers, which shall be determined by adding to the whole number of free persons, including those bound to service for a number of years, and excluding Indians not taxed, three-fifths of all other persons. The actual enumeration shall be made within three years after the first meeting of the Congress of the United States, and within every subsequent term of ten years, in such a manner as they shall by law direct. The number of representatives shall not exceed one for every thirty thousand, but each state shall have at least one representative; and until such enumeration shall be made, the state of New Hampshire shall be entitled to choose three; Massachusetts, eight; Rhode Island*

---

[1] See Journals of Congress.

and Providence Plantations, one; Connecticut, five; New York, six; New Jersey, four; Pennsylvania, eight; Delaware, one; Maryland, six; Virginia, ten; North Carolina, five; South Carolina, five; and Georgia, three.

§ 43. It is to be observed that the *representative population* is not the *whole* population of the United States; after including "all free persons," excluding "Indians not taxed," it includes "three-fifths of all other persons." The *other persons* here mentioned are *slaves*, and conseqently the states holding slaves have a representation for three-fifths of the whole number: thus, in some of the states, the slaves exceed the whites in number, and as these slaves exercise no political privileges themselves, it follows that their masters hold double the political power held by the citizens of the non-slaveholding states. Of this, however, they do not, and ought not to complain, as it was the *necessary result* of the *compromise*, without which it is probable the Union could never have been formed.

§ 44. It is said that the *electors* must be the same as those for "the most numerous branch of the state legislature." Some of these electors, as in North and South Carolinas, must have a *property qualification*, and others again come in under *universal suffrage;* hence, the qualifications for electors are not uniform.

§ 45. In all the states, the mode of electing representatives to Congress is by districts.

§ 46. Under this section has arisen a question in

respect to the mode of apportioning representatives. Congress passed a law,[1] giving a number of representatives equal to the *whole population* of the United States, *divided* by 30,000. This gave a larger number than would arise by dividing the population of the *respective states* by the same number, and adding together the quotients. The additional members were given to the states having the *largest fractions*. This principle was objected to by General Washington, who was then president, and the bill returned with his reasons. The objection was, that the Constitution required that the representation should be apportioned among the *several states*, and not according to the whole population of the Union. The bill was returned to Congress, the matter again discussed, and the objectionable feature struck out. The same principle came up under the census of 1830.[2] The House of Representatives passed the apportionment-bill in the usual form, and the Senate inserted a provision, making the number for a single representative *a divisor of the* whole representative population of the United States, and giving a representative to the largest fraction. The House would not agree to the principle, and the Senate finally receded from their ground. "Notwithstanding this decision, Congress, by the Act of May 23, 1850, adopted the principle contended for by the Senate. That Act provides: 1. That 233 is to be the number of representatives. 2. That the whole *aggre-*

---

[1] Pitkin's Civil Hist., 351.

[2] Journals of Congress, 1832.

gate representative population of the United States shall be divided by the number 233, and the quotient (disregarding fractions of a unit) shall be the *ratio* or rule of apportionment." 3. With this ratio, the *representative population* of each state is to be divided, which gives the number of its representatives. 4. The number of representatives wanting are to be given to the states *having the largest fractions;* till the number is made up.

§ 47. This section likewise requires, that an enumeration should be taken every ten years of the inhabitants of the United States. This commenced in 1790, by Act of Congress, and has been continued ever since. The *ratio* of representation has been altered at each census. The ratio, that is, the common divisor, or number which is entitled to a representative, has been constantly increasing, but the increase being in a less proportion than that of the population, the number of representatives has likewise increased.[1]

§ 48. Clause 4th. *When vacancies happen in the representation from any state, the executive authority thereof shall issue writs of election to fill up such vacancies.*

§ 49. The necessity for this clause frequently arises, by virtue of the death or resignation of members of

---

[1] In 1790 the *ratio* was 33,000, and the number of representatives 106. In 1800, the same ratio, but 140 members. In 1810, ratio 35,000, members 181. In 1820, ratio 40,000, members 210. In 1830, ratio 47,700, members 240. In 1842, the ratio was raised to 70,000. It was raised to 93,000, —making 233 members,—by a permanent law, enacted in 1850.

Congress. In some states, as in Massachusetts and Vermont, repeated elections have to be held before a choice can be made, in consequence of a majority of the votes being required to elect.

§ 50. 5th clause. *The House of Representatives shall choose their Speaker, and other officers, and shall have the sole power of impeachment.*

§ 51. The power of impeachment is one of the most important under the Constitution. It is the only mode in which the *judiciary* is made responsible, and it is a salutary and necessary check upon the President and his officers.

§ 52. The most prominent examples of impeachment under the Constitution are those of Judges Chase and Peck.[1] In March, 1804, the House of Representatives, by resolution, impeached Samuel Chase—one of the judges of the Supreme Court—of malversation, improper and arbitrary conduct in office. In 1830, they did the same in relation to James H. Peck, district judge for the state of Missouri. They were both acquitted.

§ 53. The *mode* of impeachment is this: the House pass a resolution to impeach, and then appoint a *committee* to manage the impeachment, and prepare the *articles;* articles making a plain statement of the case, in the manner, but with less formality than an indictment, are then adopted by the House. The Senate are then officially informed that such charges are pre-

---

[1] See Journal of the 8th Congress.

ferred by the House, and *resolve*, that on a given day the Senate will sit as a Court of Impeachment. In the mean time, a summons to appear and answer is served upon the party, and as many subpœnas for witnesses are issued as the managers or the party accused may direct. On the day appointed for trial, the appearance or non-appearance of the party is recorded, and at twelve o'clock, the secretary of the Senate administers an oath to the president of the Senate, that "he will do impartial justice, according to the Constitution and laws of the United States." The same oath is then administered by the president to each senator present.[1] Counsel are then heard for the respective parties; all motions are addressed to the president, and decisions are made by *ayes* and *nays* without debate. Witnesses are examined and cross-examined, in the usual manner. Questions put by senators are reduced to writing, and put by the president. It requires *two-thirds* to make a conviction.

§ 54. SECTION 3d. 1st clause. *The Senate of the United States shall be composed of two senators from each state, chosen by the legislature thereof, for six years, and each senator shall have one vote.*

§ 55. In the Senate each state is *equally* represented. It has been said by an eminent jurist,[2] that this feature of the Senate, and the mode of its election by the legislatures, are evidences of the *separate* and *inde-*

---

[1] Rules adopted by the Senate on the trial of S. Chase.

[2] 1 Kent's Comm., 211.

pendent existence of the states. If by *separate* and *independent* be meant any thing more than *local* and *municipal* independence, the truth of the proposition is not readily seen. The counties of Great Britain were till recently equally represented in the House of Commons; so also are the counties of the state of Maryland[1] in the state legislature; yet, who would attribute a *separate existence*, or independent power, to these counties, beyond mere local county purposes? The very contrary of this position, as it respects the United States, is shown from the fact, that the Senate votes, not by *states*, but by *persons:* hence, the members from a given state may, and often do, vote on opposite sides of a question. Here the representation of the state is neither separate nor independent, but mixed up with the whole mass. It is no doubt true, that this provision was intended to secure to the people of each state an equality of political power in the Senate; but it no more proves the *separate* existence, *independence*, or sovereignty of the states, than the government of Maryland acknowledges the *separation* and *independence* of its *counties*. As to the election of the senators by the state *legislatures*, it is only the *mode* by which the *people* of the state exercise their power. In the same manner, the counties in Maryland send an equal number of delegates to a convention, which convention choose the state Senate; now the convention is the mere *form* through which the *people express*

---

[1] Such was *formerly* the case as to Maryland and Great Britain.

their will;—it is no acknowledgment of any separate authority in those counties.

§ 56. As it is provided, that the *senators* shall be *chosen by the legislatures*, it is settled by the practice of most of the states, that they may be chosen by *joint ballot* of *both houses*, voting by individuals, and *not* necessarily by the legislature in its official capacity, each house having a negative on the other.

§ 57. 2d clause. *Immediately after they shall be assembled, in consequence of the first election, they shall be divided, as equally as may be, into three classes. The seats of the senators of the first class shall be vacated at the expiration of the second year, of the second class at the expiration of the fourth year, and of the third class at the expiration of the sixth year, so that one-third may be chosen every second year; and if vacancies happen by resignation or otherwise, during the recess of the legislature of any state, the executive thereof may make temporary appointments, until the next meeting of the legislature, which shall then fill such vacancies.*

§ 58. The members of the first Senate were, in conformity to the Constitution, divided *by lot* into three classes, the terms of service of which expired in two, four, and six years, and ever since one third has been removed every second year. In drawing the lots, care was taken that but one vacancy should occur at the same time in the representation of any one state.

§ 59. It has been decided[1] under this clause, that the

---

[1] Gordon's Digest of the Laws of the U. States, 1827; Appendix, note 1.

governor cannot make an appointment during the recess of the legislature, in *anticipation of a vacancy.* Thus, the term of James Lanman, senator from Connecticut, expired on the 3d of March, 1825. The President had convoked the Senate to meet on the 4th of March. The legislature of Connecticut did not meet till May. The governor, in February, appointed Mr. Lanman to sit after the 3d of March. The Senate decided that such an appointment cannot be constitutionally made; the *vacancy* must first *occur.*

§ 60. 3d clause. *No person shall be a senator who shall not have attained to the age of thirty years, and been nine years a citizen of the United States, and who shall not, when elected, be an inhabitant of that state for which he shall be chosen.*

§ 61. All these limitations are manifestly founded upon propriety. It is probable they might have been made still stronger without injury to the public interests.

§ 62. 4th clause. *The Vice President of the United States shall be president of the Senate, but shall have no vote unless they be equally divided.*

§ 63. Legislative bodies have generally the power of choosing their own presiding officer; in this instance, however, the Constitution conferred the office of presiding over the Senate to the Vice President; one reason may have been that he has no other duties to perform, and the chair of the Senate conferred dignity upon him. The *casting vote* of the Vice President has been frequently given, and in some very important cases.

§ 64. In 1826,[1] a question arose whether the Vice President had the power of preserving order independent of the rules of the Senate? The then Vice President, Mr. Calhoun, decided that he had not. In 1828, however, the Senate made a rule, that "every question of order shall be decided by the president without debate, subject to appeal to the Senate."

§ 65. 5th clause. *The Senate shall choose their other officers, and also a president pro tempore, in the absence of the Vice President, or when he shall exercise the office of President of the United States.*

§ 66. The power of choosing a president pro tempore is constantly exercised, the Vice President being frequently absent.

§ 67. 6th clause. *The Senate shall have the sole power to try all impeachments. When sitting for that purpose, they shall be on oath or affirmation. When the President of the United States is tried, the Chief Justice shall preside; and no person shall be convicted without the concurrence of two-thirds of the members present.*

§ 68. The impeaching power, and some of the rules of conducting an impeachment, have been heretofore noticed.[2] This mode of impeachment and trial under the Constitution is derived from the British Parliament, where the Commons have the sole power of impeachment, and the House of Lords the power of trial. It seems, however, to have been introduced into the Com-

---

[1] American Annual Register, i., 86, 87; 3 Idem, 99.

[2] Sections 51, 52, 53.

mon Law from the customs of the Germans; among them, however, the people were both accusers and judges.

§ 69. In the trial of the President, the Chief Justice presides, in order to preclude the Vice President, who, in case of a vacancy, succeeds to the presidency, from having any part in the creation of that vacancy.

§ 70. 7th clause. *Judgment in case of impeachment shall not extend further than to a removal from office, and disqualification to hold and enjoy any office of honor, trust, or profit, under the United States; but the party convicted shall, nevertheless, be liable and subject to indictment, trial, judgment, and punishment according to law.*

In England, the judgment upon impeachments extends, not only to removal from office, but to the whole penalty attached by law to the offence. The House of Lords may, therefore, inflict capital punishment, banishment, or forfeiture of goods, according to its discretion.[1]

§ 71. In another place[2] we have stated the mode of procedure in the Senate upon the trial of impeachments. When the evidence is gone through, and the parties have been heard, the Senate proceed to consider the case. If debates arise, they are in secret; a day is then assigned for a public decision by *yeas* and *nays*. When the court has met, the question is propounded by the president of the Senate to each individual member by name: whereupon the member rises and an-

---

[1] Com. Digest. Parliament, I., 44.

[2] Section 53.

swers, guilty or not guilty, as his opinion is. If upon *no one* article the party is found guilty by two-thirds of the Senate, he is declared acquitted by the president of the Senate. If guilty, the Senate proceed to fix and declare the punishment.

§72. Section 4th. 1st clause. *The times, places, and manner of holding elections for senators and representatives shall be prescribed in each state by the legislature thereof; but the Congress may, at any time, by law, make or alter such regulations, except as to the places of choosing senators.*

§73. Under this section *Congress* has the power to appoint the *times* and *modes* of choosing representatives and senators. This power they have never exercised, and the time and mode of choosing them is consequently very various. In some states, as New York and Ohio, members of the House of Representatives are chosen in the year previous to the dissolution of Congress; in others, as New Hampshire and Virginia, in the spring following; and in others again, as in Indiana, in the following summer. Congress has, except on two occasions, met on or about the first Monday in December; but suppose, that from the emergency of the case, they should appoint a day early in the spring; in what manner would those states now electing representatives in the summer be represented? The power of regulating the times and places of electing representatives, was thus given to Congress, in order that it might have the means of its own preservation; otherwise, the states might prevent an election.

§ 74. 2d clause. *The Congress shall assemble at least once in every year; and such meeting shall be on the first Monday in December, unless they shall by law appoint a different day.*

§ 75. This provision was inserted in order to establish, beyond the possibility of prevention, the *annual sessions* of Congress; the time of meeting within the year has been fixed, but Congress may change it, and on two or three occasions they have held extra sessions.

§ 76. SECTION 5th. 1st clause. *Each House shall be the judge of the elections, returns, and qualifications of its own members; and a majority of each shall constitute a quorum to do business; but a smaller number may adjourn from day to day, and may be authorized to compel the attendance of absent members, in such a manner and under such penalties as each House may provide.*

§ 77. Some number must be fixed to constitute a *quorum;* it is here fixed at a majority, upon the general principle recognized in all the institutions of the United States, that *the majority must govern.* If any less number were required to make a quorum, the *minority*, by acting in the absence of the majority, might govern; and if a larger number were required, the minority might prevent legislation by absenting themselves.

§ 78. The House and Senate regularly appoint committees on *elections*, which investigate all contested claims to seats, and all doubtful returns, qualifications, &c. The committees report to the House, which makes the ultimate decision. From this decision there is no appeal, and it is obvious there ought not to be, for the power could be nowhere else lodged so safely.

§ 79. 2d clause. *Each House shall determine the rules of its proceedings, punish its members for disorderly behavior, and, with the concurrence of two-thirds, expel a member.*

§ 80. The *rules of proceedings* enacted are numerous, and will be considered in another place.

§ 81. The power to "punish its members for disorderly behavior," has been frequently exercised. Thus, in 1797, William Blount, a senator from Tennessee, was *expelled* for "a high misdemeanor, entirely inconsistent with his public trust and duty as a senator." His offence was, an attempt to seduce an Indian agent from his duty, and alienate the affections of the Indians from the authorities of the United States. The offence was not statutable, nor committed in his official character, nor committed during the session of Congress, nor at the seat of government. Yet he was expelled from the Senate, and afterwards impeached.[1]

§ 82. It is, therefore, settled by the Senate, that expulsion may be for any misdemeanor, though not punishable by any statute, which is inconsistent with the trust and duty of a senator.

§ 83. Although there is a power enumerated given to Congress to punish *disorderly behavior*, yet there is none expressly given to *punish contempts*. Yet this

[1] 2 Story's Commentary, 299.

power, being absolutely necessary to the order and security of the House, has been adjudged, both by Congress and the Supreme Court, to be a necessary incident to the powers of Congress.

§ 84. This power was exercised by the House of Representatives in the case of Robert Randall, in 1795, for an attempt to corrupt a member.

§ 85. The same point was solemnly decided by the Supreme Court in the case of Anderson *vs.* Dunn.[1] One Anderson was committed for a contempt of the House, and placed in the custody of the sergeant-at-arms. An action of trespass was brought against the officer, and the case carried to the Supreme Court. That tribunal decided that the House had the power, and that it extended no further than imprisonment, and continued no longer than the *duration* of the power that imprisoned, and consequently terminated with the dissolution of Congress.

§ 86. The same power was exercised in 1800, by the Senate, in the case of William Duane, who was found guilty of a printed libel on the Senate, and punished with imprisonment.[2] So, also, by the House of Representatives, in the case of Samuel Houston, who assaulted a member for words spoken in debate, and was found guilty of a contempt, and reprimanded.[3]

§ 87. 3d clause. *Each House shall keep a journal of its proceedings, and from time to time publish the same,*

---

[1] 6 Wheaton, 204.

[2] Journal of the Senate, March, 1800.

[3] Other authorities. 1 Dall. Rep., 296. 4 Johnson's Reports, 417.

excepting such parts as may in their judgment require secrecy; and the yeas and nays of the members of either House, on any question, shall, at the desire of one-fifth of those present, be entered on the journal.

§ 88. The *yeas* and *nays*, being the means by which the constituents discover the conduct of their representatives, are often called for, and generally granted. No important question is agitated upon which the yeas and nays are not recorded. This provision is very important; for, as the periods of elections are short, the representative is constantly held responsible to the people, and there is no scrutiny which he dreads more than that into his recorded votes.

§ 89. 4th clause. *Neither House, during the session of Congress, shall, without the consent of the other, adjourn for more than three days, nor to any other place than that in which the two Houses shall be sitting.*

§ 90. By this provision, it is impossible that either House should prevent the progress of business, and each has a complete negative on the other.

§ 91. Section 6th. 1st clause. *The senators and representatives shall receive a compensation for their services, to be ascertained by law, and paid out of the Treasury of the United States. They shall in all cases, except treason, felony, and breach of the peace, be privileged from arrest during their attendance at the session of their respective Houses, and in going to or returning from the same; and for any speech or debate in either House, they shall not be questioned in any other place.*

§ 92. The *compensation* allowed by Congress for their own service was, and is now, a *per-diem* allowance, with *mileage* for the distance travelled, going and returning. Congress, several years since, enacted that each member should receive a fixed compensation, thus, in fact, making themselves salary officers. This was received by *the people* with so much *censure* and *condemnation*, that the next Congress was obliged to *repeal* the law.[1]

§ 93. The *privilege* from *arrest* during attendance upon *legislative* business, is derived from the Saxon institutions. It was the privilege of the members of the Saxon Wittenagemot,[2] or assembly of wise men, and thence has descended through all the systems of English and American law.

§ 94. The *effect* of this privilege is, that the arrest of a member is unlawful, and a trespass for which he may maintain his action. He may also be discharged upon a writ of habeas corpus,[3] and the arrest may be punished as a contempt of the House.

§ 95. In going to and returning from Congress, ample time is allowed, and a little deviation does not take away the privilege.

§ 96. The privilege from arrest takes place by force of the election, and before the member has taken his seat, or is sworn.

§ 97. This privilege does not extend to *felony*, *treason*,

---

[1] Congress has since enacted, and the people sanctioned, a salary to members of Congress.

[2] Hume, vol. i., p. 155.

[3] 2 Wilson's Rep., 151.

or *breach of the peace;* and the terms *breach of the peace*, being general, have been decided to extend to all *indictable offences*, as well as those which are only constructive breaches of the peace.[1]

§ 98. The privilege of speech and debate does not extend beyond the limits of legislative or parliamentary duty. Thus, for a speech merely delivered in the House, a member cannot be questioned; yet if he *publish* the speech, and it contain a *libel*, he is liable to an action for it, as in any other case.[2]

§ 99. 2d clause. *No senator or representative shall, during the time for which he was elected, be appointed to any civil office under the authority of the United States which shall have been created, or the emoluments whereof shall have been increased, during such time, and no person holding any office under the United States shall be a member of either House during his continuance in office.*

§ 100. The first part of this clause was inserted as a safeguard against *venality;* yet were there really any danger from such a source of corruption, it would not seem to be prevented by this provision, for it extends only "during such time,"—the time *for which he was elected*, which is so short as to leave the full force of promised reward beyond it.

§ 101. The second provision, which prevents office-holders from holding a seat in Congress, is very unlike

---

1 Blackstone's Commentary, 166.

2 1 Maule and Selwyn's Reports, 273.

the constitution of the British Parliament, by which any member of the ministry may hold a seat in the House of Commons. By this means *there is certainly a degree of responsibility on the part of the ministry*, which is unfelt by the executive officers of our government, who communicate with Congress only through the details of a report, or the columns of a newspaper. The provision was inserted, however, for the purpose of preventing an undue influence of the government upon the action of Congress.

§ 102. Section 7th. Clause 1st. *All bills for raising revenue shall originate in the House of Representatives, but the Senate may propose or concur with amendments, as on other bills.*

§ 103. This provision is borrowed from the British constitution, where the *Commons*, or Lower House, are the exclusive representatives of the people. In the United States it has been continued, in consequence of the senators being rather the representatives of the state governments than of the people.

§ 104. *Bills for raising revenue* do not include every bill which brings money into the treasury; for, bills for establishing the *Post-office*, and the *Mint*, originated in the Senate; so also bills for the sale of public lands, though directly productive of money, are not included in this phrase: its proper meaning is confined to *bills to levy taxes.*

§ 105. 2d clause. *Every bill which shall have passed the House of Representatives and the Senate shall, before it become a law, be presented to the President of the United States; if he approve, he shall sign it; but if not, he shall return it with his objections to that House in which it shall have originated, who shall enter the objections at large on their journal, and proceed to reconsider it. If, after such reconsideration, two-thirds of that House shall agree to pass the bill, it shall be sent, together with the objections, to the other House, by which it shall likewise be reconsidered, and if approved by two-thirds of that House, it shall become a law. But, in all such cases, the votes of both Houses shall be determined by yeas and nays, and the names of the persons voting for and against the bill shall be entered in the journal of each House respectively. If any bill shall not be returned by the President within ten days* (Sundays excepted) *after it shall have been presented to him, the same shall be a law, in like manner as if he had signed it, unless the Congress, by their adjournment, prevent its return, in which case it shall not be a law.*

§ 106. The power of the President to return bills with his objections has been repeatedly exercised. It was exercised, we have seen, by General Washington, in respect to the bill fixing the ratio of representation; by President Monroe, in 1817, on the Internal Improvement Bill; by President Jackson, on the Maysville road, the United States Bank, and in other cases.

§ 107. This power, and the mode of its exercise, are so clearly defined by the Constitution as to admit of little doubt or misconception. If the President abuse the veto, it is presumed the representatives of the people will pass the bill in question, by the constitutional majority of *two-thirds*.

§ 108. If a bill be not presented to the President more than *ten days* before the end of the session, the President has it in his power to defeat it, by simply withholding his signature, for he is obliged to return it with objections (if he has any) only within ten days; of course, if Congress by adjournment prevent that return within that time, the bill must fail, if not signed by the President.

§ 109. 3d clause. *Every order, resolution, or vote to which the concurrence of the Senate and House of Representatives may be necessary (except on a question of adjournment), shall be presented to the President of the United States, and before the same shall take effect, shall be approved by him, or, being disapproved by him, shall be repassed by two-thirds of the Senate and House of Representatives, according to the rules and limitations prescribed in the case of a bill.*

§ 110. The "order, resolution, or vote" to which the President's signature is, by this section, required, are not those orders, resolutions, and votes which relate to the separate and internal government of each House. Rules of order, resolutions in respect to their own conduct, judgments upon their own elections, votes of censure and thanks, being matters exclusively relating to themselves, do not come within the scope of this provision.

§ 111. SECTION 8th. Clause 1st. *The Congress shall have power to lay and collect taxes, duties, imposts, and excises; to pay the debts and provide for the common defence and general welfare of the United States; but all duties, imposts, and excises shall be uniform throughout the United States:*

§ 112. This clause, divided by the semicolon, does *not* confer upon Congress *two separate powers*, one "to lay and collect taxes," &c., and the other to "provide for the general welfare;" but it is the grant of *one power*, viz., "to lay and collect taxes," &c.—limited by the *object*, which is *for the purpose* of "providing for the general welfare."[1]

§ 113. *Taxes* are of two kinds,—*direct* and *indirect.* Direct taxes are all burdens imposed immediately upon the person or estate of the citizen; thus, a tax upon houses, lands, money, &c., is a direct tax: indirect taxes are the burdens imposed upon articles of consumption, and chiefly upon imported articles; thus, the revenue, or duty levied upon each yard of broadcloth, or cotton sheeting, brought to this country from *abroad*, is an indirect tax.

§ 114. Indirect taxes increase the price of imported articles, and thus act as a burden upon those who purchase them. The difference between the two modes of taxation is this: *direct* taxes act *directly* upon the person and property of the citizen, and are *independent* of his *will; indirect taxes*, by being imposed upon articles imported from *foreign countries*, or used in consumption, leave the people at liberty to pay them or not,

---

[1] Jefferson's Opinion on the Bank of the United States, 1791; Monroe's Message, May, 1822; Hamilton's Report, Dec., 1791; 9 Wheaton's Rep., 199.

by *using* or *not using* the articles upon which they are imposed. Thus, a farmer cannot avoid the payment of a tax levied upon his land, but he may avoid the payment of the duty upon coffee, by not using it. And previous to the Revolution, such was the fact, as we all know, in relation to the duty upon tea. The people, by a patriotic impulse and common consent, abstained from the use of tea, and thus prevented the levying of the duty.

§ 115. In general, all the necessaries of life, such as coarse clothing, bread, meat, fruit, wood, and iron, are the productions of our own country,—so that the whole import duty, or nearly the whole revenue of the country, as now levied, is a mere matter of voluntary contribution upon the part of each and every citizen; hence it is that *indirect taxes*, being in a measure unfelt and voluntary, are comparatively popular, while *direct taxes* are more or less odious.

§ 116. The terms *imposts* and *duties*, as now used, are nearly synonymous;[1] but originally the word *duty* had a general signification, as it respects taxes, of which *imposts* was a particular application. Now they are applied indiscriminately to the revenue obtained from imported articles.

§ 117. The term *excise* is defined to be a duty on *commodities*, but of late it has been confined to a tax on *domestic distilled liquors*. In this sense it is a tax, not only on the *productions* of the country, but also a

[1] Madison's Letter on the Tariff.

tax on the *manufacture* of them: it is a tax, at once, upon the raw material and the *labor* put upon it. Such a double duty, it is obvious, could never be imposed by the legislature, nor borne by any people, but from a conviction in a large portion of the community of the *disastrous influence* of *spirituous liquors*, and a strong desire to repress their use. Even with this conviction among the intelligent, an *excise duty* has never been imposed but in time of great public emergency, and then at the risk of civil war. In the year 1793, Congress laid an excise duty on distilled spirits, and appointed inspectors, officers, &c., to collect it. This law became so excessively odious to a portion of the people, that notwithstanding the unrivalled popularity and commanding influence of General Washington, who was then President, they were excited, especially in the neighborhood of Pittsburgh, Pennsylvania, into open acts of violence. The inspectors were attacked in their houses, the mails robbed, the marshal resisted, and numerous other outrages, amounting to open insurrection, were committed.[1] At length, the President called out the militia, and by the display of superior force, and the determination to use it, quelled the insurgents. In this brief history, we see the *effect* of *excise duties*, of which the chief cause, next to the appetite for spirituous liquors, may be found in the *onerous* nature of a tax both upon labor and production.

§118. But all duties, imposts, and excises, must be

---

[1] Marshall's Washington, vol. v., p. 585.

uniform. In the case of Hylton *vs.* United States,[1] the Supreme Court decided that a duty levied indiscriminately upon *all carriages* was not a *direct* tax, and was therefore properly laid, and *uniform.* Had it been a direct tax, it must, according to a previous provision of the Constitution (§ 42), have been apportioned in proportion to the population of the several states.

§ 119. In the case of Loughborough *vs.* Blake,[2] the court decided that the power of Congress to tax extended over the District of Columbia, and all other territories; that the power of taxation was coextensive with the government, but that when exercised, direct taxes must be in proportion to the population. The court decided that Congress were not obliged to extend taxation to the territories, although when they did so, the Constitution gave a rule of assessment.

§ 120. 2d clause. *To borrow money on the credit of the United States:*

This power has been constantly exercised, and for the plain reason that no state or government could subsist without it. Every war, especially under a frugal and economical government like ours, imposes upon the government the necessity for greater revenues than the ordinary taxes can supply; the consequence is a *national debt.* But the same simplicity and frugality which keep the revenue below the lavish demands of war, furnish the means of speedily *extinguishing the debts* which result from it. Thus, in our country, the

---

[1] 3 Dallas, 171. [2] 5 Wheaton, 317.

year 1816 found the nation more than 120 millions in debt; the year 1834,—eighteen years afterwards,—found it not only out of debt, but its statesmen actually contending about the *surplus revenue!*

§ 121. Clause 3d. *To regulate commerce with foreign nations and among the several states, and with the Indian tribes:*

§ 122. The power given in this paragraph has been the origin of many important legislative provisions, of which some have given rise to judicial decisions, and others to frequent and severe political discussions. In a very celebrated case, Gibbons *vs.* Ogden,[1] arising under the Steamboat Laws of New York, the Supreme Court of the United States have solemnly decided the meaning of the phrase *to regulate commerce.*

§ 123. The term *commerce*, in that decision, is decided to comprehend *navigation*, and the power to *regulate* navigation is as expressly given as if it had been added to the word *commerce.*

§ 124. The power to *regulate commerce* extends to every species of commercial intercourse between the United States and foreign nations, and among the several states. But it does not comprehend that commerce which is *internal*, as between man and man, and between different parts of the same state. It does not, however, stop at the jurisdictional lines of the several states, but extends wherever the subject of it exists.

§ 125. The power to regulate commerce is the power

---

[1] 9 Wheaton, 189, 193.

to *prescribe the rule* by which commerce is to be governed.

§126. The power to regulate commerce extends as well to *vessels* employed in carrying *passengers* as to those in transporting goods, to vessels navigated by fire and *steam* as to those by sails.

§127. The law regulating the *coasting-trade*, in relation to which these decisions were made, was passed in February, 1793. From that day to this, Congress have been in the constant exercise of the power to regulate commerce. They have passed laws to regulate commerce, as such, to lay embargoes, navigation acts, &c.

§128. By the Embargo act, December, 1807, a *prohibition* was laid of *exportation* from the United States, either by land or water, of any goods or wares, either foreign or domestic. In the case of the United States against the Brigantine William,[1] this act was controverted, as *unconstitutional;* but the court *decided* that the Embargo Act was *constitutional;* that non-intercourse and embargo laws are within the range of legislative discretion; and that the power of *Congress was sovereign* relative to commercial intercourse.

§129. Within a few years, another question has arisen under the power to regulate commerce. Political zeal and party spirit have originated an idea, which certainly, so far as authentic history goes, never entered into the heads of the framers of the Constitution.

---

[1] 2 Hall's Law Journal.

This notion is, that a law *imposing duties for the protection of domestic manufactures is not constitutional.* It is admitted, that any amount of imposts and duties may be levied upon *any articles* for the purpose of *revenue*, and that the protection arising from this impost, being *incidental*, is *constitutional*,—but that these same imposts being imposed for *protection so called*, are not constitutional. This is in reality *a distinction without a difference;* for, according to the theory itself, Congress, without transcending their powers, may levy the whole revenue from particular articles, and thus create not only a protection against, but an absolute prohibition of them. But, suppose the bill was enacted for protection merely, and let us examine briefly the principles and authorities applicable to it. It is neither necessary nor proper here to enter into a detailed argument upon the subject, but the matter may be stated in a few propositions with sufficient force to make the conclusion irresistible.

§130. The avowed *objects* of the Constitution, as expressed in the preamble, are to provide for the *common defence*, and *promote the general welfare;* for this purpose various means are provided, and among others the express power given "to lay imposts, duties, and excises, to provide for the common defence, and promote the general welfare." Now, it is perfectly apparent that neither of these provisions can be carried into effect without such discriminating duties as will encourage and *protect* the domestic manufacture of *the munitions of war*, and of *necessary clothing.*

§ 131. The power to *regulate commerce* includes every thing in relation not only *to the mode of carrying it on*, but also to the *terms upon which* it shall be carried on.[1] *Those terms*, therefore, may be arranged either for the purpose of *raising revenue* or *protecting manufactures*, as suits the legislator. The government has a *discretion*, which it may exercise as it pleases.

§ 132. The meaning of the phrase, to *regulate trade*, must be gathered from the use of it among commercial people, and the manner in which it was understood by those who used it in making and adopting the Constitution.[2] In both these cases it was understood to include the encouragement of manufactures.

§ 133. The Supreme Court is vested with power to decide upon the *constitutionality* of all laws: this point has not been directly before them, but they may be considered as having decided it *upon principle*, by the application of certain rules which they have laid down.

§ 134. The court have decided[3] that the power to *regulate commerce* is the power to *prescribe the rule by which commerce shall be governed;*

§ 135. That, like all other powers vested in Congress, *it is complete in itself*, and has no other limits than such as are prescribed in the Constitution;

§ 136. That the power to regulate implies in its nature full power *over the thing to be regulated.*

§ 137. Now, if Congress have power to tax *all arti-*

---

[1] Madison's Letter on the Tariff. [2] Idem.

[3] Gibbons *vs.* Ogden, 9 Wheaton, 189.

cles in all modes (as they have, under the clause to *lay duties, imposts*, &c.), and have besides the power to regulate commerce without limitation as to the *subject-matter*, then it is impossible to avoid the conclusion, that they have the power to make *any discrimination whatever*, in the *duties* to be levied, no matter for what *purpose*, whether of *revenue* or *protection*, is answered thereby.

§ 138. But if any thing were wanting to make conviction perfect, it would be found in the *uniform practice* of the government, whether administered by those who were colaborators in its formation, or by those who grew up under it from the adoption of the Constitution to the present day; in the opinions often expressed, of the wisest and most distinguished statesmen; and finally, in the admissions of the ablest opponents of the protective policy.

§ 139. The power to regulate commerce is *exclusive* in the general government.[1] The full power to regulate a particular subject implies the *whole power*, and leaves no *residuum*. A grant of a power to regulate necessarily excludes the action of all others who would perform the same thing.

§ 140. The power to regulate trade and commerce *extends* to the *coasting trade* and *fisheries*, within or without a state, wherever it is connected with other states, or with foreign nations; it extends to the *regulation* and *government* of American *seamen* on board

---

[1] Brown *vs.* Maryland, 12 Wheaton, 419, 445.

of American ships, and to conferring *privileges* upon *American ships* in domestic as well as in foreign trade.[1]

§ 141. It extends also to *quarantine*, *pilotage*, and *salvage* laws; to the construction of *light-houses;* to the *removal of obstructions* in creeks, harbors, and sounds; and to the establishment of *ports of entry* for the purposes of foreign commerce.

§ 142. These powers have all been exercised in the enactment and enforcement of various laws regulating the collection of the revenue, the government of seamen, the mode of navigation, and the improvement of harbors.

Persons are not the subjects of commerce,—within the meaning of the Constitution,—granting power to "regulate commerce."[2] Hence, state laws, affecting the introduction of foreign persons,—so far as they are *police* regulations,—are *constitutional.* For example, the law of New York, requiring masters of vessels to make a report of the names, ages, places of birth, &c., of their passengers, and affixing a penalty to its violation, is constitutional. So is a state law prohibiting the introduction of slaves as merchandise for sale.[3] But a state law requiring masters of vessels to pay a *tax* on each passenger is *not* constitutional; for this is a tax on commerce, and not a police regulation of persons.[4]

---

[1] 2 Story's Comm., 518.
[2] New York *vs.* Milne, 11 Peters', 102.
[3] Groves *vs.* Slaughter, 15 Peters', 449.
[4] Passenger cases, 17 Curtis, 122.

No state can grant an exclusive use of *navigable* waters lying between two states, or between the United States and foreign states. But the grant by a state to an individual of an *exclusive right* to navigate a river impassible to general navigation, *lying wholly within a state*, and not making *part of a continuous trade* between two states, or of a state and foreign country, is *not* repugnant to the Constitution of the United States.[1]

A regulation of "pilots and pilotage" is a regulation of commerce within the meaning of the 8th section of the 1st Article of the Constitution; *but* the mere grant of such power to Congress does not prevent the states from regulating pilots.[2]

A state may *become* the retailer of foreign liquors,—and it is not repugnant to the Constitution of the United States. So a state may *prohibit* the sale of liquor when it is *imported* from another state.[3]

§ 143. This section of the Constitution contains also the power, which has been often exercised, of regulating intercourse with the Indian tribes. The Supreme Court have decided[4] that Congress have the exclusive right of *pre-emption* to all the *Indian lands* within the territories of the United States. This right the United States have constantly exercised; neither the states nor any individuals are allowed to purchase lands from the Indians.

---

[1] Veazie *vs.* Moore, 20 Curtis, 305.

[2] Cooley *vs.* the Port Warden of Philadelphia, 19 Curtis, 143.

[3] License cases, 16 Curtis, 513. [4] 2 Wheaton, 543 · 6 Cranch, 142.

§ 144. In the case of the Cherokee Nation *vs.* Georgia,[1] it was decided that *a tribe*, situated within the territorial limits of a state, but exercising the powers of government and national sovereignty, under the guarantee of the general government, is *not a foreign state* in the sense of the Constitution; but is entitled to sue in the courts of the United States. Such a tribe is to be deemed politically a *state*, that is, a distinct political society, but is not a foreign state.[2] It is a domestic dependent nation, and is to be deemed in a state of *pupilage*. Its relation to the United States is that of a *ward* to a *guardian*.

§ 145. As it respects *foreign nations*, the Indian tribes within the limits of the United States are considered as completely within the control and protection of the United States; so that the interference of any foreign nation with those Indian tribes, or an attempt to seduce their good will from the United States, would be considered as a cause of war.

§ 146. 4th clause. *To establish a uniform rule of naturalization, and uniform laws on the subject of bankruptcies throughout the United States:*

§ 147. This provision vests the power of *naturalization* exclusively in the United States.[3] In pursuance of this power, Congress have passed a series of laws prescribing the *mode of naturalization*. Of the *classes* of persons who may come under these provisions there

---

[1] 5 Peters' R., 1, 16, 17; 9 Wheaton, 203, 209.
[2] Worcester *vs.* Georgia, 6 Peters', 559.
[3] 2 Wheaton, 259, 269.

are *three*,—1st. Aliens of full age; 2d. Aliens, minors; 3d. Children of citizens born in foreign countries.

§ 148. 1st. The laws provide[1] that any *alien of full age* shall be admitted to citizenship in the following manner. 1. He shall *declare* on oath, or affirmation, before any *court of record*, having common-law jurisdiction, a seal and a clerk, in any state or territory, or a circuit or district court of the United States, or before the clerks thereof, *two years* at least before his admission, that it is bona fide his intention to become a citizen of the United States, and renounce forever all allegience to any foreign prince or state of which he may at the time be a citizen or subject. 2. That he shall, at the time of his application to be admitted, declare on oath, before the aforesaid courts, that he will support the Constitution of the United States, and does absolutely renounce and abjure all allegiance to any foreign prince or state whatever; and particularly that prince or state whereof he was before a citizen or subject, which proceeding shall be recorded by the clerk of the court. 3. That the court admitting such alien shall be satisfied that he had resided within the United States the *continued term of five years next preceding* his admission, without being during that time out of the United States, and one year at least within the state or territory where such court is held; and that, during that time, he has behaved as a man of good moral character, attached to the principles of the

[1] Act of April, 1802, as amended by the acts of 1804, 1813, 1816, 1824, and 1828.

Constitution, and well disposed to the good of the same,—provided the oath of the applicant shall not be allowed to prove his residence. 4. That if the alien applying to be admitted shall have borne any hereditary title, or been of any of the orders of nobility in the kingdom or state whence he came, he shall, in addition to those requisites, expressly renounce his title or order of nobility, in the court to which his application shall be made, and it shall be recorded; provided, no alien who shall be a citizen or subject of any country at war with the United States at the time of his application, shall be admitted as a citizen of the United States.

§ 149. 2d. Free white *minors*,[1] who have resided in the United States *three years next preceding* their arrival at twenty-one years, and who shall have continued to reside therein till the time they make application, may, after their arrival at twenty-one years of age, and after they shall have resided *in the country five years*, within the United States, including three years of their minority, be admitted without having made the declaration first required; provided they shall make such declaration at the time of their admission, and shall further declare on oath, and prove to the satisfaction of the court, that for three years next preceding, it has been the bona-fide intention of such alien to become a citizen of the United States, and shall otherwise comply with the laws relative to naturalization.

---

[1] Act of May, 1824.

§ 150. The *children of naturalized persons*, or of those who have become citizens previous to the passage of any law upon the subject, and were under twenty-one at the time of their parents' admission to citizenship, shall, if dwelling in the United States, be considered citizens of the United States.

§ 151. 3d. The *children* of those who now are or have been *citizens of the United States* shall, though born out of the limits and jurisdiction of the United States, be considered as citizens; provided the children of those who have never resided within the United States shall not be so considered.

§ 152. And it is further provided,[1] that if an alien make the declaration in the first condition, and pursue the other requisitions as far as may be, and die before he is actually naturalized, the widow and children shall be considered as citizens, and entitled to all the rights of citizens, upon taking the oaths prescribed by law.

§ 153. An *alien* is, by the common law,[2] without power to hold real estate. Several of the western states, as Ohio, &c., have abrogated this part of the common law by statute, for the encouragement of emigration.

§ 154. The power to pass a general Bankrupt Law is, by this section, vested in Congress. This power was exercised by Congress in April, 1800; but the law was repealed in 1803. In August, 1841, a Bankrupt Law was again passed, which was repealed in

---

[1] Act of March, 1804. [2] 2 Blackst. Comm., 249, 298.

1843. A Bankrupt Law has, therefore, existed but *four* years in sixty. The several states have frequently passed Insolvent Laws; but as another part of the Constitution, of which we shall speak hereafter, renders all acts *impairing the obligations of contracts* void, there has been much doubt as to the constitutionality and effect of these laws.

§ 155. The Supreme Court have now determined, by a series of decisions, the following points:[1]

1st. That state insolvent laws cannot discharge the *obligation of antecedent contracts;*

2d. That the power of Congress to pass bankrupt laws is not an *exclusive* grant; it may, therefore, be exercised within constitutional limits by the states;

3d. That a state may pass valid laws discharging the *person* of the debtor and his after-acquired property from debts contracted *after* the passing such law;

4th. That such a discharge is valid only *between the citizens of the state* by which the law was passed.

5th. That the insolvent law of one state does not discharge the debtor from debts which he has incurred in another state.

§ 156. 5th clause. *To coin money, regulate the value thereof, and of foreign coin, and fix the standard of weights and measures:*

§ 157. The power conferred by this paragraph has been long and efficiently exercised, so that the American coinage has supplied much of the currency of the

---

[1] 4 Wheaton's R., 122; 12 Idem., 278.

country, and holds a high rank among foreign nations. The *Mint* of the United States is an office, with the proper officers, created by Congress in 1792,[1] and has been in operation ever since. Every person may bring gold and silver to the mint to be coined, and if it is of the standard value, is assayed and coined free of expense; but if below the standard, enough is retained to pay the expense of coinage. The coinage of the United States is entirely *decimal*, and therefore in practice more convenient than that of any other nation. Thus, the Spanish milled *dollar* is taken as the *unit*, and all smaller coin is in *tenth* parts of that, and all gold coin in *tens above;* as the *dime* is the *tenth* part of a dollar, and the *eagle ten dollars.* That part of this clause which relates to the standard of weights and measures, has never been acted upon, although nothing could conduce more to the accuracy of trade, or the convenience of commerce. Several elaborate and scientific treatises have been produced upon the subject, for the information of Congress, among which is the able Report of Mr. J. Q. Adams. In the mean time, the power is sometimes exercised by the states. Double eagles, *twenty dollars*, have also been coined; and a semi-coinage established, by marking gold bars.

§ 158. 6th clause. *To provide for the punishment of counterfeiting the securities and current coin of the United States:*

Congress have exercised this power by making the

---

[1] Act of April, 1792.

crime of counterfeiting a felony, punishable by imprisonment, fine, &c. This power is consequential to the preceding,—that of coining money and regulating its value.

§159. 7th clause. *To establish post-offices, and post-roads:*

The establishment of post-offices and post-roads has existed since, and before, the organization of the present government. Being a branch of public administration co-existent with commerce, social intercourse, and the diffusion of knowledge, it has grown with the increase of the general prosperity, and has become, from small beginnings, an immense and complicated machinery. In 1848 the number of post-offices was 16,000, and the number of miles in post-roads 152,865; and this number is constantly increasing.

§160. To *establish* post-roads and post-offices means simply to make any given road a *post-route*, and appoint in any given place a *postmaster*. The *routes* are *established* by act of *Congress;* but it is the duty of the postmaster-general to appoint postmasters at all such places as he may judge best, and expedite the mail as frequently, on established routes, as the public interest may require.

§161. The power to establish post-offices and post-roads being given, the *consequential* powers necessary to carry it into execution are likewise given; as, for example,[1] the power to secure the *safety and speedy*

---

[1] Act of April, 1810.

transportation of the mail. Congress have accordingly made the *robbery* of the mail a *felony*, and prohibited, under high penalties, the *obstruction* of the mail. Under this act the Supreme Court[1] have decided, that even a stolen horse found in the mail stage could not be seized, and that the driver could not be arrested on *civil process* in such a way as to obstruct the mail. But it was subsequently decided, that this was not to be carried so far as to endanger the *public peace* by interfering with *criminal process*.[2] Thus, a felon may be arrested in the mail stage, or the driver, if he had committed murder.

§ 162. Under the power to establish *post-roads* has arisen the question of *internal improvements*. Though much agitated, it is not settled; and I shall give here merely the different authorities upon the subject, whether legislative, executive, or judicial.

§ 163. 1st. Of the *legislative opinions* upon the subject. By the act of March 3, 1803, Congress concluded a compact with the state of Ohio, by which *three per cent.* of all the moneys derived from the sale of *public lands* within the state of Ohio were reserved for the construction of roads within that state. The consideration was, that the lands of the United States in that state should not be taxed. Whether by inadvertence or intention, this act clearly acknowledged the power of the general government to make internal improvements; for the appropriation was made by the

---

[1] 3 Hall's Law Journal. [2] 1 Peters' Rep., 390.

United States, and the funds were derived from the property of the United States. It could be no objection to this reasoning, that the work was to be done by the state; for it is an established principle, that "he who acts by another, acts by himself." Neither is it an argument, to say there was a consideration; for "what one cannot do directly he cannot do indirectly." This was so understood by Congress; for in several subsequent acts they authorized the construction of roads within the Northwest Territory.

§ 164. The next step taken by Congress[1] was the construction of the *Cumberland Road.* This road was commenced in 1806, and in a few years finished from Cumberland, on the Potomac, to Wheeling, on the Ohio. In 1820, Congress resumed the construction from Wheeling westward, and continued it partly through the western states. This work was undertaken on the ground of the compact with Ohio. By the terms of a compact made between that state and the United States, *five per cent.* of all the moneys arising from the sale of public lands within that state were to be applied to the making of roads "leading from the navigable waters of the Atlantic to the Ohio." This, however, falls within the same principles already stated, in reference to the *three per cent. fund;* and as the sum drawn from the *reserved funds* was soon greatly exceeded, the work has since been conducted simply on the ground of *internal improvement.*

---

[1] Act of March, 1806.

§ 165. The next act[1] was the opening of the road from Athens, in Georgia, to New Orleans, and from Nashville to Natchez. In 1809, the canal of Carondelet[2] was extended to the Mississippi by the general government.

§ 166. In 1811, Congress directed[3] the survey and making of two roads: one from the rapids of the Maumee to the Western Reserve, and another from Sandusky to the Greenville line.

§ 167. By several successive acts in 1812, 1816, 1817, and 1818, Congress confirmed their former decisions, by making surveys of, and authorizing the construction of roads; till it would seem that, *practically*, there was no doubt in the national legislature upon the subject. The matter has, however, been several times tested by the interposition of the executive veto.

§ 168. A bill to set apart a portion of the bank bonus and dividends for the purpose of internal improvement was passed in 1817, and returned by *Mr. Madison*, who denied the power of Congress to construct roads and canals, or improve water-courses. The House of Representatives, however, reaffirmed their power by a vote of sixty to fifty-six.

§ 169. At the succeeding session, Mr. Monroe, in his message, also denied the constitutional power of Congress to make *internal improvements*. The House soon after passed a resolution, ninety to seventy-five, declar-

---

[1] Act of April, 1806. [2] Act of February, 1809.
[3] Act of December, 1811.

ing that Congress, under the Constitution, *had power* to construct roads and improve water-courses.

§ 170. From this period internal improvement seemed the settled policy of the government for several years. In 1822, Mr. Monroe, indeed, interposed his veto on the bill providing for the collection of tolls on the Cumberland road; but, the objection was not to the *power of making* roads, but to the *collection of tolls* upon it, as being inconsistent with the jurisdiction and sovereignty of the soil. This, however, was not deemed an impediment to the construction of public works, for Congress immediately took measures to organize a system of surveys and reports, in relation to such roads and canals as the public interest might require; and in April, 1824, what is called the Survey Bill became a law. It appropriated $30,000 for the purpose of making surveys of different parts of the country, and authorized the employment of the engineer corps in that service. Soon after the passage of this bill, the accession of a new administration, decidedly favorable to internal improvement, gave the system a new impulse, and from that time forward Congress enacted many laws affirming and enlarging these powers. They subscribed a large amount of stock to the Ohio and Chesapeake canal, to the Dismal Swamp canal, and the Louisville and Portland canal. They made appropriations for the improvement of numerous harbors, rivers, &c., &c.,—for the making of military roads,—for the continuance of the Cumberland road, and various other public works. A practical check was given to this system by President Jackson, in his veto on the Maysville road bill, of which I shall speak hereafter. Congress, however, remained unchanged. By the passage of the Harbor bills, and numerous other items for roads and improvements in other bills, they have manifested a fixed opinion in favor of their power to construct roads and other public works.

§ 171. The *result* deduced from this legislative history is, that *Congress have uniformly asserted their power, under the Constitution, to construct and hold, with the public funds, public works, under the denomination of internal improvements.* We shall now examine the opinion of another branch of the government.

§ 172. 2d. Of the *executive opinions.* During the administration of Washington and the elder Adams, the power of Congress in respect to internal improvements was neither exercised nor much examined, and therefore no executive opinions were formally advanced. Under the administration of Mr. Jefferson, we have already seen the compact was made with Ohio, and the Cumberland road undertaken. To both these acts Mr. Jefferson gave his assent, and it is difficult to see in what respect these works differ from other public improvements; yet, by his message of December 2d, 1806, he denied the power of Congress to make roads and improve water-courses, though he earnestly recommended the grant of such powers by the states. The reason given was, that this power was not enumerated among the powers of Congress. The authority of *Mr.*

Jefferson, therefore, may be considered as decidedly *against* the power to make internal improvements, though he was most earnestly in favor of granting such a power to the government.

§ 173. *Mr. Madison*, in 1796, spoke in favor of a resolution relative to a survey of a road from Maine to Georgia; yet, in 1815, in his message to Congress, while strongly recommending to Congress "the great importance of establishing throughout our country the roads and canals which can best be executed under national authority," intimated that any *defect in the constitutional power* might be supplied in the mode provided by the Constitution.

In 1817, Mr. Madison placed his *veto* upon the bill providing means for the *construction of roads and canals*, and the improvement of *water-courses*. He denied the constitutional power of Congress to make such works, and thus gave his judgment also in the *negative*.

§ 174. In Mr. Monroe's first message to Congress,[1] he declared his agreement with his predecessors, and doubt of the constitutionality of such works. After the passage of the resolution of Congress, in 1818, affirming the power, he is understood to have withdrawn his opposition, and during his administration, appropriations for such purposes greatly increased. In 1822, however, he placed his *veto*[2] upon the act for the erection of toll-gates and the collection of tolls on the Cumberland road. This he considered as requiring the

[1] December, 1817.

[2] May, 1822.

jurisdiction and sovereignty of the soil, which the general government did not possess.

§175. Mr. John Quincy Adams strongly recommended and encouraged internal improvements. During his administration, the system seemed to have become a part of the permanent policy of the country. Numerous surveys were completed, and large sums appropriated for various public works.

§176. General Jackson, while a member of the Senate, is understood to have had no constitutional scruples upon the subject; but, by his veto upon the well-known Maysville road bill,[1] he gave his influence in the *negative.* In whatever manner this document may be judged of, during the heat of temporary party controversies, there can be no doubt that it contains a temperate and judicious review of the question, and a correct decision upon the particular point submitted to him. That point was, the propriety of constructing by the general government a *local road entirely within one state.* There is no doubt that if the power of making internal improvements exist in the general government, it must be confined to *national, not local* objects. General Jackson, however, went further than this, and deemed that all the power which had been uninterruptedly exercised upon this subject, viz., that of *appropriating money, was insufficient and unsafe for the successful prosecution* of national works. He regarded it, notwithstanding the usage was admitted, as improper

[1] Message, 27th May, 1830.

to exercise powers not granted, and which might easily be conferred.

§ 177. Since this message, the executive influence has been altogether opposed to internal improvements, and they have made little progress.

§ 178. We have now seen that the opinions of Presidents Jefferson, Madison, Monroe, and Jackson were opposed upon *constitutional grounds* to the exercise of such a power by the general government; but that all of them, except the latter, were in favor of the measures themselves, and under all their administrations, except also the last, many national works were undertaken. President Adams alone conceded both the *theory and practice.*

The conclusion of the whole then is, that *the weight of legislative authority has been uniformly in favor of the power, while that of executive authority has been against it.*

§ 179. 3d. Of *judicial opinions* we have none except general decisions upon the *indirect powers of Congress.*

The Supreme Court decided, that a contemporary exposition of the Constitution practised and acquiesced in for a number of years, fixes the construction of the Constitution, and *the court will not shake or alter it.*[1] Also, that there is nothing in the Constitution of the United States which excludes incidental or implied powers.[2]

---

[1] Cranch, 299. [2] 4 Wheaton, 316.

The two principles here cited might be considered as showing an inclination in the Supreme Court to sustain the power claimed by Congress. Yet, as it may be long before the question will come before that tribunal, it may be considered as open to discussion.

§180. Clause 8th. *To promote the progress of science and the useful arts, by securing, for limited times, to authors and inventors, the exclusive right to their respective writings and discoveries:*

§181. In England it was solemnly decided,[1] that an author had, by common law as well as by statute, an exclusive right to his own works. In this country, *copyrights* and *patent-rights* are derived from *Acts of Congress*, founded on this provision of the Constitution.

§182. The acts[2] relative to patents, direct that "Patents may be obtained for any new and useful art, machine, manufacture, or composition of matter not known before the application." The *term* for which a patent may be obtained is *fourteen years*. Such a law would seem to be an effectual protection to inventors against an infringement of their rights, yet we may see in the Life of Whitney[3] of how little avail it is against the pressing interests of society. In Georgia, no jury could be found to give him a verdict of damages for the open violation of his patent for the Cotton Gin,—an invention which had doubled the value of cotton!

§183. *Copyrights* were formerly secured for *fourteen years;* now, by the Act of February, 1831, in

[1] 4 Burrows' Rep., 2303.
[2] Acts of February, 1793, and April, 1800.
[3] See Silliman's Journal.

every respect better than the former, the *term* is prolonged to *twenty-eight years*, and at the expiration of that time, the author (or, if he be dead), his wife or children, may renew it for fourteen years longer.

§184. Clause 9th. *To constitute tribunals inferior to the Supreme Court:* Clause 10th. *To define and punish piracies and felonies committed on the high seas, and offences against the law of nations:*

§185. In another place we shall consider what relates to the Supreme and inferior courts.

By the law of nations, and by the common law, *piracy* is defined to be *robbery on the high sea*, that is, the *same crime* which, *when committed on the land* is denominated *robbery*.[1] *Piracy* is against all nations, and punished by all. A plea which would be good in one civilized state, would be good in all.

An *alien* under the sanction of a *national commission*, cannot commit piracy while he pursues his authority.[2] Hence, the Barbary states are regarded as lawful powers, and not pirates.

§186. *Felony*, at common law, comprises *every species of crime which occasions the forfeiture of lands and goods.* These, under the English law, were most crimes punishable with death, such as murder, forgery, theft, &c. But this does not include all offences on the high seas; for example, Lord Coke says that *piracy* is not felony, because punishable by the *civil* and not the common law.

---

[1] 4 Blackst. Comm., 71, 72. [2] 1 Kent's Comm., 176.

§187. The *high seas* means *all the waters of the ocean*, whether within the territorial boundaries of a foreign nation or of a domestic state.[1]

Between high-water mark and low-water mark, where the tide ebbs and flows, the common law and the admiralty hold alternate jurisdiction; one upon the water when it is full sea, the other upon the land when it is ebb.

The high seas, here defined, however, do not extend to creeks and inlets, but, as it respects the states, means that part of the ocean which washes the sea-coast, and is not included within any county.

§188. Congress, by various enactments, have exercised the powers vested in them by this section, and have affixed various punishments to the crimes of treason, murder, robbery, piracy, &c.

§189. Congress has power to provide for the punishment of offences committed by persons serving on board a ship of war of the United States, wherever that ship may be: but Congress has not exercised that power in the case of a ship lying in the waters of the United States.[2]

§190. Clause 11th. *To declare war, grant letters of marque and reprisal, and make rules concerning captures on land and water:*

§191. These powers are attributes of *sovereignty;* they are vested in the *national* government, and not in the *states.* The power of declaring war is the highest

---

[1] 5 Wheaton's Rep., 184, 200, 204. [2] 8 Wheaton, 336.

which the government possesses, and involves directly the happiness and existence of the people: as it is called the *last resort of kings*, so it is certainly the last *appeal of nations.*

§ 192. To grant letters of marque and reprisal is but a part of the power to declare war; for such an act would unquestionably produce war.

§ 193. The power of "making rules concerning captures on land and water," which is superadded in the Constitution to that of declaring war, is not confined to captures which are *extra-territorial*, but extends to rules respecting enemies' property found within the territory, and is an express grant to Congress of the power of confiscating enemies' property found within the territory at the declaration of war, as an independent power, not included in that of declaring war.[1]

§ 194. Clause 12th. *To raise and support armies, but no appropriation of money to that purpose shall be for a longer term than two years:*

§ 195. The United States have always had a small standing army, to keep up the forts on the seaboard and awe the Indians. The provision preventing an appropriation for a longer period than *two years* was for the obvious purpose of keeping the standing army always within the immediate *control of the people.*

§ 196. Clause 13th. *To provide and maintain a navy:*

This, like the provision to maintain an army, is a

---

[1] 8 Cranch, 110.

consequence of the general power to declare war, and is absolutely necessary to national existence. The United States have long had a respectable navy, and all the provisions necessary to its organization, support, and increase, have been provided for by law.

§ 197. Clause 14th. *To make rules for the government and regulation of the land and naval forces:*

Congress have established, by law, rules and articles of war for the government of the army,[1] and rules and regulations for the government of the navy.[2] These rules provide for the discipline of the service, the mode of trial, and the punishment for offences. The rules and articles of war must be read at the head of each corps every six months, and are to govern as well the militia in service as the regulars, but the militia are to be tried by their own officers.

§ 198. Whatever crimes are committed on board of public ships of war of the United States, whether in port or at sea, are exclusively cognizable and punishable by the government of the United States.[3] The public ships of sovereigns, wherever they may be, are deemed to be extra-territorial, and enjoy the immunities from the local jurisdiction belonging to their sovereign.[4]

§ 199. It is plain that the government must have power to *govern* all persons in the military and naval service. If it had not, all military power is at an end.

---

[1] Act of April, 1806.
[2] Act of April, 1800.
[3] United States *vs.* Bevans, 3 Wheaton, 336.
[4] Idem.

The war power is one of necessity, given for the security of the nation. Full authority on this head is given to Congress, in the power to raise an army and navy, and make military and naval regulations. The government of the army is exercised through these regulations, and the common usage of nations. This is called martial-law. Now, it is plain that this constitutes a distinct code of law, applicable only to the military service. It is equally plain that there are many points on which it must apparently conflict with the civil law. Shall the civil law have no effect within military jurisdiction? Shall the martial law withdraw criminals, debtors, or minors from civil jurisdiction? Practice, in many years, has settled many of these questions on principles of justice and common sense. *Criminal* process may be executed within military jurisdiction. Judgments of courts against military debtors will have the same effect against their property as in other cases. Minors cannot be enlisted under a certain age, without consent of their guardians. But the main point to be settled was, whether a civil court can arrest the proceedings of a military court, or interrupt its ministerial officers in the performance of their military duty? The Supreme Court has decided that a court-martial has jurisdiction over offences against martial law, and an action of false imprisonment will not lie against the ministerial officer who executes its sentence.[1] This decision makes the military

[1] 20 Howard, 65.

courts entirely independent in the adjudication and execution of martial law.

§ 200. Clause 15th. *To provide for calling forth the militia to execute the laws of the Union, suppress insurrections, and repel invasions:*

Clause 16th. *To provide for organizing, arming, and disciplining the militia, and for governing such part of them as may be employed in the service of the United States, reserving to the states respectively the appointment of the officers, and the authority of training the militia according to the discipline prescribed by Congress:*

§ 201. Upon these two provisions, and a subsequent one, that the President shall be commander-in-chief of the militia when called into actual service, rest the whole power of the national government over the militia. Upon two occasions only has the power to "call forth the militia to execute the laws, suppress insurrections, and repel invasions," been exercised,—one the insurrection in Pennsylvania in 1794, the other to repel the invasion of the enemy during the war of 1812. Some serious questions have arisen under this power. In consequence of a requisition made by President Madison on the governors of Massachusetts and Connecticut for their quotas of militia, a question arose between the general and state governments in relation to this power. In that and following discussions, these questions were made:

1. *Who* is to determine *when* the exigency pointed out by the Constitution *has happened?*

2. Whether the President can place the militia under the command of any one but himself?

3. Whether he can detach *parts* of the militia corps?

§ 202. On the first question, the governors of Connecticut, Massachusetts, and Rhode Island, with the Supreme Court of Massachusetts, held[1] that the *governors of the states* were to judge *when* the exigency contemplated by the Constitution had happened. This doctrine, however, was denied by President Madison in his message to Congress, and the question has since been solemnly settled[2] by the Supreme Court of the United States. It was then settled that the authority to decide belongs exclusively to the President. The act of 1795, providing for the mode of calling out the militia, was framed on this principle. The law contemplates that, in certain exigencies, orders shall be given to carry the powers into effect, and no person can have a right to disobey them. No provision is made for an appeal from, or review of, the President's opinion. And whenever a statute gives a discretionary power to any person, to be exercised by him upon his own opinion of certain facts, the general rule of construction is, that he is thereby constituted the sole and exclusive judge of the existence of those facts.[3]

§ 203. The power to *govern* the militia, when in the service of the United States, is an *exclusive one;* for any such power concurrent in other authorities would destroy all unity of action and command.

---

[1] Martin *vs.* Mott, 12 Wheaton's Rep., 30, 31.

[2] 1 Kent's Comm., 245, 246.

[3] 12 Wheaton, 19, 31, 32.

§ 204. There is nothing in the Constitution to prohibit a state from calling forth its own militia to assist the United States, when that militia is not in the service of the United States, to suppress insurrections and repel invasions. Such a concurrent exercise of power does not interfere with, or obstruct the exercise of, the powers of the Union.

§ 205. Upon the questions whether the President can *delegate his authority*, or detach *parts* of the militia corps, different opinions have been advanced by the state and national authorities. Thus, Connecticut and Massachusetts, during the war, asserted that he could not; President Madison, that he could. The latter seems the general opinion, and is certainly most consonant to reason.

§ 206. By the act of May, 1792, Congress provided for the organization, arming, and disciplining of the militia. By that act, directions were given as to the mode in which the President was to give his orders; and refusal or neglect to obey them was declared a public offence, and the mode of trial, by court-martial, was pointed out. In relation to this act, the Supreme Court have decided[1] that the militia, when called into actual service, were not to be considered in *that service*, or as *national militia*, till they were mustered at the *place of rendezvous;* and that *until then*, the state retained a right, concurrent with the government of the United States, to punish their delinquency. If the

---

[1] Huston *vs.* Moore, 5 Wheat. Rep., 1.

militia, when called into the service of the United States, refuse to obey the order, they remain within the military control of the *state*, and it is competent for the state to provide for trying and punishing them by a state court-martial.

§ 207. In addition to the act of 1792, Congress have passed several other acts upon this subject. In February, 1795, a law was passed, calling forth the militia, in contemplation of the well-known Whiskey Insurrection. In May, 1820, they passed an act providing that the system of *discipline* observed by the *militia* throughout the United States should be the same as observed by the *regular army*.

§ 208. A *court-martial* that imposes a fine upon a man *not liable* to militia duty are *trespassers*, as well as the officer who distrains for such fine.[1]

§ 209. Clause 17th. *To exercise exclusive legislation in all cases whatsoever, over such district (not exceeding ten miles square) as may, by cession of particular states, and the acceptance of Congress, become the seat of government of the United States, and to exercise like authority over all places purchased by consent of the legislature of the state in which the same shall be, for the erection of forts, magazines, arsenals, dock-yards, and other needful buildings: And*

Clause 18th. *To make all laws which shall be necessary and proper for carrying into execution the foregoing powers, and all other powers vested by this Consti-*

[1] 8 Cranch, 331.

tution in the government of the United States, or in any department or officer thereof.

§ 210. In pursuance of the power to exercise exclusive jurisdiction, &c., &c., Congress, in July, 1790, accepted of a grant from Virginia and Maryland, of *ten miles square*, on the Potomac, for the seat of government, which is the present District of .Columbia. Over this territory Congress have exclusive jurisdiction, and exercise all legislative powers.

§ 211. The jurisdiction over various other sites, as West Point, &c., has been granted by the legislatures of the respective states in which they lie, for military and naval purposes.

§ 212. The power to exercise exclusive jurisdiction includes the power to tax.[1]

§ 213. Congress shall have the power of *general* as well as *local* jurisdiction, in reference to acts committed within that jurisdiction.[2]

§ 214. The states cannot take cognizance of any acts done in the ceded place after the cession; and on the other hand, the inhabitants of those places cease to be inhabitants of the states, and can no longer exercise any political rights under the laws of the state.[3]

But there is commonly reserved by the states a right of executing criminal process within the limits of ceded places, and this may be exercised in perfect consistency with the right of jurisdiction on the part of the United States.

---

[1] 5 Wheaton's Rep., 317. [2] 1 Kent's Comm., 403; 6 Wheaton, 426.
[3] 3 Story's Comm., 103; 8 Mass., 72.

§ 215. The clause giving Congress power to make all laws which shall be *necessary and proper to carry the foregoing into execution*, has given rise to more diversity of sentiment, discussion, and controversy, than any other in the Constitution. The reason is obvious; about the direct provisions of that instrument, men of ordinary comprehension could have but little difference of opinion; but as to what is *necessary and proper*, different men might form very different judgments: so it happened; the Constitution had scarcely gone into operation under the administration of Washington, when a radical difference of opinion arose, in relation to the charter of the United States Bank.

§ 216. In 1791, the secretary of the treasury recommended the establishment of a national bank, as necessary to the proper administration of the financial concerns of the nation. A bill for that purpose was introduced into the House of Representatives, and warmly opposed on constitutional grounds. Mr. Giles, Mr. Madison, and Mr. Jackson, of Georgia, were among the opponents of the measure, and Mr. Ames, Mr. Boudinot, and Mr. Gerry, among its advocates. The former denied its constitutionality, on the ground that Congress could not exercise any powers not expressly granted; that no power was anywhere given to charter a bank; and that if such implied powers were exercised, there would be *no limits* to the powers of the general government.[1] Their opponents contended

[1] 4 Elliott's Debates.

that Congress had power to pass all laws *necessary and proper* to *effect the ends* proposed by the Constitution; that in a confused state of the general currency, such a bank was *necessary* to the power of *levying and collecting taxes;* and that it was implied in the *power to borrow money*, which also includes the power to *lend;* and that *without* the exercise of *implied* powers, the government could do nothing. After much debate, the bill passed[1] both Houses of Congress. The President (Washington), on receiving the bill, called a cabinet council, in which it was again debated. The secretary of state (Mr. Jefferson) and the attorney-general denied its constitutionality; while the secretaries of the treasury and war (Hamilton and Knox) agreed with the majorities in Congress. The President, after deliberation, gave it his signature and the weight of his favorable judgment.

§217. In 1811, the charter of the United States Bank expired, and it was *not rechartered.* In the debate upon the question of its constitutionality, it was advocated by Mr. Crawford, and opposed by Messrs. Clay and P. B. Porter, upon the same grounds as it had formerly been advocated and opposed by Messrs. Ames and Madison.[2]

§218. In 1816, a new bank was chartered, with a much larger capital. The currency of the country was then in a very depreciated and bankrupt condition. The effect of the establishment of the bank was

---

[1] 1 Kent's Comm., 234. [2] 4 Elliott's Debates, 268, 276.

to restore a healthy action to the money market, and resuscitate credit.

§ 219. In 1832, in anticipation of the expiration of the charter in 1836, an application was made for its renewal, and a bill passed both Houses of Congress, but was rejected by the interposition of the executive veto, by President Jackson.[1]

§ 220. The action of the Supreme Court upon the subject, has been direct and distinct. In the case of McCullough *vs.* State of Maryland,[2] that tribunal decided,—

1st. That Congress has power to incorporate a bank.

2d. That there is nothing in the Constitution which excludes incidental or implied powers; and that if the *end* be within the *scope* of the *Constitution*, all the *means* which are appropriate, and are *adapted* to the *end*, and not prohibited, may be constitutionally employed to carry it into effect.

3d. That the bank of the United States has a constitutional *right* to establish *offices* of discount and deposit *within the states.*

4th. That the states *cannot tax* the branches: they have no right to tax any of the constitutional *means* used by the government to effect constitutional ends.

5th. That the last rule does not extend to any of the *real property* held by the bank in particular states, nor to the *proprietary interests* of any citizen of that state in the bank.

---

[1] Journals of Congress, 1832.

[2] 4 Wheaton's Reports, 316.

§ 221. In the case of Osborne *vs.* Bank of the United States,[1] the court decided, 6th, that the bank may *sue in the federal courts.*

§ 222. These several decisions gave validity to the charter and the acts of the United States Bank; and so far as its constitutionality could be established by judicial authority, it was so. The authorities upon this subject stand thus:—*Congress* passed acts in its favor in 1791, 1816, and 1832. On the other hand, in 1811, they rejected a bill for its recharter. Of the *executive*, Presidents Washington, Adams, Madison, and J. Q. Adams, approved of it; President Jackson alone disapproved. The *supreme judicial* tribunal of the Union has given a solemn decision in its favor. The *constitutionality* of a national bank is therefore settled, as far as it can be, by *decision*, *precedent*, and *authority*. The *expediency* of such an institution may at any time be questioned by the representatives of the people, and so, as a matter of *argument* or *theory*, may its constitutionality, simply because all things are open to discussion at the *ultimate tribunal* of *public opinion;* but the *existence* of the bank being once supposed, *nothing* can shake its *validity* while the decisions of the Supreme Court remain unimpaired, and the Constitution unviolated. In reference, however, to the decision of the Supreme Court in the case of McCullough against the State of Maryland, it may well be *doubted* whether the Constitution contains any

---

[1] 9 Wheaton, 733.

power to perform any acts which are merely *appropriate* and *adapted* to the *end*, as stated in the second proposition; for most assuredly an act *may* be *appropriate* and *adapted* which is not both *necessary* and *proper*. The constitutionality of the United States Bank was maintained, by Hamilton and others, upon the ground of its *necessity* to the *fiscal* operations of the *government*.

§ 223. Another *incidental power* claimed and exercised by the government is to create a *priority of payment* in their favor, in case of the death or insolvency of the debtor. Congress, by their acts of 1789, 1790, 1792, 1797, and 1799, gave this priority of payment over private creditors, in cases of insolvency, and the distribution of the estates of deceased debtors.[1] In the case of Fisher *vs.* Blight,[2] the power thus vested in the government by act of Congress was declared to be constitutional, and coming within the legitimate scope of *means* adapted to an *end* which is constitutional. The government must pay the debts of the Union, and therefore is vested with the *most eligible* means of doing it.

§ 224. The principle is, that the government of the United States are *preferred creditors* to citizens, or even to states; but no lien is created by this preference; a prior *bona-fide* conveyance is *valid*. The same principle came up and received a further exposition in several other cases.[3]

---

[1] 1 Kent's Comm., 230. [2] 2 Cranch, 358.
[3] 3 Cranch, 73; 5 Idem, 289; 8 Idem, 431; 2 Wheaton, 396.

§ 225. The *limits* of this priority are thus defined:

1. It exists in the case of the death of the debtor without sufficient assets.

2. In the case of bankruptcy, or legal insolvency, manifested by some act pursuant to law.

3. In case of the *voluntary assignment*, by the insolvent, of all his property to pay his debts.

4. In case of an *absent*, concealed, or absconding debtor, whose effects are attached by process of law. This prerogative of the United States must be strictly construed, for it is in derogation of the rights of creditors.

§ 226. The United States have likewise, by *implication*,[1] the right of suing in their own courts; and suits may be brought in the name of the United States, or of any artificial person, as the Postmaster-general, for their benefit.[2]

§ 227. Another exercise of implied power by the government is found in the acquisition of Louisiana and Florida by treaty. No provision is made in the Constitution for acquiring foreign territory; and even in the opinion of President Jefferson, there was no constitutional power to make the treaty for the acquisition of Louisiana. The President and Congress, however, approved the act, and the nation acquiesced.[3] This power is, however, an incident of sovereignty. The subsequent annexation of Texas and portions of Mexico, were made by no direct grant in the Constitution, but by the ultimate and reserved sovereignty of the

[1] 1 Kent's Comm., 233. [2] 3 Story's Comm., 155.

[3] 3 Story's Comm., 162; 4 Elliott's Debates 255.

nation; without which, such acquisitions cannot be defended on constitutional grounds.

§ 228. Another exercise of *implied* authority was the passage of the celebrated Alien and Sedition Laws.[1] The first gave the President the power to order out of the country such aliens as he should deem dangerous to the peace and safety of the country; and the second made it a public crime for persons to combine and conspire together, with intent to oppose any of the measures of the United States, or to write, print, or publish, or to disseminate any false, scandalous, and malicious writings against the government of the United States, Congress, or the President. These acts soon expired by their own limitations, and never received a judicial sanction. They excited general odium, and have not been revived.

§ 229. Section 9th. 1st clause. *The migration or importation of such persons as any of the states now existing shall think proper to admit, shall not be prohibited by the Congress prior to the year one thousand eight hundred and eight; but a tax or duty may be imposed on such importation, not exceeding ten dollars for each person.*

§ 230. The *persons* here spoken of were *slaves*, and the effect of this clause was to permit the slave-trade till 1808. After that time arrived, Congress prohibited it in every direction, and affixed to it the *penalties of piracy.*

---

[1] Alien and Sedition Acts, 1798.

§ 231. 2d clause. *The privilege of the writ of habeas corpus shall not be suspended, unless when in cases of rebellion or invasion the public safety may require it.*

§ 232. The term *habeas corpus* is a Latin phrase, signifying "You may have the body." The writ of *habeas corpus* is a judicial writ, *grantable by any court of record or judge thereof*, and commands the sheriff, or other officer named in it, to have the body, and *bring it before said judge, or court.* The object of the writ is, by bringing a person, confined *by any means whatever*, before a competent authority, to have his confinement, and the cause of it, investigated; and if it be not strictly legal, to discharge him.[1] The writ is grantable upon the application of *any person whomsoever*, upon behalf of the prisoner, and is the only mode by which a person illegally detained may at once obtain his liberty. The privilege of the writ of *habeas corpus* is, therefore, an invaluable privilege, and is a part of the essence of liberty inserted in the Constitution, where it can neither be mistaken nor evaded.

§ 233. Our writ of *habeas corpus* is derived from the English Statute of the 31st Charles II., which was passed in consequence of frequent invasions of the personal rights and liberties of the citizen during the reign of Charles I.

§ 234. The writ may be suspended in case of *rebellion* or *invasion ;* yet no suspension has ever yet taken place. An attempt to suspend it was made during the

---

[1] 1 Blackst. Comm.

administration of Mr. Jefferson, on the occasion of Burr's conspiracy; but it failed in the House of Representatives by a large majority.[1]

§ 235. 3d clause. *No bill of attainder, or ex post facto law shall be passed.*

The terms bill of attainder and ex post facto have already been defined.[2] The very definition of these explains the meaning of the clause in the Constitution. The former, by which judgment should be passed and punishment inflicted upon the citizen without trial, and the latter which makes an act criminal which was not criminal when committed, were obviously inconsistent with any thing like justice to, or liberty in, the citizen. They were, therefore, expressly prohibited.

§ 236. 4th clause. *No capitation or other direct tax shall be laid, unless in proportion to the census or enumeration hereinbefore directed to be taken.*

This clause is nearly the same with a part of the third clause of the 2d section, 1st article. The only difference is the insertion of the word *capitation*,—but this, by the following words, *or other direct tax*, is evidently included under the head of *direct taxes.* The meaning of both clauses then is, that *direct taxes*, as well as representation, should be in proportion to the *census* in each state,—as directed to be taken in the 2d section.

§ 237. 5th clause. *No tax or duty shall be laid on articles exported from any state. No preference shall*

[1] 1 Senate Journal, 1807; Journal of the House of Representatives, 1807.

[2] Definitions, 33 and 34.

be given by any regulation of commerce or revenue to the ports of one state over those of another; nor shall vessels bound to or from one state, be obliged to enter, clear, or pay duties in another.

These prohibitions explain themselves so clearly, as to require little exposition by commentary or authority. The first clause, preventing duties upon exported articles, is rendered necessary by the fact, that without it, the agriculture and commerce of some states might, at any time, be destroyed by such duties. Some states, as South Carolina and Alabama, derive their whole wealth from the exportation of particular articles, and others again, as Virginia, and North Carolina, and Maine, a great part of it: so that by means of such duties the government might at any time make the most odious distinctions among the states; nor would it derive any advantage to itself, for duties upon *exports* can at no time be advantageous, for the obvious reason that it is by such means only a nation is enabled to procure either the money or produce of other nations.

It is also forbidden to give any preference to the ports of one state over those of another, or to oblige vessels bound from one state to enter, clear, or pay duties in another. The reason of this is yet more clear than that of the other. If the reverse of this were true, and such preference was allowed, and such duties imposed on vessels, it is plain the states would be in the relation of foreign states to each other. There would be no reciprocity of interests between them, and the unity of the government would be destroyed.

§ 238. 6th clause. *No money shall be drawn from the treasury, but in consequence of appropriations made by law; and a regular statement and account of the receipt and expenditures of all public money shall be published from time to time.*

The object of this provision was,—

1st. To place the *public moneys* beyond the reach of the *executive:* however limited the powers of the executive in other respects, it is obvious that if he has *control of the purse*, he would be *unlimited* in the most essential attribute of power. It is, therefore, wisely provided, that the people, who alone bear the burdens of taxation, should, through their representatives, alone have the power of appropriating the *resulting revenue.* The administrations of General Washington and Mr. Jefferson were minutely strict in the observance of this injunction of the Constitution; but many instances might be cited since their time, in which money has been applied to objects different from those to which it had been specifically appropriated.

§ 239. 2d. The other part of this clause, requiring a strict account of receipts and expenditures, was made to insure fidelity and accuracy in the disbursement of public moneys. In the treasury department, as will be seen hereafter, various checks and balances, in respect to the transfer of money from the treasury, have been devised.

§ 240. 7th clause. *No title of nobility shall be granted by the United States, and no person holding any office of profit or trust under them shall, without the consent of Congress, accept of any present, emolument, office, or title of any kind whatever, from any king, prince, or foreign state.*

§ 241. The first clause, in reference to titles of nobility, is the constitutional barrier against those odious personal distinctions which arise from, and originate aristocracies in other countries.

The second clause, in reference to offices and titles from foreign powers, is made as a check against the corruption of the officers and citizens of this government, by the princes and ministers of foreign states.

§ 242. Section 10th. Clause 1st. *No state shall enter into any treaty, alliance, or confederation; grant letters of marque and reprisal; coin money; emit bills of credit; make any thing but gold and silver coin a tender in payment of debts; pass any bill of attainder, ex post facto law, or law impairing the obligation of contracts; or grant any title of nobility.*

§ 243. The power to enter into any treaty, alliance, or confederation, is one of the most important attributes of *national sovereignty:* when the states parted with it, they parted with one of those characteristics which made them *independent* as it respects each other. This should be borne in mind, as it will be seen in the end that they parted with them all, and thus divested themselves of all that *national sovereignty*, which in modern times is the sole foundation of the strange and fanciful theories put forth under the name of *state rights.*

This right to make separate treaties and alliances was yielded up by the *old articles of confederation;*

for it was perfectly plain and palpable that the states could not retain it and form one *united nation:* the latter was their object, and they yielded the former.

§ 244. Letters of marque and reprisal are a commission from the *sovereign authority* to a citizen or subject to make *reprisals* on the vessels or property of foreign nations who have injured the one granting them.[1] The right of issuing these is *prohibited* to the several states. It lies in the government of the Union. The reason of this also is obvious. Letters of marque[2] are merely introductions to war; and if one state had the right to issue them independent of the rest, all the others might immediately be involved in war by the instrumentality of that one. It will be remarked, that this right again is, by the definition, an attribute of *national sovereignty*, and is therefore taken from the states and vested in the government of the nation.

§ 245. The right of *coining* money is also a right[3] of *sovereignty*, and is vested in the general government. If the right of *coinage* was vested in the several states, then there would be no uniformity in the *standard of value*, and spurious coin might be circulated.

§ 246. The next prohibition is that against issuing "bills of credit." What is a bill of credit? A bill of credit[4] is defined to be *paper intended to circulate through the community for its ordinary purposes, as money, which paper is redeemable at a future day.*

§ 247. Is it necessary to constitute a bill of credit,

---

[1] Vattel, book II., chap. xviii., § 346.

[2] Vattel, book I., chap. x., §§ 106, 107.

[3] 3 Story's Comm., 819.

[4] 3 Story's Comm., 227.

that it should be made a legal tender? In the case of Craig *vs.* The State of Missouri,[1] the Supreme Court decided that it was *not necessary* that they should be made a legal tender in order to constitute them a bill of credit. In that case the state of Missouri made loans on certain *certificates*, issued by the auditor and treasurer of the state, of various denominations, and which were made receivable at the treasury in payment of taxes and debts, and by public officers in payment of their salaries. They bore interest, and were redeemable by the state. Such *certificates* were decided by the court to be bills of credit, and as such unconstitutional.

§ 248. The object of the prohibition was to prevent the flood of depreciated currency which had so embarrassed the states during and subsequent to the revolutionary war. It is plain that without this and the accompanying clauses in relation to coins and currency, there could be no fixed standard of value, and commerce and property would be constantly exposed to all the hazards of an uncertain and fluctuating currency.

§ 249. The states are also forbidden to make any thing but *gold* and *silver coin* a legal tender in payment of debts. If they could have made any thing else a good tender, there is no species of depreciated currency which might not be paid for debts; and the difficulties, dishonesty, and bankruptcies attendant upon such a state of things will be easily understood. Any thing

---

[1] 4 Peters' Supreme Court Reports, 410.

may be borne in civil society with more ease than that which interrupts the regular course of business, obstructs the due administration of justice, and prevents the just payment of debts. The emission of bills of credit, and the making any thing but coin a legal tender by the states, would produce all these mischiefs. During the Revolution,[1] and both subsequent and anterior to it, the resort to such means had reduced public credit to utter contempt, and ruined thousands of honest and industrious citizens. It was the recent *experience* of these evils, and the inconsistency of such powers in the states with the existence of a national government, which prompted the prohibitions we have just recited.

§250. It is prohibited to the states, as well as to the general government, to pass any *bills of attainder* or *ex post facto laws*. The reason is the same. The same injustice would be worked in either case. Such laws, at all times unjust and inexpedient, are peculiarly so in a country where the whole basis of the government is right and justice.

§251. The states cannot impair the *obligation of contracts*. This is one of the most important provisions of the Constitution, and has already occasioned much discussion, and been illustrated by several judicial decisions.

§252. The first inquiry is, what is a contract? *A contract is an agreement*[2] *to do or not to do a particular*

---

[1] Pitkin's Civil History, vol. ii., pp. 156, 157. [2] 2 Blackst. Comm., 443.

thing. It must be made between *two* or more persons.[1]

§ 253. Contracts may be either *executory* or *executed.*[2] An *executory contract* is one in which a party binds himself to do or not to do *something hereafter.*[3] Thus, if two men agree to exchange horses next week, or one of them agrees to do work to-morrow, and the other to pay money for it, these contracts are *executory*, because they are to be performed at a *future time.*

§ 254. But, a contract *executed* is one in which the act to be done is *performed at once.* As, if two men agree to exchange horses now, and do it on the spot, or one agrees to convey land, and makes and delivers the deed on the spot, such contracts are *executed*, because the act required to be done is done *at once.*

§ 255. A *grant* and a contract executed are the same thing.[4] A contract executed conveys a *thing in possession.* A contract executory conveys a *thing in action.*

§ 256. Contracts are also *express* or *implied.*[4] *Express contracts* are those of which the terms are *expressed* in the agreement; *implied* contracts are those which are necessarily inferred from the *nature* of the agreement. An agreement that I shall pay so much for an ox is an express contract. If a man work for me, for my benefit, reason, justice, and the law all imply a contract that I shall pay him for it. Both these

---

[1] 2 Blackst. Comm., 443; 3 Story's Comm., 241. [2] Idem.
[3] Wheaton, 197; 12 Idem, 256. [4] 2 Blackst. Comm., 443.

kinds of contracts are included in the general words of the Constitution.

§ 257. The Supreme Court have decided, that a contract and a *compact* are one and the same thing.[1]

§ 258. As the term contract in the Constitution is not limited, it signifies both contracts executed and executory. A *grant*, therefore, is such a contract as cannot be *impaired* by the states. Such was the decision in Fletcher *vs.* Peck.[2] There the state of Georgia had granted away certain lands to Peck, who had conveyed them to Fletcher for a valuable consideration; subsequent to which, the state of Georgia cancelled their grant to Peck. Fletcher sued on the covenant of *warrantee*, and the court held that the law cancelling the grant was unconstitutional, because *impairing a contract*, which had already vested in Fletcher a right to the land.

§ 259. The next inquiry is, what is *the obligation of contracts?* There are two kinds of obligations to contracts,—*moral* and *legal*. The obligation contemplated by the Constitution is a *legal* obligation;[3] it is one arising under *civil laws;* for a moral obligation cannot be *impaired* or enforced by *human laws.* The obligation, then, meant by the Constitution, must be one which arises either from the enactments of a state, or can be influenced by those enactments. If, then, a contract is, by the laws of the place where it is made, illegal and void, that contract has no *civil* obligation,

---

[1] 6 Cranch, 136. [2] Idem. [3] Ogden *vs.* Saunders, 12 Wheaton, 257.

and no action can arise upon it.[1] When it arises from civil laws, and is not by these laws illegal and void, then it is such an obligation as may be *impaired*, and consequently such a one as comes within the scope of the Constitution.

§ 260. The *obligation*, therefore, must be a *civil* one, and it must be *valid* according to the municipal law. It cannot then subsist *contrary* to the *positive* law. But may it exist *independently* of it? May it exist without a remedy? Thus, if two persons make a contract of a kind which, though by the laws of the state it is perfectly valid to make, yet by the laws of the state cannot be enforced, has that contract an obligation within the meaning of the Constitution? If it has, what is it? The only obligation which it would seem to have is a *moral one*. That undoubtedly it has. But a moral obligation, it is conceded on all hands, cannot be *impaired*, and consequently is not the obligation meant.

§ 261. On this point there is great diversity of opinion. It is stated on high authority[2] that the obligation may exist independently of positive law, and be perfect without a remedy. The examples given, however, do not appear to confirm the principle laid down. Thus it is said,[3] that a state may have taken away "imprisonment for debt, and the debtor may have no property; but still the *right* of the creditor remains, and he *may* enforce it against the future property of the debtor. So a debtor may die without leaving any known estate,

---

[1] 3 Story's Comm., 215. [2] Idem, 247. [3] Idem.

or without any known representative. In such cases we should not say that the right of the creditor was gone, but only there was nothing on which it could presently operate. But, suppose an administrator should be appointed, and property in contingency should fall in, the right might then be enforced to the extent of the existing means." These examples are cited by the learned commentator, to show that *right may exist without a remedy.* With due deference to an opinion which is at once authoritative and respected, it is thought that he has, in these examples, manifestly *confused* the *remedy* given by the law, with the *object* upon which that remedy acts. What is a *remedy* at law? We are told by an authority,[1] at least as high as the one above cited, that "the law consists of several parts, one *declaratory*, whereby the *rights* and *wrongs* are clearly classified and laid down; another *directory*, whereby the subject is instructed to observe these rights, and abstain from these wrongs; a third *remedial*, whereby a method is pointed out to recover his rights, or redress his wrongs."

§ 262. Here the *remedy* in law is defined to be the *method* whereby a man may recover his rights, or redress his wrongs. Now, in the example first cited above, of a debt, the *remedy*, or the *method* given by law is, first the *action of debt*, next the *judgment* upon that action, and lastly the *execution* under that judgment; now the person or property of the debtor con-

[1] 1 Blackst. Comm., 58, 54.

stitutes the *object* upon which that remedy acts: both may be *out of the reach* of the remedy, and yet the remedy exist, and be *perfect at law.* It is not perfect in its *consequences*, merely because other circumstances, *disconnected* from the *remedy*, have prevented that remedy from attaching to the object. The *remedy* in the example above stated attaches to the property; that property, by one of the conditions of human life, whether poverty or misfortune, does not exist. Here, then, the *right* to a remedy is perfect: the remedy itself, viz., *action*, *judgment*, and *execution*, is perfect; but the *object* upon which the remedy is to attach is out of reach. The case is the same in the second example, of an intestate dying without an estate or representative. The municipal laws of almost every civilized state either require that the Probate Court should appoint an administrator, or give power to the *creditor* to have one appointed. The administrator being appointed, the second example is precisely the same as the first: the administrator, as the representative of the intestate, is the debtor, and the right, the remedy, and the object the same as in the other case. The *remedy* here spoken of is the remedy *at law.* The circumstance of the existence of property or not, on which the remedy can attach, is one which constitutes *no part* of the remedy at law; for it is obviously one which no human law can regulate. If human intelligence could have devised a means by which the debtor should always have property to answer the demands of his creditor, it would be an act of wisdom which never would have been neglected. We may conclude, then, that if a right can exist without a remedy to enforce it, these are not examples of it. Are there any other examples, either real or imaginary, by which such a principle can be illustrated?

§ 263. The meaning of the term *obligation* always implies a *power to enforce it.* To *oblige* is to *compel.* According to Justice Blackstone,[1] the strict sense of obligation is such a constraint as *makes it impossible for a man to act otherwise.*

§ 264. Civil obligation, then, consists in the *remedial power of enforcement.* This seems to have been the opinion of several eminent judges in the celebrated case of Ogden *vs.* Saunders.[2] In that decision the judges gave their opinions *seriatim;* and in respect to the obligation of contracts, as well as several other points, were widely different in their judgments. These questions are, therefore, far from being settled, although the *decision upon the facts of that case* is doubtless permanent law.

§ 265. Justice Washington said that "the obligation of a contract is the *law which binds the parties to perform their agreement.*" While he admitted that the common law of nations, or the moral law, might form a part of the obligation of a contract, he insisted that this law is to be taken in strict subordination to the municipal law of the land where the contract is made, or is to be executed.

---

[1] 1 Blackst. Comm., 57.

[2] 12 Wheaton, 260.

§ 266. Justice Thompson said: "for it is *the law which creates the obligation*, and whenever, therefore, the lex loci provides for the dissolution of the contract in any prescribed mode, the parties are presumed to have acted subject to such contingency."

§ 267. Justice Trimble said: "It may be fairly concluded, that the obligation of the contract consists in the power and *efficacy* of the *law*, which applies to and enforces performance of a contract, or the payment of an equivalent for non-performance. The *obligation* does not inhere and subsist in the contract itself, *proprio vigore*, but in the law applicable to the contract. This is the sense, I think, in which the Constitution uses the term *obligation*."[1]

§ 268. Chief-justice Marshall then said:[2] "*Obligation* and *remedy* then are not identical. They originate at, and are derived from, different sources;—it would seem to follow that law might act on the remedy without acting on the obligation."

Enough of these *dicta* have been cited to show that while the majority of the court agreed in the decision which was made, the individual judges held very different opinions upon the main question, the obligation of the contracts.

§ 269. The next great question in respect to the impairing the obligation of contracts, arose in respect to the insolvent laws of the several states. The principal cases upon this point are those of Sturges *vs.* Crownin-

---

[1] 12 Wheaton, 318. [2] Idem, 850.

shield;[1] M'Millan *vs.* M'Niell,[2] and the case just cited, of Ogden *vs.* Saunders. The substance of these decisions has already been given in another place.[3]

§ 270. The next decision upon this subject was in regard to *grants.* In the case of Terrett *vs.* Taylor,[4] the Supreme Court decided, that a legislative grant, competently made, vested an *indefeasible and irrevocable title.* A state cannot revoke what it has once granted away; nor can the legislature repeal statutes creating private corporations, and divest the rights under them, without the consent or default of the corporators.

§ 271. One of the most important cases upon the subject is that of Dartmouth College *vs.* Woodward.[5] A charter was granted by the British crown in 1769 to the trustees of Dartmouth College, who acted under it, established the college, and acquired property. The legislature of New Hampshire made material alterations in the charter, transferred the government of the college to the government of the state, and made the will of the donors subservient to their own.[6] The Supreme Court decided that such a *charter* was a *contract* within the meaning of the Constitution; that the college was a private institution, not liable to the control of the legislature; and that, therefore, the act of the legislature was an act impairing the obligation of contracts, and void. The court said, that charters of an eleemosynary kind, for the benefit of religion, educa-

[1] 4 Wheaton, 122. [2] 2 Idem, 209. [3] Page 125. [4] 9 Cranch, 43.
[5] 4 Wheaton, 518. [6] 1 Kent's Comm., 390.

tion, or charity, administered by trustees, was within the purview of the Constitution; and that rights acquired under them were vested and protected by it. No doubt such is the clear dictate of reason; and such institutions, if any, ought to be protected from the ruthless hands that are too often laid upon them.

§ 272. As the prohibition in relation to *ex post facto* laws is confined to retrospective *criminal* laws,—and as there is a class of *retrospective* laws which are not criminal,—this last class is restricted only by the prohibition against the impairing the *obligation* of contracts, and there is therefore a large class of retrospective laws which it is constitutional for the states to pass. Thus, a law abolishing imprisonment for debt, as well to *past* as to future contracts, may be constitutionally passed by the state legislatures.[1] All retrospective laws are, however, unjust and impolitic; for they destroy the relation of circumstances under which the parties upon whom the law acts stood at the time they made the contract, or performed the act in question.

The last prohibition of this clause is, that the state shall grant no *title of nobility*. The reason of this is the same as that in regard to the national government: it was an exclusion of every thing like nobility and aristocracy.

§ 273. Under the 1st clause of the 10th section of the 1st article, the Supreme Court has given several recent

---

[1] 2 Peters' Supreme Court Rep., 870.

decisions, which will throw light on the terms used. "Bills of credit, notwithstanding the prohibition in the Constitution, have repeatedly been issued by the states, in forms which it was supposed would *evade* that prohibition. In the case of Missouri, they were in the form of *certificates*, made receivable at the treasury in payment of taxes. Such certificates were bills of credit. In the case of the *Bank of the Commonwealth* (Ky.),[1] the Supreme Court decided, that to constitute a "bill of credit" it must be *issued* by a state, involve the *faith* of the state, and be designed to circulate, as money, *on the credit of the state.* The Bank of the Commonwealth was a purely state bank. But it had some capital assigned it; and its notes made *no promise on the part of the state*, and were therefore *not* "bills of credit."

§ 274. The prohibition upon the states against the "impairing the obligation of contracts," has, as we have seen, led to a great amount of litigation, and to numerous elaborate decisions of the Supreme Court. These decisions have, in some instances, given a construction to the phrase "*impairing* the obligation of contracts" which would not be arrived at by other than judicial minds, but which seem clear to legal reason. The first of these was, that a *grant* was a contract. This principle carried with it a long train of consequences which could not at first have been

---

1 Briscoe *vs.* The Bank of the Commonwealth of Kentucky, 12 Curtis, 418.

foreseen. The legislatures of the several states are in the constant habit of *granting* to companies and individuals powers and privileges which they afterward wish to withdraw. Among this class of cases are bank charters, or banking laws.

A banking law is not merely *declaratory of intention*, but amounts to a contract.[1] If a *grant* be a contract, a banking law must be, for it prescribes the *conditions* which, being accepted, constitute a contract between the state and the bank.

A legislature of a state, not restrained by its own constitution, may make a contract in the charter of a bank corporation, that no more than a certain rate of taxes shall be levied; and a subsequent legislature has no power to pass an act impairing that obligation.[2]

On the same principle, when the legislature accepts a *bonus*, in consideration of a bank corporation, and agrees not to impose any further tax or burden on the corporation, a tax upon the *stockholders* is a violation of the contract, and illegal.[3] We have said that the *legal remedy* was a part of the *obligation* of a contract. To take away that remedy or diminish it is, therefore, to *impair* the obligation of a contract. When a mortgage contained a *power to sell*, and thereby pay the debt, and was valid by the state laws, and a *subsequent* law gave the debtor *twelve months'* time, and

---

[1] State Bank of Ohio *vs.* Knoop, 21 Curtis, 190. [2] Idem.
[3] Gordon *vs.* Appeal of Tax Court, 15 Curtis, 333.

prohibited a sale under *two-thirds* the value: this law impaired the obligation of contracts, and was unconstitutional.[1]

On the dissolution of a corporation, its effects are a trust fund for the benefit of its creditors, which they may follow into the hands of others. A state law depriving the creditors of those rights, impairs the obligation of contracts, and is void. A law which deprives the creditors of a corporation of their legal remedy, is void.[2] So, a law prohibiting a trial by jury in cases arising upon contract, is void.[3]

On the other hand, an *appointment* to office is *not* a contract, which may be impaired by repealing the law creating it, and removing the officer.[4]

§ 275. The Supreme Court has also reviewed many cases, involving the validity of *retrospective* laws. An *ex-post-facto* law prohibited to the states, being a retrospective *criminal* law only, it follows that other retrospective laws, *not* impairing the obligation of contracts, may be valid. A state law may be retrospective, and *divest* "vested rights," and yet not violate the Constitution of the United States.[5] Rights may be *vested*, and yet not matter of contract.

A retrospective law enabling banking corporations to sue in their own names, on notes payable to the cashier, does not impair the obligation of contracts.[6]

---

[1] Bronson *vs.* Kinzie, 14 Curtis, 628. [2] Curran *vs.* Arkansas, 20 Id., 524. [3] Webster *vs.* Reed, 18 Id., 678. [4] Butler *vs.* Pennsylvania, 18 Id., 435. [5] Charles River Bridge *vs.* Warren Bridge, 12 Id., 496. [6] Crawford *vs* Branch Bank of Mobile, 17 Id., 120.

An act of a state, *making valid* deeds of land (void from some defect), though *retroactive*, does not impair the obligation of contracts,—is not *ex post facto*, and therefore not repugnant to the Constitution of the United States.[1]

The right to *imprison* a debtor, constitutes no part of a contract; and a discharge therefrom does not impair its obligation.[2]

§ 276. Clause 2d. *No state shall, without the consent of Congress, lay any imposts or duties on imports or exports, except what may be absolutely necessary for executing its inspection laws; and the net produce of all duties and imposts laid by any state on imports and exports, shall be for the use of the Treasury of the United States; and all such laws shall be subject to the revision and control of the Congress. No state shall, without the consent of Congress, lay any duty on tonnage, keep troops or ships of war in time of peace, enter into any agreement or compact with another state or with a foreign power, or engage in war unless actually invaded, or in such imminent danger as will not admit of delay.*

§ 277. The Constitution had already restricted Congress in the power to lay taxes, by requiring that *direct taxes* should be in proportion to the *census*, and *indirect* taxes *uniform*; that no duties should be laid on exports, and no preference given to the commerce of one state over another. If such restrictions were found necessary for the general government, much more were

---

[1] Watson *vs.* Mercer, 11 Curtis, 38. [2] Beers *vs.* Stoughton, 11 Id., 376.

they for the several states, who, by local regulations, were at all times liable to collision, and might destroy the commerce of each other. In fact, the *revenue* from commerce is another *attribute of national sovereignty*, and could safely be trusted only to that body in whom the national sovereignty resided, and to whom was intrusted the *national defence* and the *general welfare.* Sufficient power over internal commerce is left to the states, with *the consent of Congress*, to execute their *inspection laws*,—all the rest is taken away.

§278. Inspection laws are not strictly regulations of *commerce*, though they may have an influence upon it.[1] The object of inspection laws is to improve the *quality* of articles produced in the country, and fit them for use and exportation.

§279. In the year 1821, the state of Maryland enacted, that all importers of foreign articles, commodities, &c., by bale, package, &c., and those persons selling the same at wholesale by bale, package, &c., shall, before they are authorized to sell, &c., take out a *license*, for which they shall pay *fifty dollars*, &c. This act was resisted as a violation of the Constitution, and the Supreme Court decided that *it was unconstitutional.* The ground of the decision was, that although an import duty is generally secured before the goods are landed, yet a tax is not the less an *impost*, though levied on them after they were landed; that *a duty on imports is not merely a duty on the act of importation*,

---

[1] 3 Story's Comm., 472.

but is *a duty on the thing imported.*[1] Nor does it make any difference whether the duty was imposed by way of license upon the occupation, or as a direct duty on the article.

§280. It has already been seen that a state has no power to tax the Bank of the United States, because they have no power to restrain the constitutional *means* given to the government to execute constitutional ends.

§281. In the same manner it has been decided that a state has no power to tax stocks issued for loans to the United States.[2]

§282. *Tonnage duties* are taxes laid on vessels at so much *per ton.* After what has been said upon the propriety of imposts on imports and exports by the states, the reason for prohibiting a duty on tonnage will be evident. If the states could have laid duties on tonnage, they could have effected, indirectly, all the mischiefs flowing from a power in the states to tax imports and exports.

§283. The states shall not keep troops or ships of war in time of peace: this again is founded on the same principles as the other prohibitions relative to the exercise of national sovereignty; to keep troops, make war, &c., are attributes of *national sovereignty,* which could not exist at once in both the general and state governments, without constituting them *separate nations,*—a result which it was the very object of the

---

[1] 12 Wheaton's Rep., 419.

[2] Warton *vs.* The City Council of Charleston, 2 Peters' R., 449.

Constitution to prevent. The prohibition does not extend to a *municipal guard*, such as those kept to guard penitentiaries and arsenals; for these are not troops, but merely ministers of the civil law.

§ 284. The power to make treaties, alliances, and confederations had, in another place, been taken from the states; to this prohibition is here superadded that of making compacts and agreements *with another state or with a foreign power*, without the *consent of Congress*. It may be asked what compacts and agreements are here meant? As alliances, treaties, &c., had before been mentioned, this clause refers[1] to "private rights of sovereignty; such as questions of boundary, interest in land situated in the territory of each other, and other internal regulations for the mutual comfort and convenience of states bordering on each other." The compact between Virginia and Kentucky is of this class.

§ 285. No state can control the exercise of any authority under the general government.[2]

§ 286. The state courts cannot annul the judgments, or determine the extent of the jurisdiction, of the courts of the Union.[3]

§ 287. No state tribunal can interfere with seizures of property made by revenue officers under the laws of the United States.[4]

§ 288. No state can issue a *mandamus* to an officer

---

1 3 Story's Comm., 272.

2 1 Kent's Comm., 382.

3 5 Cranch, 115.

4 2 Wheaton, 1.

of the United States. The official conduct of an officer of the government of the United States can only be controlled by the power that created him.[1]

§ 289. State laws, as, for example, statutes of limitation, insolvent laws, &c., have no operation upon the rights or contracts of the United States.[2]

Article II.

OF THE EXECUTIVE.

§ 290. Section 1st. Clause 1st. *The Executive power shall be vested in a President of the United States of America. He shall hold his office during a term of four years, and, together with the Vice President, chosen for the same time, be elected as follows:*

§ 291. The chief points laid down in this clause are, 1st. The *unity* of the executive; 2d. That he shall be *elected;* 3d. He shall hold his office for a *limited time;* and, 4th. That he be styled *President.*

1st. As to the *unity* of the executive, common sense, as well as the agreement of the best writers,[3] unite in the opinion, that the office which is entirely *ministerial*,—and in our government the executive is so,—is better filled by one head than by several. History has in all instances condemned the vesting executive power in the hands of a council, and whenever the

---

[1] 6 Wheaton, 598. [2] 8 Idem, 258.

[3] Montesquieu's Spirit of Laws, book II., chap. 6; De Lolme on Constitution of England; 1 Kent's Comm., 253, 255; 3 Story's Comm., 282.

experiment has been tried among the states, it has proved disastrous.

2d. The next principle laid down is, that the executive shall be *elective;* and this is the distinguishing characteristic of our government from that of England, France, and other governments of Europe, where some portion of constitutional liberty is enjoyed. It is not the power possessed by the executive so much as it is the *authority* whence, and the *mode* in which, it is derived, that constitutes the difference between these governments and ours. The *hereditary* and *perpetual* principles which prevail in all the governments of Europe, forever destroy all *accountability* on the part of the executive to the people; hence the English maxim, "The king can do no wrong." He is, by their constitution, placed above *inquiry* and *accountability.* In this country, however, there is accountability in all the departments of the government. The executive is *elective*, and his office of limited duration; so that if he err or offend, he may soon be held amenable at the bar of public opinion.

3d. The office is *limited.*—This principle, like that of election, is necessary to give a full and perfect control of the public opinion over the executive, and make it responsible.

4th. The style of *President* is very appropriate to the office of one whose duty it is to *preside* over the administration of public affairs.

Of the Vice President we shall speak hereafter.

§ 292. Clause 2d. *Each state shall appoint, in such*

a manner as the legislature thereof may direct, a number of electors equal to the whole number of senators and representatives to which the state may be entitled in the Congress; but no senator or representative, or person holding an office of trust or profit under the United States, shall be appointed an elector.

§ 293. The electors are to be appointed in the *manner* which the legislatnre shall direct. In the different states, different modes of electing the electors have prevailed. In one state, South Carolina, they are elected by the legislature itself; but generally they are elected by general ticket. The district system has been found to fritter away the power of the state, and election by the legislatnre seemed to take it away from the people.

The number of electors a state is entitled to, is equal to the whole number of senators and representatives; thus, Ohio has twenty-one representatives and two senators; consequently she is entitled to twenty-three electors.

No qualification is required of an elector, except he shall *not* hold an office of profit or trust under the government of the United States.

§ 294. The next clause in the Constitution has been abrogated by an amendment, passed by the constitutional number of states in 1801, which we shall presently recite.

That clause of the Constitution required that the electors should vote for *two persons*, without designating either of them, for President or Vice President. That the person having the greatest number of votes, if that be a majority of the electors, shall be President; and if there be more than one who has such a majority, and have also an *equal number* of votes, then the House of Representatives shall immediately choose by ballot one of them to be President; but if no one has the majority, then from the *five highest* the House shall choose the President. Each state in the House shall have *one vote.* After the choice of President, the person having the highest number of votes shall be Vice President; and if two have an equal number of votes, the Senate shall choose between them.

§ 295. As in the mode here pointed out, there was no distinction made between President and Vice President, it follows that, in party conflicts, where the whole party support one ticket, it must necessarily happen, that unless a vote be dropped, two persons would have an equal number of votes, and consequently the election devolve upon the House of Representatives. This difficulty actually occurred at the election of 1801, at which *Jefferson* and *Burr* received the same number of votes. The House of Representatives, being divided by violent party feelings, protracted the election through thirty-six ballotings, and at last made the election only in consequence of the danger of vacating the executive office. The result of that canvass gave rise to an amendment of the Constitution prescribing the present mode of election.

The following is the amendment:

§ 296. 12th Amendment to the Constitution. *The electors shall meet in their respective states, and vote by ballot for President and Vice President, one of whom at least shall not be an inhabitant of the same state with themselves;* they shall name in their ballots the person voted for as President, and in distinct ballots, the person voted for as Vice President; and they shall make distinct lists of all persons voted for as President, and of all persons voted for as Vice President, and of the number of votes for each, which lists they shall sign and certify, and transmit, sealed, to the seat of the government of the United States, directed to the president of the Senate; the president of the Senate shall, in the presence of the Senate and the House of Representatives, open all the certificates, and the votes shall then be counted; the person having the greatest number of votes for President shall be the President, if such number be a majority of the whole number of electors appointed: and if no person have such a majority, then from the persons having the highest numbers, not exceeding three, on the list of those voted for as President, the House of Representatives shall choose immediately, by ballot, the President. But in choosing the President, the votes shall be taken by states, the representation from each state having one vote; a quorum for this purpose shall consist of a member or members from two-thirds of the states, and a majority of all the states shall be necessary to a choice. And if the House of Representatives shall not choose a President whenever the right of choice shall devolve upon them, before the fourth day of March next following, then the Vice President shall act as President, as in case of the death or other constitutional disability of the President.

§ 297. The person having the greatest number of votes as Vice President, shall be the Vice President, if such a number be a majority of the whole number of electors appointed; and if no person have a majority, then from the two highest numbers on the list the Senate shall choose the Vice President: a quorum for that purpose shall consist of two-thirds of the whole number of senators, and a majority of the whole number shall be necessary to a choice.

§ 298. But no person constitutionally ineligible to the office of President, shall be eligible to that of Vice President of the United States.

§ 299. By this arrangement, the competitors for the vice presidency were no longer candidates likewise for the presidency; different persons are to be distinctly voted for as candidates for each office. This is said to diminish the dignity of the office of Vice President; but it seems to be absolutely necessary, to destroy the very confusion of persons and offices which occurred before.

The Senate are at liberty now to choose the Vice President, immediately after counting the votes, which before they could not have done without a choice of President. This is certainly an improvement.

§ 300. The mode of choosing the President does not yet seem to be perfect. A discussion might arise, on opening the certificates, as to the competency of the electors, the authority of the votes, &c., for which the Constitution has made no provision.[1]

An instance of *defect* is put in the case in which an *equality* of votes should be given for more persons than the number from which the choice is to be made.[2]

§ 301. 3d clause. *The Congress may determine the time of choosing the electors, and the day on which they shall give their votes; which day shall be the same throughout the United States.*

The reason of this clause is obvious. Were the time of giving the votes different in different states, there would be the greatest possible room for intrigue among the electors, and as their body is small, some of them might be influenced by undue means.

The power of determining the time of choosing the electors is also given to Congress. They have not, however, so exercised it as to appoint the same time. In 1792, they enacted that the states should choose their electors within thirty-four days of the first Wednesday in December. The consequence is, that within that time the elections are still made at *different periods.* It would seem that, to prevent all possibility of improper influence over the people, the elections should all have been held on the same day. As it is, those which are held last must be more or less influenced by those which are held first, upon the principle of a common desire in human nature to be on the strong side.

§ 302. 4th clause. *No person, except a natural-born*

---

[1] 3 Story's Comm., 327. [2] Idem.

citizen, or a citizen of the United States at the time of the adoption of the Constitution, shall be eligible to the office of President; neither shall any person be eligible to that office who shall not have attained to the age of thirty-five years, and been fourteen years a resident within the United States.

That the chief executive officer should be a citizen of the United States, and a native, is unquestionable. The age of *thirty-five is young enough.* The Presidents elected have all been more than that; most of them between sixty and seventy. Indeed, there will always be enough of the fire of human passions infused into the executive by partisans, without the aid of the warmth and ambition of youth.

§ 303. By *residence* in the United States is not meant an absolute *inhabitancy* in the United States during the whole period, but such an inhabitancy as constitutes *a permanent domicile.* Any other construction would take away the citizenship of any public *officer resident abroad* in pursuance of his duty.

§ 304. 5th clause. *In case of the removal of the President from office, or of his death, resignation, or inability to discharge the powers and duties of said office, the same shall devolve on the Vice President; and the Congress may by law provide for the case of removal, death, resignation, or inability, both of the President and Vice President, declaring what officer shall then act as President, and such officer shall act accordingly, until the disability be removed, or a President shall be elected.*

Congress, on this head, have provided, that in case of the removal, death, or resignation, or inability of the President and Vice President, the president pro. tem. of the Senate, and in case there shall be no such president of the Senate, then the speaker of the House of Representatives for the time being, shall act as President, until the disability be removed or the vacancy filled.

§ 305. The case of a vacancy in the offices of President and Vice President, by reason of *non-election*, at the proper period, is not provided for in the Constitution. Congress have declared that in case of such an event, there shall immediately be held a new election. Whether this be constitutional or not is unsettled.

§ 306. 6th clause. *The President shall, at stated times, receive for his services a compensation which shall neither be increased nor diminished during the period for which he shall have been elected; and he shall not receive within that period any other emolument from the United States or any of them.*

The object of this provision is plain enough; it would not be proper to allow either the general or state governments an opportunity, by increasing or diminishing the salary of the executive to play upon its wants or its avarice. Congress have permanently fixed the salary of the President at twenty-five thousand dollars, and that of the Vice President at five thousand dollars.

§ 307. 7th clause. *Before he enter on the execution of his office, he shall take the following oath or affirmation: I do solemnly swear (or affirm), that I will faith-*

fully execute the office of President of the United States, and will, to the best of my ability, preserve, protect, and defend the Constitution of the United States.

The solemnities of an oath seem to be proper and necessary to all responsible offices, and peculiarly so to that great and sacred one, the chief magistracy of a great republic.

§ 308. SECTION 2d. Clause 1st. *The President shall be commander-in-chief of the army and navy of the United States, and of the militia of the several states, when called into the actual service of the United States, he may require the opinion in writing of the principal officer in each of the executive departments, upon any subject relating to the duties of their respective offices; and he shall have power to grant reprieves and pardons for offences against the United States, except in cases of impeachment.*

The power to command the army and navy, militia, and entire military armament, flows necessarily from the nature[1] of an *executive.* It is made the duty of the executive to enforce the laws, preserve order, and repel invasions,—duties which could not be performed without the command of requisite force.

§ 309. The power of the President to *delegate* his authority to another officer was disputed during the last war.[2] The exception, however, seems untenable, from the reason that, if no one but the President in person can command them, then the president can only

[1] 1 Kent's Comm., 264.

[2] 8 Mass. Rep., 548.

control one detachment in *one place*,—a result evidently contrary to the intention of the Constitution. During the administration of Washington, the governor of Virginia commanded several detachments from different states under the appointment of the President, without dispute.[1] The power to *require opinions in writing from the heads of departments* is the mere expression of a power which was necessarily incident to the organization of the executive.

§ 310. The power to grant *reprieves* and *pardons* is one which requires to be, and is exercised. It has been supposed by some that a perfect criminal code requires no such power; but there is no *perfect* criminal code. There is no such administration of human justice, that, after the conviction of the prisoner, it shall always be improper and unjust to pardon him. The only proper depository of such a power is the executive. The judiciary cannot pardon without first supposing itself wrong in its own decisions; nor can the legislature without relaxing the law. He, however, whose only duty it is to execute the laws, which others have made and adjudged, may very consistently be allowed to exercise a discretion in punishment.

§ 311. 2d clause. *He shall have power, by and with the advice and consent of the Senate, to make treaties, provided two-thirds of the senators present concur: and he shall nominate, and by and with the consent and advice of the Senate, shall appoint ambassadors, other*

---

[1] Marshall's Washington, vol. v., p. 580.

public ministers, and consuls, judges of the Supreme Court, and all other officers of the United States, whose appointments are not herein otherwise provided for, and which shall be established by law; but the Congress may, by law, vest the appointment of such inferior officers as they think proper, in the President alone, in the courts of law, or in the heads of departments.

Some very important political questions have arisen out of this provision, and agitated the minds of eminent statesmen, as well as the councils of the country.

§ 312. In the year 1796, a treaty was made[1] by Mr. Jay with Great Britain, containing some stipulations very offensive to the House of Representatives. The treaty was ratified by the President and Senate, but required a law to carry it into effect. On that occasion, after much debate, the House of Representatives declared by a vote of sixty-two to thirty-seven, that they had the right to withhold their assent to the *validity* of a treaty, and might, at their pleasure, withhold a law to carry it into effect. This doctrine was denied by President Washington, and the exclusive power of the President and Senate affirmed. In their final decision upon the treaty, the House deemed it expedient, by a vote of fifty-one to forty-eight, to execute the treaty, but reserved to themselves the rights they claimed.

In 1816, the same question occurred, and the House then decided that the *sole power* over treaties rested with the Senate and President.[2]

---

[1] Marshall's Washington, v., p. 650.

[2] 4 Elliott's Debates, 250, 275.

§ 313. The predominance of opinion now is, that the power to make treaties, &c., is vested only in the executive and two-thirds of the Senate. The great reason is, that the Constitution has made treaties, as well as laws, the *supreme law* of the land, and as such has made them, when ratified, a binding *contract with other nations.*

§ 314. The next power conferred on the President, with the advice and consent of the Senate, is the *appointment* of ambassadors, ministers, consuls, and other public officers. This power is necessary to, and a part of, the executive power; for the executive duties have to be performed by the officers, and if they are not appointed by, and not responsible to, the executive, he cannot be accountable for the performance of those duties.[1]

§ 315. As the Constitution gave power "by and with the advice and consent of the Senate" to make appointments, but said nothing about removals, it early became a question whether the power of *removal* was vested in the President *alone*, or in the President and Senate *jointly*. In the year 1789, the question came before Congress, on a motion to strike out of the act creating a secretary for foreign affairs, a clause vesting the President with the power of removal. After a long and animated debate, the House decided by a vote of thirty-four to twenty not to strike out the clause,—thus affirming the power of the President. In this debate,

---

[1] 4 Elliott's Debates, 250, 275.

it was expressly declared, that the decision was intended to be permanent, and act as an exposition of the Constitution; as such it has remained, and the power of the President to remove was never questioned till recently. In favor of the power were Messrs. Madison, Ames, Boudinot, and Baldwin; against it, Messrs. Sherman, Gerry, Smith, and Jackson, of Georgia.

§ 316. A learned commentator[1] has recently expressed *surprise*, that this power of removal should so long remain in the President's hands without question, and intimates that it may be liable to abuses, and is at best of questionable constitutionality. To this it may be answered, that the decision of this question was one of the most solemn ever made by Congress, and, therefore entitled to high respect. As to the question itself, any other decision than that made, may at once be reduced to an *absurdity*. Thus, suppose the power is vested in the President with the advice and consent of the Senate; the President wishes to remove an officer, and communicates his wish to the Senate: that body calls for the reason; the President gives it, and the officer, through the mouth of some senator, replies: the President is then reduced to the level of an accuser, or a defendant, in respect to one of his own officers, before a *collateral* branch of the government, which assumes to decide between them, and be superior to both! And suppose the Senate does not consent to

---

[1] 3 Story's Comm., 395, 396.

his removal,—the officer retains his place after he has become obnoxious to his superior, and it may be, obtains impunity for his offences. Is this consistent with either the dignity or the responsibility of the executive? It is supposed by some very judicious persons, that an officer is entitled to his place *during good behavior*, and that he acquires something like an *estate* in his office. But no principle like this is recognized in the Constitution. On the contrary, every thing there is made *directly* or *indirectly elective*, and consequently nothing is placed on a more permanent footing than *public opinion*. When that changes, minor things must change with it.

§ 317. Such *inferior offices* as they may think proper, Congress may vest in the President alone, in the courts of law, or in the heads of departments. A learned commentator[1] supposes, in consequence of this clause, that Congress may require the consent of the Senate to such appointments: now this is not at all obvious; for the Constitution, after giving the appointment of *superior* officers to the President and Senate, may give the appointment of *inferiors* to whom? to this same President and Senate? No, but to the President *alone*, *the courts* of *law*, or the *heads* of *departments*. After this *express* designation of these persons, it is not in the competency of Congress to confer the appointment on others.

§ 318. It is decided, in reference to the power of

---

[1] 3 Story's Comm., 397.

appointments, that the Supreme Court cannot issue a mandamus to compel the delivery of a commission to an officer after it is made out. This was so decided in a case[1] in which the commission had been made out and deposited in the secretary of state's office, during the administration of Mr. Adams, and on the accession of Mr. Jefferson he withheld it,—deeming[2] that *delivery* was necessary to its perfection, and being himself unwilling to appoint the man. The case went off for want of *original* jurisdiction, but the court expressed the opinion, that the withholding the commission was *a violation of a legal right.*

§ 319. 3d clause. *The President shall have power to fill up all vacancies that may happen during the recess of the Senate, by granting commissions which shall expire at the end of their next session.*

The appointments thus made expire at the end of the next term of the Senate by the constitutional *limitation.* Suppose the President should fill a vacancy during the recess of the Senate, and should then nominate this officer to the Senate, and the Senate should reject him; and the President should, on the first day of the next recess, *appoint him again* to fill the vacancy, may he not in this manner perpetuate an appointment without the consent of the Senate? Certainly this cannot be the intention of the Constitution, for it would defeat the co-ordinate power of appointment which it has vested in the Senate. Yet such a prac-

---

[1] 1 Cranch, 137. [2] Jefferson's Correspondence, vol. iv.

tice[1] has in some instances recently obtained. Where is the remedy? Nobody is vested with power to annul the appointment; but it can be effectually restrained by withholding the *appropriations*. Here, then, is an instance of the signal virtue of powers, effective and restraining, vested directly in the representatives of the people.

§ 320. Does the power to fill up *vacancies* give the President authority to *appoint* and *commission* ambassadors during the *recess* of the Senate? In this manner President Madison appointed the commissioners to negotiate the Treaty of Ghent. But this is not a *vacancy*, neither does it *happen*, and the Senate held accordingly, in 1822, and decided, that the President could not create the office of minister during the recess of the Senate without the consent of the Senate.

§ 321. Section 3d. *He shall, from time to time give the Congress information of the state of the Union, and recommend to their consideration such measures as he shall judge necessary and expedient; he may, on extraordinary occasions, convene both Houses, or either of them, and in case of disagreement between them with respect to the time of adjournment, he may adjourn them to such time as he may think proper; he shall receive ambassadors, and other public ministers; he shall take care that the laws be faithfully executed; and shall commission all the officers of the United States.*

---

[1] See the Journals of the Senate, 1830, 1831, 1832, 1838; cases of Gwynn and Gardner.

§ 322. The President, in conformity with the first part of this section, lays before Congress, at the first day of their session, a *message*, in which is exhibited the operations of the government during the past year, and which is accompanied with reports from the chief officers of government, illustrating the condition and prospects of each department of the government. In addition to which the President gives his opinion upon all the measures which, in his opinion, ought to be acted upon. During the administration of Presidents Washington and Adams, the President met Congress in person, and delivered oral speeches, to which answers were returned, similar to the mode still adopted by the constitutional governments of Europe. President Jefferson, however, abolished that custom, and ever since the message has been sent to Congress, and no answer returned. The President communicates to Congress all the new circumstances, views, or information which may from time to time occur; and Congress, by calls upon the different departments, obtain all the documentary facts which they may desire.

§ 323. The power to call an extraordinary session of Congress may become absolutely necessary to the public safety. There have been five extraordinary sessions called: one in 1797, by President Adams, on the occasion of the difficulties with France; another in 1809, by President Madison; another in 1813, by the same; one by Mr. Van Buren, in 1837; and one by Gen. Harrison, in 1841.

§ 324. The President has a general authority to

execute the laws; and in the exercise of his political duties, independent of the specific limitations imposed by the law and the Constitution, he is subject to no control, but is amenable only to his conscience and his country.

§ 325. As incident to the power of *receiving*[1] ambassadors, the President has the power to *reject* and *dismiss*[2] them.

§ 326. Incident to the executive functions is the power to perform them without let or hindrance.[3]

§ 327. Section 4th. *The President, Vice President, and all civil officers of the United States, shall be removed from office on impeachment for, and conviction of treason, bribery, or other high crimes and misdemeanors.*

In what mode this impeachment is to be made and tried, we have seen elsewhere. *All officers* are liable to this impeachment for offences, although there is no prohibition against other kinds of removal.

Article III.

JUDICIARY.

§ 328. Section 1st. *The judicial power of the United States shall be vested in one Supreme Court, and in such inferior courts as the Congress may from time to time ordain and establish. The judges, both of the Supreme and inferior courts, shall hold their*

---

[1] Federalist, 69.

[2] Case of Genet, 5 Marshall, 443.

[3] 3 Story's Comm., 419.

offices during good behavior, and shall, at stated times, receive for their services a compensation which shall not be diminished during their continuance in office.

§ 329. The Supreme Court is *instituted* by the *Constitution*, but receives its *organization* from Congress.[1] The Constitution left the number of the judges, the mode of its proceeding, and the character of its officers, to be subsequently determined by the legislature. By successive acts,[2] Congress have organized the Supreme Court by creating a chief-justice and eight associate justices, and five of whom make a quorum. It holds one annual term at the seat of government, and though five judges are necessary for general business, yet any one of them may make all the necessary orders preparatory to trial, and one judge attends annually at the city of Washington for that purpose.[3]

§ 330. The inferior courts organized by Congress are the Circuit and the District Courts.[4] The Circuit Court is composed of one Judge of the Supreme Court and the District Judge, except when the District Judge is interested, when it may be held by the Circuit Judge. The number of Circuits is equal to the number of Supreme Judges, and are composed of two or three districts generally, but some of the western states, as Indiana, Illinois, Missouri, &c., have no Circuit Courts.

§ 331. Another court, inferior to the Supreme Court, is the District Court.[5] This is composed of a single judge, who holds annually four terms, and special courts

---

[1] 1 Kent's Comm., 279.
[2] Acts of April, 1802; Feb., 1807.
[3] There are now *nine* judges.
[4] Kent's Comm., 282.
[5] Idem, 283.

at his discretion. The districts are composed generally of a single state, but sometimes of a part of a state, as in New York and Pennsylvania.

The judges hold their offices *during good behavior.* Any other provision than this would place them at the mercy of the other branches of the government. It is plain that the members of distinct branches of the government must be wholly independent of the other branches, or the whole would soon become mixed up into one absorbing power. In the state of New York, sixty is the age at which a judge's office expires, and in Connecticut, seventy. These were both, however, provisions made to answer a temporary and party purpose. They are as anomalous in jurisprudence as they are contrary to the maxims derived from uniform experience. Youth for energy, and age for judgment, are rules everywhere illustrated in human life. The ablest judges that ever adorned England and America, Mansfield and Marshall, gave their best decisions after the age of seventy.

§ 332. Their compensation shall *not be diminished* while in office. This is obviously necessary. Life depends upon sustenance, and to take from the judges their salaries would drive them from office.

§ 333. SECTION 2d. Clause 1st. *The judicial power shall extend to all cases in law and equity arising under this Constitution, the laws of the United States, and treaties made, or which shall be made, under their authority; to all cases affecting ambassadors, other public ministers, and consuls; to all cases of admiralty and maritime jurisdiction; to controversies to which the United States shall be a party; to controversies between two or more states; between a state and citizens of another state; between citizens of different states; between citizens of the same state, claiming lands under grants of different states; and between a state, or the citizens thereof, and foreign states, citizens, or subjects.*

The 11th amendment to the Constitution declares, that *The judicial power of the United States shall not be construed to extend to any suit in law or equity commenced or prosecuted against one of the United States by citizens of another state, or by citizens or subjects of any foreign state.*

§ 334. The *jurisdiction* of the Supreme Court is here made coextensive with *national objects*, and *independent* of *other branches* of the government. "There is no liberty if the judiciary power be not separated from the legislative and executive powers."[1] The *Constitution* and *the laws of the United States* are to be construed and adjudged of by the Supreme Court. How could they be adjudged by the state courts without at once making the states superior to the Union? Yet it must be observed, that the state, as well as the other courts, have the power to construe United States and all other laws, when they come *incidentally* in question upon the trial of a cause.

§ 335. All matters in relation to treaties, public ministers, and consuls, admiralty and maritime juris-

---

[1] Montesquieu's Esprit de Loix, book XI., chap 6.

diction, come under the sole cognizance of the Supreme Court. These things belong to the *laws of nations;* hence, only a *national court* can sit upon them. The Supreme Court is the national court of the United States; and, in this single clause, we see at once the wide distinction placed by the Constitution between the United States' courts and the state courts. By this, taken in connection with the other clauses upon the jurisdiction of the Supreme Court, and restrictions upon the states, the Supreme Court is made a *national*, while the state courts are merely *municipal courts.*

§336. The next sentence is in perfect conformity to this principle, for if the Supreme Court be *national*, it is the proper *arbiter* between the different states, in relation to all controversies which involve the rights and laws of different states. Accordingly, the Constitution gives the court jurisdiction of *controversies* between *two or more states;* between a *state* and the *citizens* of other states, or foreign states when the *state is not defendant:* and between citizens of the same state, claiming under *grants of different states.* The simple reading of these provisions is a sufficient answer to every theory which supposes that the *states* have sufficient power to *annul* the laws of the *Union.* In this article a tribunal is erected superior to all state courts, and by the express direction of the Constitution, a competent *arbiter* between the states themselves. "There must be some tribunal than which there can be no higher," is a maxim self-evident in all governments which purport to have system and stability; for without it they must become mere anarchies. In the Supreme Court, the Constitution has established that tribunal in the United States; and it is manifest that, within its jurisdiction pointed out by the Constitution, it is above all others. When we go behind this, there is nothing left but *the people*, whose work the Constitution itself is; but who cannot be appealed to against their own laws, till they have first resolved those laws to be a *nullity*, and themselves into a *state of nature*. This is a right which is left to all people of all nations, savage and civilized,—the *right of rebellion*,—never to be exercised till sufferance is exhausted. Provision is made, as we shall see hereafter, for *amending* the Constitution; but this presupposes *a constitution* and *a government:* this amendment, then, in the forms prescribed by the Constitution, is not the exercise of that ultimate right we have spoken of above.

§ 337. But, while it is affirmed that the Supreme Court is the ultimate tribunal, it must be borne in mind, that the functions of a court are to say *what the law is, and not to make it*. They are judges, and not lawgivers. "The judicial department has no will in any case. Judicial power, as contradistinguished from the power of the laws, has no existence. Courts are the mere instruments of the law, and can will nothing."[1]

---

[1] Osborn *vs.* Bank of the United States, 9 Wheaton's Rep., 866.

§338. It will be observed, that by the 2d section of the 3d article of the Constitution, the jurisdiction of the Supreme Court is expressly confined to "CASES." A *case* is a *suit* at law or equity; in other words, some kind of litigation. It follows from this conclusively, that the Supreme Court has no jurisdiction in relation to the powers of government, or to any act which is an act of the national will; or of any department of the government, acting within its constitutional powers. The Supreme Court is *not* a tribunal above the sovereignty of the people, or above the legislative or executive departments. Constitutionality of law, or of ministerial acts, come *incidentally* only in question before this court. If Congress by mistake pass unconstitutional laws, and acts are done under them, this will give rise to litigation, and the court has then jurisdiction over the validity of the law. But this gives no *original* jurisdiction over the legislative department, or of the acts of that department, which simply express the national will, and are purely political. There are such acts, of which the annexation of Louisiana, the annexation of Texas, and the Missouri compromise, are examples. In the latter case, the Supreme Court has expressed an opinion,[1] but with no such definitiveness as makes it authoritative. On the contrary, this court has expressly decided, that it has *no jurisdiction over political questions.* In the cases arising out of the Dorr Insurrection in Rhode Island, the

---

[1] Dred Scott *vs.* Sandford, 19 Howard, 393.

Supreme Court decided, that the question whether the acting government is "a duly constituted government of the state," is a *political*, not judicial question; and the courts of *the United States cannot decide it*, but must recognize the decision of the state courts.[1] The power to decide whether the organized government of a state is *duly constituted* or not, is (*quoad* the United States) delegated to the President.[2] So, when the President of the United States denies or affirms the jurisdiction of a foreign government over certain territories, *the courts must take the fact to be so.*[3]

§ 339. At this point, the conflict of courts may be considered. The *principle* established by the Constitution is very simple. In all cases in which there can legally occur a conflict between the authority of the United States and that of the state courts, *the United States' courts are supreme.* When the Supreme Court of the United States declares a state law to be in conflict with the Constitution of the United States, the courts of the state are bound to conform to that decision.[4] The state courts cannot obstruct or interfere with the process of the United States Court. When a *habeas corpus* from a state court is served on the marshal of the United States, he is bound to notice it, and make known *why* he holds the prisoner; but he must *obey the process of the United States, and not that of the state.*[5] So, also, the process of the state court

---

[1] Luther *vs.* Borden, 17 Curtis. [2] Idem. [3] Williams *vs.* Suffolk Insurance Co., 13 Id., 225. [4] Cook *vs.* Moffat, 16 Id., 405. [5] The Booth Case, 21 Howard, 506.

has no authority beyond the limits of the state.[1] At the same time, the state and United States sovereignty exist, and are independent, and may be exercised within the same territorial limits.[2]

§ 340. If the ministerial officers of the United States refuse to perform the duties imposed upon them by law, the United States Court may enforce obedience. This it may do by writ of mandamus.[3]

§ 341. In the clause above, the phrase is read "all cases in law or equity." The reference here is plainly to those *common-law* distinctions of law and equity remedies, which before existed in the jurisprudence of England and this country. So far as the remedies go, the Constitution recognizes the existence and the operation of the common law.[4] And it would seem, as the reference is direct to the remedy at common law, that the *principles* upon which the remedy is to be applied must be the same; and such is the interpretation and mode of administering justice in such cases in the courts of the United States. What is a *case* as here contemplated? "A *case* is a suit in law or equity, instituted according to the regular course of judicial proceedings; and when it involves any question arising under the Constitution, laws, or treaties of the United States, it is within the judicial power confided to the Union.[5]

§ 342. To understand the jurisdiction of the Supreme

---

[1] The Booth Case, 21 Howard, 506. [2] Idem. [3] Kendall *vs.* Stokes et al., 12 Peters, 524. [4] 3 Story's Comm., 506. [5] Idem, 507; 1 Tucker's Blk. Comm. App., 418, 420; Madison's Virginia Resolutions, 1800.

Court, we must consider the next clause of this section, which is,

Clause 2d. *In all cases affecting ambassadors, other public ministers, and consuls, and those in which a state shall be a party, the Supreme Court shall have original jurisdiction. In all the other cases before mentioned, the Supreme Court shall have appellate jurisdiction, both as to law and fact, with such exceptions and such regulations as the Congress shall make.*

§ 343. Jurisdiction may be considered, 1st. With reference to the *parties;* 2dly. In relation to the *subject-matter;* and 3dly. In respect to *realm* or *locality.*

1st. Jurisdiction in reference to the *parties.* The *parties* who come within the jurisdiction of the Supreme Court are, 1. Ambassadors, public ministers, and consuls; 2. The United States; 3. The States; 4. Citizens of different states; 5. Citizens of the same state; 6. Foreign states, citizens, or subjects.

§ 344. 1. "Ambassadors, public ministers, and consuls." The grades of public ministers, and the laws which apply to them, we shall see in another place.[1] The rights, duties, powers, and privileges of public ministers are determined, not by municipal constitutions, but by the law of nature and nations, which is equally obligatory upon all nations. Consuls are not strictly *ministers*, but merely *commercial agents.* The Constitution, however, has, in relation to the courts, placed them upon the same level as ministers. In

---

[1] Chapter on the Practical Operation of the Government.

cases *against* ministers and consuls, the jurisdiction is supposed to be exclusive.[1]

The *indictments* found against persons for offering violence to ministers, &c., and their servants, do not come within the scope of the phrase, *affecting* ambassadors, &c., &c. The minister is not a party to the record.[2] Yet, if he be not a party, the case may be one which *affects* him in interest; and the court has decided that in such a case it has jurisdiction.

§ 345. 2. *The United States.* To enforce the rights of the United States, they must sue either in their own courts, or those of the states. In the latter they would at once be subject to the states, the very end which the Constitution was formed to prevent. In their own courts they could enforce their own rights, and have a uniform rule of justice. The latter, therefore, was adopted. The clause which conferred this jurisdiction on the Supreme Court gave no power to individuals to bring suit against the United States, nor have they or the states any such power. It is inherent in the nature of *sovereignty* not to be amenable to any private person.[3] The same exception extends to every state in the Union.[4] What remedy, then, has the citizen against the national government for injustice and injury? If it be an oppression exercised by public functionaries upon the body of the people, the people have, through the Constitution, the power of removing them. If the oppression be in the exercise of unconstitutional powers,

---

[1] 1 Kent's Comm., 44. [2] 3 Story's Comm., 524. [3] Idem, 538. [4] Idem.

the functionaries who wield them are amenable for their injurious acts to the judicial tribunals of the country, at the suit of the oppressed.[1]

§ 346. The government is, *in itself*, incapable of a *personal wrong*, such as assault and battery, and personal violence.[2] In respect to property, the remedy lies against the *immediate perpetrators*, who cannot shelter themselves under an agency from the government. Such agent, like every other violator of the laws, must refund in damages to the injured party.[3]

§ 347. In the case of *contracts*, however, the agent is not responsible when lawfully made, and the government cannot be sued; hence, the only remedy is by legislative interposition,—an appeal to Congress. This may be justly considered as a defect upon the part of Congress, who have the right to provide a mode of settling private rights. In this respect, as in every other concerning justice between public and private rights, the contrast between us and the government of England is strongly against us. There the subject is allowed to bring what is called a petition of right before the chancellor, who as a matter of duty hears it, and administers right according to the fact.[4]

§ 348. 3. Another class of parties under the jurisdiction of the Supreme Court are the *States*. The provision subjecting the states to the jurisdiction of the Supreme Court, brings them at once within the sovereignty of the Union, even if all the powers before vested

---

[1] Story's Comm., 539. [2] Idem. [3] Idem. [4] Idem, 541.

in the national government had not. This jurisdiction is frequently exercised, and although the states have often been much irritated, yet they have uniformly submitted. As the amendment to the Constitution has taken the states out of the jurisdiction of the Supreme Court when the suit is *against* them by individuals, it becomes important to inquire when a state is to be deemed a party, so as to avail itself of this exemption? "A state is a party only when it is on the record as such, and sues or is sued in its political capacity."[1] It is not sufficient that it has an interest in the suit, as between other persons, or that its powers and duties come incidentally in question.[2] The same principle applies to incorporations under the state; thus an incorporated bank, in which the state is stockholder, is suable, although the state is exempt from the action.[3] "As a member of a corporation, a government never exercises its sovereignty."

§ 349. It is laid down as "a rule, which admits of no exception, that in all cases under the Constitution of the United States, where jurisdiction depends upon the party, it is the party named on the record."

§ 350. 4. The next class of *parties* are "Citizens of different States." The first inquiry here is, who is a citizen of a state, and how does he change his citizenship? Does it depend upon his domicile, or residence, or upon any other principle? Judge Story has an-

---

[1] 3 Story's Comm., 549.

[2] 3 Dall. R., 411; United States *vs.* Planter's Bank of Georgia, 9 Wheaton, 904.

[3] Story's Comm., 565.

swered these questions in his commentaries in a very satisfactory manner. "The Constitution," says the commentator, "having declared that the citizens of each state shall be entitled to all the privileges and immunities of citizens in the several states, every person, who is a citizen of one state, and removes into another, with the intention of taking up his residence and inhabitancy there, becomes in reality a citizen of the state where he resides; and he then ceases to be a citizen of the state from which he has removed his residence."[1] What circumstances constitute such a change of residence? A removal from one state into another, *with* an *intention* of *remaining*, constitutes a change of residence, and consequently of citizenship.[2] But a native citizen of one state never ceases to be a citizen thereof till he acquires a new citizenship elsewhere. Residence[3] in a foreign country does not change his citizenship. Every citizen of a state is a citizen of the United States.[4] A naturalized citizen, by a residence in any state in the Union, becomes a citizen of that state. So a citizen of a territory, by a residence in a state, acquires the character of the state where he resides.[5]

§ 351. But a naturalized citizen of the United States, or a citizen of a territory, does not become a citizen entitled to sue in the courts of the United States, by such *residence* in a *territory*, nor until he has acquired a residence in a particular state.[6]

---

[1] 3 Story's Comm., 565. [2] Idem. [3] 1 Kent's Comm., Sect. 4.
[4] 3 Story's Comm., 565. [5] Idem, 566; 6 Peters' Supreme C. R., 761.
[6] 1 Kent's Comm., 360; 1 Wheaton's R., 91.

§ 352. 5. *A corporation*, as such, is not a citizen of a state in the sense of the Constitution: but if all the members of the corporation are citizens, their character will confer jurisdiction.[1] A citizen may sue, who is trustee, executor, or administrator for another.

§ 353. Citizens of the same state may be parties, when they claim under *grants of different states.* This is the only case in which the Constitution gives jurisdiction directly to the federal courts, over cases between citizens of the same state. The reason is, that it contemplates a case in which the laws and boundaries of different states are brought into question, and upon which, therefore, the state tribunals are *not unbiassed.*

§ 354. 6. "Foreign states, citizens, and subjects" may be parties. Who is a foreign citizen or subject? or who is an alien? Any person who is not a citizen of the United States is an alien. But when he is naturalized, he is no longer an alien; for this is a case provided for by the Constitution and the laws: and it makes no difference whether he sues in his own name or as a trustee.

§ 355. A foreign corporation established in a foreign country, *all* of whose *members* are aliens, can sue in the same manner.

§ 356. The jurisdiction vests, however, only when one party to a suit is a citizen.[2] *Alien enemies*, however, cannot sue; their right is suspended until peace.

---

[1] United States *vs.* Planter's Bank, 9 Wheaton, 410; 8 Wheaton, 668.

[2] Story's Comm., 571.

§ 357. *Jurisdiction* in relation to the subject-matter is *original*, or *appellate*.

The court has original jurisdiction in all cases concerning ambassadors, public ministers, and consuls, and those in which a *state* is the party; in all others it has *appellate* jurisdiction, both as to law and fact, under such regulations and exceptions as Congress shall make. This jurisdiction cannot, by the words of the Constitution, be exercised without the intervention of Congress; but Congress are bound by that part of the clause which refers to "all cases," to confer all the jurisdiction granted by the Constitution, in some form or other, upon the Supreme Court. By the act of September, 1789, this was done, and the Supreme Court have exercised their appropriate powers uninterruptedly since.

§ 358. This original jurisdiction is confined to the enumerated cases, and cannot be enlarged by Congress. Congress cannot give it appellate jurisdiction, when the Constitution has given it original, nor original where it has appellate jurisdiction.[1] The grant of original jurisdiction is exclusive, and negatives any enlargement.

§ 359. Whether the original jurisdiction vested in the Supreme Court may not be exercised concurrently by the inferior courts, is an undecided point.[2]

§ 360. Another question is, whether the court can exercise *appellate* jurisdiction in those cases where it has original jurisdiction;[3] and it is thought it can.

---

[1] Madison *vs.* Marbury, 1 Cranch, 137; 1 Kent's Comm., 302.

[2] 11 Wheaton, 467.

[3] 3 Story's Comm., 576.

§ 361. What is appellate jurisdiction? "The essential criterion of appellate jurisdiction is, that it revives and corrects the proceedings in a cause already instituted, and does not create that cause." The appellate jurisdiction may be exercised in a variety of *forms*,—indeed in any form which the legislature may prescribe. But the substance must exist before the form can be applied. Where the object is to review a judicial proceeding, the mode is immaterial; and a writ of habeas corpus, or mandamus, a writ of error, or an appeal may be used, as the legislature may prescribe.[1]

§ 362. The most usual modes of exercising appellate jurisdiction are writs of error, appeals, or some process of removal.[2] An *appeal* removes the entire cause, fact, or will, or law for a *review* and new trial. *A writ of error* removes nothing for re-examination but the *law*.

§ 363. The appellate jurisdiction of the Supreme Court extends to the decisions of the state courts. By the act of September, 1789, sect. 25, it is declared that the final judgment or decree of the state courts may be re-examined and reversed, or affirmed in those cases in which is drawn in question the *validity* or *construction* of a *treaty*, and the decision is *against* the right, title, or privilege set up, or claimed under it; or where is drawn in question the validity of a *statute*, or an *authority* exercised under a *state*, on the ground of their

---

[1] 3 Story's Comm., 576; 6 Wheaton's Rep.; 2 Peters' Supreme C. R., 449; Ingersoll's Digest, 375.
[2] 3 Dallas, 342; 1 Wheaton, 304.

being adverse to the Constitution, treaties, or laws of the United States, and the decision is in *favor* of their validity. Such cases may be brought up on writ of error; and such writ has the same effect as if directed to the Circuit Court of the United States.

§ 364. Hence, if the highest court in a state reverse the judgment of a subordinate court, and, on appeal to the Supreme Court of the United States, the judgment of the highest court in a state be reversed, it becomes a *nullity*, and a mandate issues to the inferior court for execution.[1] The record in such cases must show the error, by showing some act of jurisdiction.

§ 365. Jurisdiction in respect to *locality*. Here we may consider: 1st. Within what boundaries the authority of the United States Courts is limited; 2d. The maritime and admiralty jurisdiction of the courts.

§ 366. 1st. What are the territorial limits of jurisdiction? The limits of jurisdiction, as it respects the Supreme Court, are the limits of the United States, for the decisions of all other courts, whether territorial, district, or state, are within the rules as to subject and parties already laid down and are subject to revision in that tribunal; except that, in the *territorial courts*, no appeal lies from their decisions without a *special statutory provision.* The territories are under the sole and absolute control of Congress.[2]

§ 367. The district court has cognizance of crimes and offences, which are cognizable by the United

---

3 Dallas, 342; 1 Wheaton, 304.   [2] 1 Kent's Comm., 360.

States tribunals, and which are committed within the respective districts, or on the high seas.

§ 368. The district courts have also admiralty and maritime jurisdiction on the *high seas*, and also within waters leading from them, and in which vessels of ten tons burden may navigate.[1]

§ 369. *The concurrent jurisdiction* of the state and national courts has also been a subject of some difficulty.

It is settled, that no part of the criminal jurisdiction of the United States can be delegated to state tribunals: and the admiralty and maritime jurisdiction is of the same exclusive cognizance. It can only be in those cases where, previous to the Constitution, state tribunals possessed jurisdiction independent of national authority, that they can now exercise a concurrent jurisdiction.[2]

§ 370. State courts may, in the exercise of their ordinary jurisdiction, incidentally take cognizance of cases arising under the Constitution, laws, and treaties of the United States: but the United States courts have appellate jurisdiction.

§ 371. Where the jurisdiction is concurrent, the *sentence* of either court, whether of conviction or acquittal, may be *pleaded in bar* of a prosecution before the other. So also the judgment of a state court in a civil case of concurrent jurisdiction, may be pleaded in bar of an action for the same cause, instituted in a Circuit Court of the United States.[3]

---

[1] Act of Sept. 1789.
[2] 1 Kent's Comm., 372; 1 Wheaton, 304.
[3] 5 Wheaton, 1.

§ 372. The conclusion then is, that in judicial matters the concurrent jurisdiction of the state tribunals depends altogether upon the pleasure of Congress, and may be revoked and extinguished whenever they think proper, in every case in which the subject-matter can constitutionally be cognizable in the federal courts; and that, without an express provision to the contrary, the state courts will retain a concurrent jurisdiction in all cases where they had jurisdiction originally over the subject-matter.[1]

§ 373. Various acts of Congress give jurisdiction to state courts and magistrates in both civil cases, and for fines and forfeitures under the laws of the United States; but the *state* courts are not bound to assume jurisdiction in such cases.[2]

§ 374. It has been questioned whether the state courts could issue a *habeas corpus*, and exercise jurisdiction in a case where the imprisonment was by an officer of the United States, or under pretext of the authority of the United States. The state courts, however, have exercised such jurisdiction, although no final decision has been had upon the question.[3]

§ 375. No state court can issue an injunction upon any judgment in a court of the United States:[4] nor can the state legislature annul the judgments, or destroy the rights acquired under them, or determine the ex-

---

[1] 1 Kent's Comm., 374.

[2] Idem, 375.

[3] Idem; 10 Johnson's Reports, 328; 5 Hall's Law Journal, 82; 11 Mass. Reports, 68.

[4] 3 Story's Comm., 624; 7 Cranch, 279.

tent of their jurisdiction.[1] Nor can a state court, or authority, prescribe the rules or forms of proceedings, nor effect of process in the courts of the United States:[2] nor issue a mandamus to an officer of the United States to compel him to perform duties devolved upon him by the laws of the United States.[3]

§ 376. On the other hand, the national courts have no authority (in cases not within the appellate jurisdiction of the United States), to issue injunctions upon judgments in the state courts; or in any manner to interfere with their jurisdiction and proceedings.[4]

§ 377. It is a question unsettled, whether the United States Courts have a common-law jurisdiction? In the case of the United States *vs.* Hudson & Goodwin,[5] tried for a libel on the President, the Supreme Court decided, by a majority, that they had no common-law jurisdiction. In the case of the United States *vs.* Coolidge,[6] the Circuit Court for Massachusetts decided it had such *jurisdiction in admiralty cases.* The Supreme Court, however, adhered to their former opinion. In consequence of this division, and the opinions of different commentators, this point is not wholly settled.[7]

§ 378. 2d. Another extensive subject of discussion in the courts of the United States, is the *admiralty* and *maritime* jurisdiction of the district courts.

The *district courts* act as courts of common law, and

---

[1] 5 Cranch, 115. [2] 10 Wheaton, 21, 22, 51. [3] 6 Wheaton, 598.
[4] 3 Story's Comm., 626. [5] 7 Cranch, 32. [6] 1 Gallison, 188.
[7] 1 Kent's Comm., 315.

also as courts of admiralty. In England a difference existed between the *instance* and *prize courts.* The former is defined[1] to be the *ordinary* admiralty court, and the latter an *extraordinary* one, having jurisdiction only in time of *war*, and in *prize* cases. In the United States, however, the Supreme Court have determined that the district courts have all the powers of courts of admiralty, whether as instance or prize courts.[2]

§ 379. Chancellor Kent, who has made law classical in our country, has given a brief review of the powers of these courts, which may be stated in the following propositions.

1. *As to the jurisdiction of prize courts.* The *prize* jurisdiction extends to all *captures in war made on the high seas.* Prize goods are goods taken on the high seas by right of war, out of the hands of the enemy.[3] The prize jurisdiction also extends to captures in foreign ports and harbors, and to captures made on *land by naval forces.* It extends to captures made in rivers, ports, and harbors of the captors' own country. The prize court extends also to all *ransom bills* upon captures at sea, and to money received as ransom or commutation on a capitulation to naval forces.[4]

§ 380. If the prize be unwarrantably carried into a foreign port, and there delivered by the captors upon security, the prize court does not lose its jurisdiction over the capture and the questions incident to it. So, if the prize be lost at sea, or actually lying within a

---

[1] 1 Kent's Comm., 331.

[2] 3 Dallas, 6.

[3] 1 Kent's Comm., 334.

[4] Idem, 385.

foreign neutral territory, the court has jurisdiction.[1] Prize courts act upon the *thing* instead of the *person*, and that notwithstanding any contract between the parties.[2] Prize courts have likewise exclusive jurisdiction and discretion as to the allowance of *freight*, *damages*, *expenses*, and *costs* in all cases of capture, and as to all *torts* and *personal injuries* connected with captures.[3]

2. *Criminal jurisdiction of the admiralty.* The act of September, 1789, gives to the district courts, exclusive of the state courts, and concurrent with the circuit courts, jurisdiction over crimes and offences cognizable by the authority of the United States, and committed within their districts, or upon the high seas, where only a moderate corporal punishment, or fine, or imprisonment is to be inflicted. As this confers jurisdiction only in *minor crimes*, it was a question whether the courts had any jurisdiction over cases of *murder*, &c. In the case of the United States *vs.* M'Gill,[4] it was decided they had not. The same was decided in United States *vs.* Bevans.[5] It is now settled, that the federal courts, as courts of admiralty, are to exercise such criminal jurisdiction as is conferred upon them expressly by acts of Congress, and they are not to exercise any other.[6]

This limitation, however, does not extend to private prosecutions in the district court to recover damages for a *marine tort*.

---

[1] 1 Kent's Comm., 336. [2] Idem, 337. [3] Idem.
[4] 4 Dallas, 426. [5] 5 Wheaton, 76. [6] 1 Kent's Comm., 341.

§ 381. *As to the division between the jurisdiction of the admiralty and the courts of common law.*

On the seashore, the jurisdiction of the admiralty is limited to *low-water mark*,[1] and between that and high-water mark, where the sea ebbs and flows, the common-law and admiralty have a divided jurisdiction.

§ 382. In the Circuit Court of the United States it has also been decided, that the admiralty jurisdiction extends to all maritime contracts, torts, injuries, and offences on the *high seas*, and in *ports* and *havens*, as far *as the ebb and flow of the tide.*[2]

It has been asked what cases come within the meaning of admiralty, and what of common-law jurisdiction? It is now settled that all seizures under laws of import, navigation, and trade, if made upon tide-waters navigable from sea, are civil cases of *admiralty jurisdiction.*[3]

§ 383. The admiralty and maritime jurisdiction of the district courts is *exclusive.* The Constitution extends the judicial authority of the United States to *all* cases of admiralty jurisdiction, and the act of Congress enacts, that the district courts shall have *exclusive* original cognizance of all civil causes of admiralty and maritime jurisdiction.

4. *Jurisdiction of the instance courts.*

§ 384. The instance courts take cognizance of crimes committed, and things done, and contracts not under seal, made on the bosom of the sea.[4] The cause must

---

[1] 1 Kent's Comm., 343.
[2] 2 Gallison, 398.
[3] 1 Kent's Comm., 349.
[4] Idem, 352.

arise *wholly* upon the sea to be within the admiralty jurisdiction. If the act be done partly on land and partly on water, the common law has the preference.

§ 385. The admiralty has cognizance of maritime hypothecations[1] of vessels and goods in foreign ports, for repairs done, or necessary supplies furnished.

§ 386. If the admiralty has cognizance of the principal thing, it has also of the *incident*. Thus, goods taken by pirates and sold on land, may be recovered from the vendee by suit in admiralty.

The proceedings in admiralty are according to the course of the *civil law*, and are brief and simple.[2]

§ 387. "The Supreme Court shall have appellate jurisdiction both as to law and fact." This clause was, at first, supposed to confer the power of reviewing the *verdicts* of *juries* on matters of *fact*. This was not, however, the case. "The real object of the provision was to retain the power of reviewing the fact as well as the law in cases of admiralty and maritime jurisdiction."[3] This subject is now settled conclusively by an amendment to the Constitution, in the following words:

"*In suits at common law, where the value in controversy shall exceed twenty dollars, the right of trial by jury shall be preserved; and no fact tried by jury shall be otherwise re-examined in any court of the United States than according to the rules of common law.*"

This at once prohibits the re-examination of facts, already tried by jury, in any other manner.

---

[1] 1 Kent's Comm., 349. [2] Idem, 354; 3 Story's Comm., 629.

[3] 3 Peters' Rep., 446.

The only modes known to the common law to re-examine such facts are: 1st, the granting a new trial by the court where the issue was tried; and 2d, by a writ of error, for an *error in law*, by some appellate court: neither of these includes the power of re-examining facts already tried by another court.

§ 388. The appellate jurisdiction is to be with such exceptions and regulations as "the Congress shall prescribe." But here a question is asked, whether the jurisdiction attaches to the Supreme Court in its own nature, to be modified by Congress, or whether an act of Congress is necessary to confer that jurisdiction? If Congress have the power they may repeal it, and thus destroy the whole efficacy[1] of the court. It was formerly decided by the Supreme Court, that if Congress provided no rule to regulate their proceedings, they could exercise no jurisdiction. That decision has, however, been since overruled, and it is asserted by the Supreme Court, that without any limitation of powers by an act of Congress, it must possess all the jurisdiction which the Constitution assigns it. The appellate powers of the Supreme Court are given by the Constitution, and not by the judicial act.[2] But they are regulated and limited by that act.

§ 389. There are certain *incidental* powers which are attached to all courts without the necessity of an enactment.

The *functions* of the judges are strictly *judicial.*

---

[1] 3 Story's Comm., 648.

[2] 6 Cranch, 307, 313.

They cannot be called upon to advise the President, or to give extra-judicial opinions, or to act as commissioners, or other like matters.

Thus also the courts have power over their own officers, and the power to protect them and their members from being disturbed in the exercise of their functions. All courts have the power to *attach* for *contempts*, and by means of this they can protect themselves.

§ 390. Clause 3d. *The trial of all crimes, except in cases of impeachment, shall be by jury; and such trial shall be held in the state where the said crimes shall have been committed. But when not committed within any state, the trial shall be at such place or places as the Congress may by law have directed.*

§ 391. In connection with this must be taken the amendments on the same subject, as follows:

Amendment 5th. *No person shall be held to answer for a capital, or otherwise infamous crime, unless on a presentment, or indictment of a grand jury, except in cases arising in the land or naval forces, or in the militia when in actual service, in time of war or public danger; nor shall any person be subject, for the same offence, to be twice put in jeopardy of life or limb; nor shall be compelled in any criminal case to be a witness against himself; nor be deprived of life, liberty, or property, without due process of law; nor shall private property be taken for public use without just compensation.*

§ 392. Amendment 6th. *In all criminal prosecutions, the accused shall enjoy the right to a speedy and public trial, by an impartial jury of the state and district wherein the crime shall have been committed,*

§ 393. The right to a trial by *jury* is of very ancient date. It was firmly established, however, in the Magna Charta, granted at Runneymede.[1] In that instrument it is declared, that no freeman shall be injured in person or property except *by the judgment of his peers or by the law of the land.* From that time to this it has descended unimpaired through the governments of England and this country. It is esteemed, and correctly, the most precious right of freemen; for it enables them to appeal from the arbitrary judgments of either governments or individuals, to the disinterested verdicts of their equals. The term *peers* means equals, and a judgment by *his peers* is one by *his equals.* The verdict, then, is given by those who are not only neighbors, but taken from the same rank and circumstances of life, and influenced by all the sentiments of justice or humanity which may be supposed to actuate persons placed in similar situations, and liable to the same contingencies.

§ 394. The *trial* of all crimes must also be *in the state* where it is committed. This is to avoid the difficulty, expense, and oppression which might happen from being carried into other states, and before foreign tribunals.[2]

Before a person can be tried for a *crime*, he must first be charged by a *grand jury* with the offence. This

---

[1] 3 Blackst. Comm., 350. [2] 3 Story's Comm., 655.

charge is in the form of a *presentment*, or *indictment*. A grand jury is a number of men, not less than *twelve*, nor more than twenty-three, of whom twelve must agree in the charge, selected in the manner of other juries, from the body of the people within the *county* where they are summoned.[1] They are sworn to make diligent inquiry of all offences committed against the authority of the government, and the peace of the state within the body of their county. In the United States Courts they are sworn to inquire and present all offences against the national government, and within its jurisdiction. When the grand jury are assembled, the proper officer, commonly the district-attorney for the state, lays before them all the offences of which he has any knowledge, and the evidence by which the charges against the prisoners are supported. They examine this carefully, and, if they find the testimony probable, and sufficient to induce a rational belief in the charges, they find what is called *a bill*, or *an indictment*, and indorse on it *A true bill*. This bill or indictment is a *formal charge* of the offence against the prisoner, usually drawn up by the attorney for the state. If the grand jury do not find the bill true, they indorse on it, "*Not a true bill*," and the prisoner is discharged; but a new bill may be found by a new jury.[2] The indictment must charge person, time, place, and nature of the offence with clearness and certainty; otherwise it will be void for *uncertainty*.

---

[1] 4 Blackst. Comm., 302.

[2] 3 Story's Comm., 658.

§ 395. It is also provided, that no person shall be twice put in jeopardy of life or limb for the same offence. The meaning is, that no person shall be *twice tried* for the same offence: it is also added, that this can only be pleaded when there has been an actual verdict and judgment, and *not* when the jury have been dismissed for want of agreement, or a new trial granted.[1]

§ 396. No person can be compelled to be a witness against himself, or be deprived of life, liberty, or property, without process of law. This is merely an affirmance of the common law, as is also the former provision. In fact nearly the whole of these amendments in relation to trial by juries, were *common-law* privileges, but inserted, no doubt, for more absolute certainty, and that no doubt should ever be permitted to enter the minds, as to this subject, of either lawgivers or judicial expositors.

§ 397. One of these re-enactments of the common law is, that no *private property shall be taken for public use without just compensation:* yet plain justice as this is, it is frequently violated in this country by indirect means, and shows how difficult it is to preserve private rights when the *people at large* are interested against them: thus, private land is frequently taken for public works, streets, highways, canals, &c.; the owners are remunerated by an *appraised valuation*, not of what the property *is worth in itself*, but with

---

[1] 3 Story's Comm., 659.

the additional circumstances of its *increased value*, by an improvement which the owner never desired, and in his judgment, is injurious to his interests. The plain rule of justice is, to pay the *actual value*, without reference either to the increase or diminution of value in the residue.

§ 398. The trial by jury is public, in the presence of both the prisoner and the witnesses. The accused is entitled to compulsory process to obtain witnesses, and is also entitled to have counsel. This provision was inserted because, by the ancient common law the prisoner had not that privilege, but acquired it by a statute of William and Mary.[1] Indeed, the criminal jurisprudence of England, previous to that time, was, except the trial by jury, conducted with the greatest disregard of justice. Neither had the prisoner the benefit of counsel, though as the maxim ran, the judge is his counsel, and bound to see him have equal advantages with the accuser. This discreditable injustice on the part of the common law is, however, entirely done away by these provisions of the Constitution.

§ 399. Section 3d. Clause 1st. *Treason against the United States shall consist only in levying war against them, or in adhering to their enemies, giving them aid and comfort. No person shall be convicted of treason, unless on the testimony of two witnesses to the same overt act, or on confession in open court.*

Clause 2d. *The Congress shall have power to declare*

---

[1] 3 Story's Comm., 663.

the punishment of treason; but no attainder of treason shall work corruption of blood, or forfeiture, except during the life of the person attainted.

Treason is some act whose object is the overthrow of the government; hence, it is the highest crime against society, and universally regarded with odium and resentment. The definition of what is treason, and what is necessary to conviction, is of vast importance to the peace of society and the liberty of the citizen. *Constructive* or implied treason, from suspicious circumstances, is dangerous wherever it exists. In the reign of Edward III., in England, a statute was passed declaring and defining treason in its different branches.[1] This was confirmed by the statute of Mary I. Our Constitution has used the very words of this statute, and thus adopted its definition, with the interpretation which it has received during several centuries. The war must be *actually levied*, to constitute treason. A *conspiracy* to levy war, is not treason.[2]

§ 400. The *punishment* of treason in our country is simply *death* by hanging; at the common law, it was accompanied by many barbarities, which would not now be tolerated.

§ 401. By *corruption of blood*, is meant the *destruction* of all *inheritable qualities;* so that no one can claim any thing from a person *attainted*, or through him. A son could not claim from a grandfather, deriving title through a father that was attainted.[3]

---

[1] Hawkins, p. 6, book I., chap. 1-7.

[2] 4 Cranch, 126.

[3] Story's Comm., 171.

§402. A state cannot take cognizance of or punish the crime of treason[1] against the United States. As treason is a crime whose object is to *overthrow* the government, and the government of the state is guaranteed by that of the United States, it follows there can be no treason against a state, which is not also treason against the United States; and, consequently, the crime of treason cannot be punished by the states.

Article IV.

MISCELLANEOUS.

§403. Section 1st. *Full faith and credit shall be given in each state to the public acts, records, and judicial proceedings of every other state. And the Congress may, by general laws, prescribe the manner in which such acts, records, and proceedings shall be proved, and the effect thereof.*

§404. The *laws* and *acts* of *foreign nations* are not judicially taken notice of by other nations, but must be proved, like other facts, when they come under examination. The mode of proof varies in different countries. As to the *effect* to be given foreign *judgments*, all civilized nations are agreed they shall have some effect; but what, they are not agreed upon. In England and the United States, *foreign judgments* are what is called *prima-facie* evidence of what they

---

[1] Story's Comm., 173.

decide. This means, that they shall be taken as true till the contrary is proved. A *domestic judgment*, however, is true *conclusively*, and cannot be contradicted.

§ 405. The *full faith and credit* mentioned in the Constitution, was inserted to place the judgments of the different states upon a different footing from those of foreign nations. The latter were already *prima-facie* evidence; the former, then, must be *conclusive*. They have absolute verity, so that they cannot be denied, any more than in the state where they originated.[1] If a judgment is conclusive in the state where it is pronounced, it is conclusive everywhere; if re-examinable there, it is so elsewhere. It is placed upon the same ground as a *domestic judgment.*

§ 406. SECTION 2d. Clause 1st. *The citizens of each state shall be entitled to all privileges and immunities of citizens in the several states.*

Clause 2d. *A person charged in any state with treason, felony, or other crime, who shall flee from justice, and be found in another state, shall, on demand of the executive authority of the state from which he fled, be delivered up, to be removed to the state having jurisdiction of the crime.*

Clause 3d. *No person held to service or labor in one state, under the laws thereof, escaping into another, shall, in consequence of any law or regulation therein, be discharged from such service or labor, but shall be*

---

[1] 3 Story's Comm., 180; 1 Peters' C. R., 74, 80.

delivered up on claim of the party to whom such service or labor may be due.

§407. The object of the first part of the clause is plain enough. If each citizen was not a citizen of the United States in other states, then the states would be completely *foreign* to each other, and their citizens *aliens* in each other. This clause makes each citizen of a state a *citizen of the United States*, and as such confers on him rights and privileges throughout the whole Union.

§408. The subject of delivering up *fugitives* from justice, is one which, among different nations, has involved some doubts. In the United States, however, it is firmly fixed by the above provision, which requires them always to be given up to those who have a right to require it.

§409. The next clause, relative to persons *held to service or labor*, plainly refers to the slaves of the southern states who may take refuge in the non-slave-holding states. The *delivery*[1] in the case of fugitives and slaves is to be made, *not* after a *full trial*, which would manifestly defeat the end in view, but after a summary investigation before a magistrate, in which it shall appear *probable* that the circumstances charged are true. By an act of Congress, 1793, it is provided, that such proof may be made before any magistrate, by the principal or his attorney, and may be either by affidavit or oral testimony to *his satisfaction*. The

---

[1] 3 Story's Comm., 677.

magistrate is then authorized to give a certificate of the facts to the party or his agent, which certificate is sufficient warrant of removal. Heavy penalties are laid on those who hinder or resist such proceedings, or harbor any of the fugitives or slaves.

§410. "Full faith and credit," refers to the judgment or record transferred, and *not to the process under it.* The reason is plain. All process of state courts, or acts of state officers, are limited by the state boundaries. When the judgment or record is verified, and transferred to another state, it is to have *full credit*, but no process from the state in which it originated can be used to give it effect. A judgment in one state has the force of a domestic judgment in another, under the Constitution of the United States, only so far as to preclude all inquiry into the merits of the subject-matter of the judgment.[1]

§411. *Citizenship* is the foundation of all national rights, and the basis of all that sovereignty which appertains to a nation. It was much higher valued in the Roman Republic than in ours, because a much more rare and valuable quality. Citizenship in Rome belonged to a Roman only, and not to the provincial and miscellaneous population which came in by conquest or migration. PAUL, when carried before the Roman officers, was about to be delivered up to the Jews, when he asked, "Is it lawful for you to scourge a man who is a Roman and uncondemned?" This at

[1] M'Elmoyle *vs.* Cohen, 13 Curtis, 169.

once placed him under the protection of the Roman government. The commander of the guard was alarmed, and said: "Are you a Roman?" "Yes." The Roman officer said: "With a great sum obtained I this freedom." "But," said Paul, "I was born free." He was born in Tarsus, a city of Cilicia. This transaction shows the sacred nature of citizenship among the Romans. It was a freedom or privilege of native-born Romans. The case is different in the United States, where all persons have the power to become citizens; those of foreign birth by naturalization. Notwithstanding this, it is not settled to this day, what are *the distinctive characteristics of a citizen.* It cannot be doubted that a citizen means practically *one of the nation*, and therefore entitled to *act with it*, and *be protected by it.* But, the main question is, *who is to recognize* the fact, that an individual is a citizen or not? Is it the state government? Is it the United States government? Is it the judiciary or the executive? The 2d section of article 4th of the Constitution settles one principle, that the *citizens of one state shall be recognized as citizens in all the states.* If John Smith is bona fide a citizen of Ohio, he must be recognized as a citizen in New York. If the state of Ohio, therefore, chooses to make John Smith a citizen, under conditions of color, character, or property,—which are inadmissible by the laws of New York,—undoubtedly he cannot vote, or do acts, which can only be done by virtue of New York laws. But how can New York deny that he is a citizen of the United States? She cannot do it under the Constitution, if this clause of the 4th article is to be obeyed. *Who* are citizens of the United States? They can be no other than the citizens of each and all the states; the citizens of Ohio, Virginia, New York, &c. If the Supreme Court can deny the rights of citizens of one state to be citizens of the United States, it can annihilate the whole citizenship of the United States; a practical absurdity, which is the logical consequence of denying to one whom Ohio or Virginia has made a citizen, the rights of citizenship in the United States. The Supreme Court has *apparently* decided that a state cannot make a citizen of the *United States*.[1] How then (except in case of naturalization) came any one to be a citizen of the United States?

The Supreme Court decided, in the case of Dred Scott, that a "free negro, of the African race, whose ancestors were brought to this country and sold as slaves, is *not* a 'citizen,' within the meaning of the Constitution."[2]

A state law, punishing a person for harboring or secreting a slave, and preventing his master from arresting him, is not in conflict with the Constitution of the United States. It is merely a cumulative remedy. The same act may be an offence against the law of the state, and of the United States.[3]

§ 412. SECTION 3d. Clause 1st. *New states may be admitted by the Congress into this Union; but no new state shall be formed or erected within the jurisdiction*

---

[1] Dred Scott *vs.* Sandford, 19 Howard, 393.

[2] Idem.

[3] Moore *vs.* Illinois, 20 Curtis, 6.

of any other state; nor any state be formed by the junction of two or more states, or parts of states, without the consent of the legislatures of the states concerned, as well as of the Congress.

Clause 2d. *The Congress shall have power to dispose of and make all needful rules and regulations respecting the territory, or other property belonging to the United States; and nothing in this Constitution shall be so construed as to prejudice any claims of the United States, or of any particular state.*

§ 413. These two clauses are the foundations upon which Congress erect and administer the territorial governments, and subsequently admit them into the Union. Under the old confederation, no such provision existed; and so little anticipation was had of the growth and prosperity of those wild regions, whose population and territory have since nearly doubled the states, and more than quadrupled their strength, that no provision existed on the subject of forming or admitting new states. Since the adoption of the Constitution, however, twenty new states have been added to the Union; and six territories will soon still further increase that number. The power given by the Constitution to do this, is one of the *new principles*[1] introduced into our system, and is perhaps the most anom-

[1] All the nations of antiquity held immense *provinces*, which constituted a part of the state, for purposes of revenue and armies, but were never admitted upon terms of *equality*, and whose inhabitants were never *citizens*. The idea of constituting a *government*, to be increased as to the *source* of *law*—by its own *colonization*, or by *recruits* from abroad, is wholly *new*.

alous, and most influential upon its future destiny of any. The *principle* is simply this, that a colony settled upon an adjacent territory, and within the jurisdiction of the United States, whether it be composed of citizens of the Union or emigrants from foreign nations, Europeans, or Asiatics, shall, on enumerating a specific population, be admitted to equal rights, privileges, and powers with the original states. This principle is likewise unlimited in respect to the number, distance, or settlement of the colonies. The consequence is, that the original states may ultimately, as they soon must, be left in a minority as to power in that government which they formed, and of which they were the sole possessors. They make the whole world partners with themselves in an inheritance of liberty and power and wealth. The grant thus made to the world, of an asylum for all mankind, is noble and benevolent, and the more so, as it seems to have had no former example among nations. It may be said, that the states thus added are not *foreign*; it is true they were not *conquered*, but they are just as subversive of the powers of the old states as if they had been taken from foreign countries. In the case of Louisiana, which was purchased, it was the accession of foreign territory; and at the time the territory of Orleans was erected into a state, its inhabitants were almost wholly Spanish and French. In the same manner, the territory of Florida is an accession from a foreign country; and so also, should the government hereafter acquire any district or territory whatever, according to the existing laws, it would first become an organized territory of the United States, and then a state. No such policy as this was ever adopted by any other country; and it succeeds and could succeed only by that nice system of *balances* and *toleration* by which one sect, or party, or state, is constantly checked by others, and the elements of discord and opposition kept from any general union against the laws and the government. It must be observed, however, as what may hereafter be of importance, that the term used in the Constitution, as to the admission of states, is *may*, and not *shall*. Hence, it is not *imperative* in the government of the United States to admit *new states* whenever *they* may demand it. The Constitution has, in the next clause, provided for the government of *territories;* and the Congress may undoubtedly keep all, not provided for by the ordinance of 1787, as territories forever.

§ 414. In respect to the formation of states and the territorial governments, the power was exercised by Congress before the Constitution was formed, and without any article in the confederation to authorize it. The whole of what was called the Northwestern Territory, ceded by Virginia to the United States, and out of which have been carved the states of Ohio, Indiana, Illinois, Wisconsin, and Michigan, was placed under a territorial government, and governed by the ordinance of 1787.[1] That ordinance was, in many respects, wisely

[1] Act of Congress, 1787.

drawn, and has had great, and not less certain because unseen, influence upon the prosperity and happiness of that immense and now populous district.[1]

§415. The articles of *compact* solemnly tendered to the people of the states about to be formed, and thus far accepted by them, contained some remarkable provisions. Among these articles are,

1st. An agreement that said territory and the states which may be formed therein, *shall forever remain a part of this confederacy*, subject to the articles of confederation, and to *such alterations as may be made therein.* This part of the compact, as will be seen hereafter, has an important bearing upon the recently agitated question of *secession.*

2d. And it is further provided, that there shall be *neither slavery* nor *involuntary servitude* in the said territory.

3d. And further, that whenever any of the said territories shall contain sixty thousand free inhabitants, it shall be admitted into the Union upon an equal footing with the original states.[2]

§416. The power of Congress over the public territory, is *exclusive* and *universal*, except so far as they

---

[1] The Northwest Territory, ceded by Virginia to the United States, and included within the ordinances of 1787, contained the states of Ohio, Indiana, Illinois, Michigan and Wisconsin. They now contain more than 7,000,000 inhabitants, and have derived the whole vigor and spirit of their institutions, and the direction of their policy and views, from the ordinance above cited. How important and lasting are the acts of early legislators!

[2] The entire ordinance will be found, page 299, of this book.

are restrained by stipulations in the cessions, or by the ordinance of 1787.[1] This is not the case, however, with merely *national property*, such as forts and arsenals, where the states have not ceded the jurisdiction: in such cases the jurisdiction of the state continues; subject, however, to the just exercise of the proper powers of the national government.

§417. In the year 1820, upon the admission of the state of Missouri into the Union, a question was raised, whether a clause *restricting* the admission of *slaves* into the state, was constitutional. That question was not directly decided; but it was indirectly, by the act passed,[2] which declared that in all the territory north of lat. 36 deg. 30 min., not included within the limits of Missouri, slavery and involuntary servitude should for ever be prohibited.

§418. The question may, however, be considered as settled long before, by the enactment of the ordinance of 1787, under the confederation, and the subsequent adoption and continuance of its provisions under the Constitution.

§419. An objection involving the same principle, was made to the compact between Virginia and Kentucky, but at once overruled by the Supreme Court.[3]

SECTION 4th. *The United States shall guarantee to every state in this Union a republican form of government, and shall protect each of them against invasion,*

---

[1] Story's Comm., 198. [2] Act of Congress, March 6, 1820.

[3] Green *vs.* Biddle, 8 Wheaton, 1, 87, 88.

and, on application of the legislature, or of the executive (when the legislature cannot be convened), against domestic violence.

This clause was unanimously adopted by the convention, and seems essential to the well-being of the republic, because the *whole* republic could not exist, if a *different form* of government was allowed to exist in either one of the states. This clause is intended to prevent such a change, either by a powerful faction, a rebellion, or any other cause.

The phrase, "guarantee a republican form of government"—"protect" against "invasion" or "domestic violence," *covers*, and was manifestly *meant* to cover, every condition of *treason*, *rebellion*, *insurrection*, *servile wars*, *or tumult*, which could possibly be imagined against the *peace* or *government* of a *state*. It covered every thing not covered by *municipal legislation*. The Constitution has already taken from the states the power to keep troops, and ships of war, and consequently, efficiently to suppress insurrections. Hence, it was necessary for the United States to assume their defence.

Article V.

§ 420. *The Congress, whenever two-thirds of both Houses shall deem it necessary, shall propose amendments to this Constitution, or, on the application of the legislatures of two-thirds of the several states, shall call a convention for proposing amendments, which, in either case, shall be valid to all intents and purposes, as part of this Constitution, when ratified by the legislatures of three-fourths of the several states, or by conventions in three-fourths thereof, as the one or the other mode of ratification may be proposed by the Congress; provided that no amendment, which may be made prior to the year one thousand eight hundred and eight, shall in any manner affect the first and fourth clauses in the ninth section of the first article; and that no state, without its consent, shall be deprived of its equal suffrage in the Senate.*

§ 421. This article provides that amendments may be made to the Constitution, and also points out the manner of making them. From this two things follow:

1st. That amendments made in accordance with the provisions of this article, become of the same binding authority as if they had formed a part of the original instrument.

2d. That no amendment can be made except in the way here pointed out.

The *amendments* do not require the assent of the President;—for, when proposed by *two-thirds of Congress*, and ratified by *three-fourths* of the *states*, they are valid.[1]

§ 422. There are three limitations to the power of making amendments:

1st. That the prohibition of Congress to pass any law prior to the year eighteen hundred and eight, for-

---

[1] 3 Dallas, 378.

bidding the introduction of slaves, should not be removed.

2d. That the mode of levying a capitation or direct tax should not be changed so long as slave property could be increased by importation.

3d. That no state should be deprived, without its consent, of its equal representation in the Senate.

The first restriction was adopted as a matter of compromise, and to insure, for a limited time, the continuance of a profitable traffic. The second necessarily grew out of the first; for it would obviously have been unjust to change the mode of laying taxes while the property exempted from taxation could have been increased at pleasure, by importation. The third restriction was intended to insure to the lesser states an effective safeguard against encroachments from the larger; and being placed in the Constitution itself, it cannot be broken down.

Article VI.

§ 423. Clause 1st. *All debts contracted, and engagements entered into, before the adoption of this Constitution, shall be as valid against the United States under this Constitution as under the Confederation.*

The obligations between a *nation* and private individuals remain the same, whatever *changes* the *form of government* may undergo.[1]

[1] Federalist, 43.

§ 424. Clause 2d. *This Constitution, and the laws of the United States, which shall be made in pursuance thereof, and all treaties made, or which shall be made, under the authority of the United States, shall be the supreme law of the land; and the judges in every state shall be bound thereby; any thing in the Constitution, or laws of any state to the contrary notwithstanding.*

§ 425. The necessity of this provision is obvious enough. If the *Constitution* were not the *supreme law* of the land it would not be a *Constitution;* it would be a *nullity:* its *supremacy* makes a part of the instrument itself; yet it was necessary to declare it, in order that all might understand it, and no room be left for controversy. *Treaties* are *supreme* laws till repealed by the legislature of the nation: the legislature has such power, though war may be the consequence of its exercise.[1] *Treaties* are compacts with foreign nations, and must be observed, or the national faith is violated.

§ 426. The *laws of the* United States, if made in pursuance of the Constitution, are as valid as the Constitution, and of course also the *supreme law.* To these provisions it is added, "*any thing in the Constitution*, or *laws of any state to the contrary notwithstanding.*" This clause gave no additional force to the foregoing provisions, but made them clearer to those who administer the laws. Another thing clearly appears from the whole clause, that the Constitution makes the *national government supreme over the state*

[1] 2 Cranch, 1; 3 Story's Comm., 695.

constitution and *laws* in all cases in which they may come in conflict. As the Constitution is thus supreme, every court has the power to declare *unconstitutional* laws *void*, when properly before them.[1]

§ 427. Clause 3d. *The senators and representatives before mentioned, and the members of the several state legislatures, and all executive and judicial officers, both of the United States and of the several states, shall be bound by oath, or affirmation, to support this Constitution; but no religious test shall ever be required as a qualification to any office or public trust under the United States.*

§ 428. This *oath* is required in all civilized nations from the officers of government; it is the most solemn obligation men can be placed under, and it is right to require it of them in a class of duties as important as any that can be performed in a social state. It is to be remarked, that this oath is required of all *state*, as well as *national* officers; for the *agency* of state officers is required to carry on the national government, and they are accordingly required to give their obligations to perform it.

§ 429. In June, 1789, Congress passed an act[2] prescribing the time and manner of taking the oath or affirmation, as well by the officers of the several states as of the United States. Some doubts were entertained of its constitutionality, but it was approved, and no doubt is now had upon it.[3]

---

[1] 1 Kent's Comm., 420. [2] Act 1st June, 1789.

[3] 4 Elliott's Debates, 139; 4 Wheaton's Rep., 415.

§ 430. The clause which enacts that *no religious test* shall ever be required for any office of trust or profit, is one of the most peculiar, as well as valuable parts of the Constitution. This is believed to be the only government in the world which permitted perfect *toleration*, and the experience of half a century has proved that it offers no hindrance to any, while it affords protection to all religious sects. While this exists, there can be no union of *Church and State*,—a union fatal to both, and disastrous to the welfare of the people. Yet Christianity flourishes and extends in the United States with the growth of the people, and the very emulation of the different sects contributes to the prosperity of the whole.

Article VII.

§ 431. *The ratification of the conventions of nine states shall be sufficient for the establishment of this Constitution between the states so ratifying the same.*

At the formation of the Constitution, there were thirteen states; nine of these ratified it immediately, three after the lapse of a few months, and the state of Rhode Island not till more than a year afterward. The instrument was, however, perfect by the ratification of nine, and if the others had not acceded, they would have stood in the relation to them of foreign nations. Since that period, twenty others have joined the union, and the whole form one great nation under a common government.

AMENDMENTS.

§ 432. Upon the adoption of the Constitution, strong objections were made to it on account of some supposed deficiencies. Among others, the want of a bill of rights was strongly urged, to which it was justly replied that the Constitution itself was a bill of rights. The people, in their conventions, however, finally thought best to accede to the Constitution, and urge upon Congress the proposal of several amendments. Accordingly, the amendments we have already mentioned, those following, and some that were not adopted, were recommended by many of the states to Congress, and by Congress to the people.

Amendment I.

§ 433. *Congress shall make no law respecting an establishment of religion, or prohibiting the free exercise thereof; or abridging the freedom of speech, or of the press; or the right of the people peaceably to assemble, and to petition the government for a redress of grievances.*

The first clause was undoubtedly meant to prohibit Congress from interfering in any manner between different sects of Christianity, and not to encourage any other religion. For nearly all the old states had laws for the encouragement of religion; at the same time, Congress has no power to do the slightest positive act to sustain or prohibit any religion whatever. It is a subject upon which they are forbidden to legislate. In this respect the United States Constitution is wholly unlike any other ever formed. It derives no aid from its connection with religion, but leaves that to be settled by conscience and its God.

§434. The next clause is, that Congress shall make no law abridging the freedom of speech or of the press. What is the freedom of speech and of the press? It is the right to speak and publish every thing in relation to every subject, *which is not in derogation of private rights.* No one has a right to injure his neighbor: this is the first law of society, and everywhere preserved in the civil state; of consequence, no one has a right to speak or publish what will injure another; hence the law of *slander* and of *libel.* Within these limits it is not perceived that there is any restraint upon the liberty either of speech or of the press.

§435. The next clause is, the people shall have the right peaceably to assemble and petition for a redress of grievances. This seems to have been altogether a work of supererogation; for the right of the people to assemble, either to petition, or for any other purpose, arises necessarily from the form of government.

Amendment II.

§436. *A well-regulated militia being necessary to the security of a free state, the right of the people to keep and bear arms shall not be infringed.*

The term *militia* is a Latin word, and signifies *the*

being a soldier. In our country it is applied only to that species of soldiery which is composed wholly of enrolled citizens, held *ready* for service, but not actually under arms. It is scarcely necessary to say, that the *right* of the people thus to bear arms is the foundation of their liberties; for, without it, they would be without any power of resistance against the existing government.

AMENDMENT III.

§437. *No soldier shall, in time of peace, be quartered in any house without the consent of the owner, nor in time of war but in a manner to be prescribed by law.*

It was an easy mode of oppression, with arbitrary princes, to quarter soldiers upon the people, so that they ate out their substance and ill-treated their families. It was to prevent the possibility of such scenes in this country that this provision was inserted in the Constitution.

AMENDMENT IV.

§438. *The right of the people to be secure in their persons, houses, papers, and effects, against unreasonable searches and seizures, shall not be violated; and no warrant shall issue but upon probable cause, supported by oath or affirmation, and particularly describing the place to be searched, and the persons or things to be seized.*

Special warrants, such as here described, are the only warrants upon which an arrest can be made according to the law of England.[1] This provision, therefore was in affirmance of the common law, and introduced into the Constitution for more abundant caution.

§ 439. Amendments 5th, 6th, and 7th, in relation to the trial by jury, and the mode of indictment, we have already considered in connection with another part of the Constitution.

Amendment VIII.

§ 440. *Excessive bail shall not be required, nor excessive fines imposed, nor cruel and unusual punishments inflicted.*

Excessive bail, and cruel punishments, were another class of means used by arbitrary governments to oppress the people; hence the insertion of this amendment.

It has been held that this clause applies only to punishments inflicted by the national government, and not to those inflicted by the states.[2]

Amendment IX.

§ 441. *The enumeration in the Constitution of certain rights, shall not be construed to deny or disparage others retained by the people.*

This was merely meant to prevent the application to the Constitution of a maxim, that the affirmation of certain things, in some cases, implies a denial of others.

---

[1] 8 Burrow's Rep., 1743; 4 Blackst. Comm., 291, 292.

[2] 3 Cowen's New York Rep., 686; 3 Story's Comm., 751.

AMENDMENT X.

§ 442. *The powers not delegated to the United States by the Constitution, nor prohibited by it to the states, are reserved to the states respectively, or to the people.*

This provision follows of course, without express insertion, from the fact that the Constitution is an instrument of enumerated powers, and those not expressly given in it, or necessarily flowing from them, are retained by the *original source of* power, or invested in collateral and inferior governments. Now, what is this *source of power?* The *people.* It must be recollected, that both national and state governments are formed by, and derive their authority from, the people; hence, whatever powers they have not invested in the national government, must either be granted to the state governments, or retained by themselves; therefore, the words of the provision, "*reserved to the states respectively or to the people.*"

§ 443. Amendment 11th, in relation to the judicial power, and 12th, in relation to the presidential election, have been already considered.

CHAPTER III.

THE RATIFICATION OF THE CONSTITUTION.

§ 444. We have now seen *what* the Constitution is, and in connection with that, what *constructions* have been put upon its various clauses, and what *decisions* have been had under it by the *judicial authority*. It is important that we should now look at the *mode* in which it was ratified, and what *opinions* were declared by the *ratifying power*, as to what were the rights vested in the national government.

§ 445. When the *convention* had formed the Constitution, they by *resolution*[1] directed it to be "laid before the United States in Congress assembled," and declared their opinion that it should afterward "be submitted to a convention of delegates, chosen in each state by the *people* thereof, under a recommendation of its legislature, for their *assent* and *ratification*;" and that each convention assenting thereto, and ratifying it, should notify Congress thereof.

§ 446. Accordingly, Congress having received *the report of the convention*,—[2]Resolved, that the report, resolutions, and letter accompanying them, be transmitted to the several legislatures, to be by them submitted to a convention of delegates chosen in each state

---

[1] 4 Elliott's Debates, 248. [2] Idem.

by the *people thereof*, in conformity to the resolve of the convention, &c., &c.

§ 447. Under this resolution of Congress, the *states* called *conventions* of the *people*, and the Constitution being submitted to them, was ratified successively by all of them, and the Constitution became the supreme law of the land.

ORDER AND MANNER OF RATIFICATION.

§ 448. 1st. [1]The first state which ratified the Constitution was Delaware, which did so on the 7th December, 1787,—without condition or the recommendation of an amendment.

§ 449. 2d. [2]The second was Pennsylvania, which, in like manner, without any declaration or recommendation, ratified it on the 12th of December, 1787.

§ 450. 3d. The next was New Jersey, which ratified on the 18th December, 1787, as is declared in their ratification, by the *unanimous* consent of all the members.

§ 451. 4th. [3]The fourth was Connecticut, which likewise ratified without any declaration, on the 9th January, 1788.

§ 452. 5th. [4]The next was Georgia, which ratified, without condition or resolution.

§ 453. 6th. The sixth was Massachusetts. In the convention of this state, there was much opposition[5] to

---

[1] 4 Elliott's Debates, 207. [2] Idem, 202. [3] Idem, 209.
[4] Idem, 212. [5] Pitkin's Civ. Hist., vol. ii., p. 266.

the Constitution, and at first a majority against it. In consequence of this, it was finally ratified with the *declaration* of the convention, that in their opinion, certain amendments and alterations were necessary to *remove the fears*, and *quiet the apprehensions* of many of the good people of that commonwealth.

§ 454. The amendments recommended were as follows, viz.:[1]

1. That[2] it be declared that all powers not *expressly* delegated by the Constitution should be reserved to the several *states*, to be by them exercised.

2. That there should be one representative to each thirty thousand persons, until the whole number of persons amounted to two hundred.

3. That Congress should not exercise the power of making *regulations for electing* members of *Congress*, unless the states neglected to make such regulations, or made them subversive of a free and equal representation.

4. That Congress do not lay *direct taxes*, but when the funds arising from impost and excise are insufficient, nor then till they have first made a requisition on each of the states for their quota, and the states have neglected or refused to pay their proportion.

5. That Congress erect no company of merchants with exclusive advantages.

6. That no person be tried for a crime, or suffer an

---

[1] 4 Elliott's Debates, 211.

[2] Whenever resolutions or other proceedings are given in this work, except in the case of the Constitution, they are set forth *substantially*.

infamous punishment, or loss of life, except in the military or naval service, without indictment by a grand jury.

7. The United States judiciary shall have no jurisdiction of causes between citizens of different states, unless the matter in dispute extend to $3000, nor the judicial power extend to actions between citizens of different states when the matter is not of the value of $1500.

8. In civil actions between citizens of different states, issues of fact at common law shall be tried by jury, if the parties request it.

9. Congress shall *not consent*, that any person holding an office of profit or trust under the United States shall receive any title or office from a king, prince, or foreign state.

§ 455. With the recommendation of these amendments, Massachusetts, after great opposition,[1] ratified the Constitution on the 7th of February, 1788.

§ 456. It will be seen in the Constitution, that the sixth recommendation in relation to *indictments* is embodied in the fifth amendment to the Constitution, and that the eighth recommendation is included in the seventh amendment. With the exception of these two, none of the recommendations were ever adopted.

§ 457. 7th. [2]The seventh state to ratify the Constitution was Maryland. This was done without any collateral resolutions, on the 28th of April, 1788.

---

[1] 4 Elliott's Debates, 212. [2] Idem, 218.

§ 458. 8th. The next was the state of South Carolina, which ratified on the 23d of May, 1788. Accompanying their recommendation also, were several resolutions, the substance of which is as follows, viz.:

1. The first resolution was the same as the third of Massachusetts, in relation to the power of *Congress to regulate* the elections of its members.

2. The second was the same as the first of Massachusetts, in relation to the powers *not expressly* granted.

3. The third was the same as the fourth of Massachusetts, in relation to *direct taxes.*

4. The fourth was a *verbal* criticism on the third section of the sixth article.

5. The fifth made it a standing *instruction* to the delegates from that state to endeavor to have these alterations made.

None of these proposed amendments were ever made.

§ 459. 9th. [1]The ninth state which ratified, and which made up the number which was necessary to put the Constitution in operation, was New Hampshire; this took place on the 21st of June, 1788. In the convention of this state, as in Massachusetts, there was great opposition to the Constitution, and their ratification was accompanied with the following recommendations.

1. The first is the same as those of Massachusetts and South Carolina, in relation to powers *not expressly* delegated.

---

[1] 4 Elliott's Debates, 214.

2. The second is the same as the second of Massachusetts.

3–9. The third, fourth, fifth, sixth, seventh, eighth, and ninth alterations proposed are the same with the corresponding ones, proposed by Massachusetts. In fact, as far as the tenth, the New Hampshire propositions seem to have been a literal copy from those of Massachusetts.

10. The tenth was, that no standing army should be kept in time of peace, without the consent of three-fourths of both branches of Congress, nor shall soldiers in time of peace be quartered upon private houses without the consent of owners.

11. Congress shall make no laws touching religion, nor infringe the rights of conscience.

12. Congress shall not disarm citizens unless such as have been in rebellion.

The latter part of the tenth alteration proposed is embraced in the third amendment to the Constitution. The eleventh is included in the first amendment to the Constitution. The twelfth is the second amendment.

§ 460. 10th. [1]The tenth state in the order of ratification was Virginia, which ratified on the 26th June, 1788. In this state also there was much opposition, and their ratification was accompanied by a declaration of rights, in substance as follows, viz.:

That the *people* may *resume* the powers of government, when they are perverted and abused to their

---

[1] 4 Elliott's Debates, 215.

injury and oppression; that every power not granted remains with them and at their will; that no *right* can be cancelled, abridged, or restrained by Congress, the President, or any department or officer of the United States, except where the power is given by the Constitution for these purposes; and that the rights of conscience and of the press cannot be so restrained, modified, or cancelled.

This declaration contained the substance of many of the resolutions offered by other states; and we shall see, in the course of this chapter, the portion of them which was adopted.

§ 461. 11th. [1]The eleventh state adopting the Constitution was New York. Their ratification was made on the 26th July, in the year 1788. It was accompanied by a long declaration of rights, and a series of proposed amendments.

In addition to the amendments already proposed by other states, there were the following:—

That Congress should not impose an *excise* on any article of the growth, production, or manuafacture of the United States.

That no person should be eligible as President, Vice President, or member of Congress, who was not a natural born citizen, or a citizen on the 4th of July, 1776, or held a commission under the United States during the war, and became citizens subsequently, and who shall be freeholders.

---

[1] 4 Elliott's Debates, 216.

That to borrow money, or declare war, two-thirds of the senators and representatives present must concur.

That the privilege of habeas corpus shall not be suspended for a longer time than six months, or until twenty days after the meeting of the next Congress.

That the right of exclusive jurisdiction over ten miles square shall not exempt its citizens from paying the same taxes that other citizens do, nor privilege them from arrest for crimes committed, or debts contracted without the district.

That the right of exclusive jurisdiction over certain public places shall not authorize Congress to prevent the operation of the state laws in civil and criminal matters, except as to persons in the employ of the United States, nor as to them, in respect to crimes.

That the compensation of members of Congress be fixed by standing laws, and no alteration operate for the benefit of members making it.

That the Journals of Congress shall be published at least once a year, except such parts as may require secrecy; that they shall keep their doors open; and that two members may require the *yeas* and *nays*.

That no capitation tax shall be laid.

That no person shall be senator more than six years out of twelve; that the legislatures may recall their senators and elect others.

That no member of Congress shall, during the time for which he was elected, be appointed to any office under the United States.

That the power of Congress to pass bankrupt laws

should only extend to merchants and traders, and that the states have power to pass other insolvent laws.

That no person be eligible as President a third time.

That the executive shall not grant *pardons* for *treason* without the *consent* of Congress, but may *reprieve* them till heard by Congress.

That the President, or person acting as such, shall not command the army in the field unless by desire of Congress.

That all letters patent, commissions, writs, &c., should run in the name of "the People of the United States," and be tested in the name of the President of the United States, or the first judge of the court out of which process shall issue.

That Congress should constitute no inferior tribunals with *appellate* power, except such as are necessary for admiralty and maritime jurisdiction, and in other cases where the jurisdiction is not original, causes shall be tried by the state courts, with a right of appeal to the Supreme Court.

That the court for the trial of impeachments shall consist of the Senate, the judges of the Supreme Court, and the chief judge of the highest court in each state.

That no judge of the Supreme Court shall hold any other office under the government of the United States, or any of them.

That the militia shall not be compelled to serve out of the state for more than six weeks, without the consent of the legislature.

None of these propositions were adopted, but taken

in connection with the amendments proposed by other states, they show what construction, was, at the time, placed upon some of the most important clauses of the Constitution.

§ 462. 12th. [1]The twelfth state which ratified the Constitution was North Carolina, on the 21st of November, 1789. In this state, also, there was great opposition, and a resolution was passed, declaring that a bill of rights should be annexed to the Constitution, and several amendments adopted.

§ 463. The ratification of New Hampshire, the *ninth* in order, was received by Congress on the 2d of July, 1788. They then appointed a committee to report an act to put the Constitution into operation. Under that act the Constitution went into operation on the 4th of March, 1789. It has been seen that North Carolina did not ratify till November, so that the first election of President was made by *eleven states.*

§ 464. Rhode Island was not represented in the Convention, and did not ratify the Constitution till the 29th of May, 1790,[2] more than a year after it had gone into practical operation. The ratification was accompanied by a Declaration of Rights, and the recommendation of many amendments. They recommended nearly all the alterations proposed by other states, and the following additional ones:

That the judicial power of the United States, in which a state is a party, shall not extend to *criminal*

---

[1] 4 Elliott's Debates, 221. [2] Idem, 225.

prosecutions, nor to authorize any suit, by any person, against a state.

That no amendment shall take effect without the consent of eleven states.

That no person shall be compelled to do military duty without voluntary enlistment.

That no standing army be kept in time of peace.

These alterations were not adopted, except the one in relation to suits by individuals against a state, which is embodied in the eleventh amendment to the Constitution.

§465. The Constitution, after its formation, was addressed to the president of Congress, and accompanied by a letter from General Washington, president of the convention, — from which the following extracts are taken.

The letter shows, in a remarkable manner, in what light the Constitution was then viewed, and what were the objects of its formation. They were very different from the fanciful constructions which metaphysical politicians have since been disposed to put upon it.

§466. [1]*It is obviously impracticable in the federal government of these states, to secure all rights of independent sovereignty to each, and yet provide for the interests and safety of all. Individuals entering into society must give up a share of liberty to preserve the rest. The magnitude of the sacrifice must depend, as well on situation and circumstance as on the object to*

---

[1] Elliott's Debates, 249.

be obtained. It is at all times difficult to draw with precision the line between those rights which must be surrendered and those which may be reserved; and, on the present occasion, this difficulty was increased by a difference among the several states as to their situation, extent, habits, and particular interests.

In all our deliberations on this subject, we kept steadily in our view that which appears to us the greatest interest of every true American, the consolidation of the Union, in which is involved our prosperity, felicity, safety,—perhaps our national existence. This important consideration, seriously and deeply impressed upon our minds, led each state in the convention to be less rigid on points of inferior magnitude than might have been otherwise expected; and thus, the Constitution, which we now present, is the result of a spirit of amity, and of that mutual deference and concession, which the peculiarity of our political situations rendered indispensable.

§467. The spirit in which our Constitution was formed, and the great object to be obtained by it, were very different from the spirit and objects entertained by some modern politicians. *Then the consolidation of our union* was the *great end*, to which all other objects were pronounced by Washington and his fellow-statesmen of *inferior magnitude. Now*, consolidation, whether of the union, of law, or of government, is the great object of fear and danger to a class of men, who either think or assert themselves to be the purest of patriots!

§468. At the first session of the first Congress, the Senate and House of Representatives, two-thirds concurring, recommended to the states the adoption of twelve amendments to the Constitution, comprising chiefly those parts of the recommendations of the states which we have already noticed as having been adopted. Ten of these amendments were adopted[1] by three-fourths of the legislatures of the states, and became a part of the Constitution. Subsequently, three other amendments were added.

§469. On the 10th of January, 1791, *Vermont*, the first of the new states, joined the union, and gave its assent to the Constitution. Since then the Constitution has been adopted, assented to, and ratified by nineteen new states, who have become integral parts of the great whole, and as we shall hereafter see, *indissolubly* connected by the Union. In this manner the Constitution was ratified, and received its binding force from *the people* in the several states, not from the state governments.

§470. The language of the ratifications is remarkably uniform, and remarkably *explicit*, as to the source whence the Constitution receives its authority and force.

All the ratifications commence with, We, the delegates of *the people thereof;* and all terminate by making the ratifications in the name of *their constituents, the people.*

---

1 4 Elliott's Debates, 227.

It is plain throughout, that some other *binding force* was thought necessary than mere state authorities. The *people*,—common constituents, it is true, of both state and national governments,—were everywhere summoned, in their *original* and *sovereign* capacity, to give authority to that Union and Constitution, which was not a compact among *state governments*, but among the *people*, who are equally *sovereign* over both national and state governments, and upon whom the Constitution acts *directly* and *personally*.

§ 471. Among the constructions given to the Constitution at the time, in the declarations of the states ratifying it, may be remarked the following fact,—that *Massachusetts* explicitly declared, that the *rights* not *expressly granted* were reserved to the *states*,—and *Virginia*, on the other hand, as explicitly held, that all powers of the Constitution were derived from *the people of the United States*, and those not granted were reserved to *them*. These states have now exactly reversed their positions, and exhibit a new evidence of the instability of human opinion. Indeed, to those who love truth more than argument, all the metaphysical subtilties of the profoundest philosopher would weigh little, in construing the Constitution, against such *facts* as the Letter of Washington, the ratifications of the states, the debates of the convention, and the declared object of all the statesmen who participated in the acts and doings of that day.

§ 472. When Congress met in December, 1859, thirty-three states had been admitted into the American

Union. The following are their names and the dates of admission, including the dates at which the original states *ratified* the Constitution:

1. Delaware ratified the Constitution, 7th of December, 1787, without condition or amendment.

2. Pennsylvania, on the 12th December, 1787, without declaration or recommendation.

3. New Jersey, on the 18th December, 1787, with the *unanimous* consent of all the members of its convention.

4. Connecticut, on the 9th of January, 1788, without any declaration.

5. Georgia, on the 2d of January, 1788, without condition.

6. Massachusetts, on the 7th of February, 1788, with a declaration that certain amendments were necessary.

7. Maryland, on the 28th of April, 1788, without any declaration.

8. South Carolina, on the 23d of May, 1788, with a recommendation of amendments.

9. New Hampshire, June 21st, 1788, with a recommendation of amendments.

10. Virginia, on the 26th of June, 1788, with a Declaration of Rights.

11. New York, on the 26th of July, 1788, with a recommendation of amendments.

12. North Carolina, on the 21st of November, 1789, after having recommended a Bill of Rights.

13. Rhode Island, on the 29th of May, 1790.

14. VERMONT was received into the Union—being the *first of the new states*—on the 10th of January, 1791, and a little more than three years from the time that Delaware (the first of the states of the Union) ratified the Constitution.

15. TENNESSEE was received by act of Congress, June 1st, 1796.

16. KENTUCKY was received into the Union, June, 1792.

17. OHIO was received into the Union, February 19th, 1803.

18. LOUISIANA was received into the Union, April 8th, 1812.

19. INDIANA was received into the Union, December 11th, 1816.

20. MISSISSIPPI was received into the Union, December 16th, 1817.

21. ILLINOIS was received into the Union, December 3d, 1818.

22. ALABAMA was received into the Union, December 14th, 1819.

23. MAINE was received into the Union, March 15th, 1820.

24. MISSOURI was admitted into the Union, August 10th, 1821.

25. ARKANSAS was admitted into the Union, June 14th, 1836.

26. MICHIGAN was admitted into the Union, January 26th, 1837.

27. TEXAS was annexed, March 1st, 1845.

28. FLORIDA was received into the Union, March 3d, 1845.

29. IOWA was received into the Union, March 3d, 1845.

30. WISCONSIN was received into the Union, March, 1847.

31. CALIFORNIA was received into the Union, September 7th, 1850.

32. MINNESOTA was admitted into the Union, May, 1858.

33. OREGON was received into the Union, May, 1858.

§ 473. If the manner in which these states have been received into the Union be historically examined, it will be found that there are *five different modes* in which the STATES of the Union have been constituted: *First.* There were the *thirteen original states*, which acquired their independence by the Revolutionary War and the Peace of 1783; *Secondly.* There are the states *formed* out of territory which belonged to the original states; *Thirdly.* The states formed out of *territory acquired by purchase; Fourthly.* A state *annexed by virtue of a joint resolution* of Congress; *Fifthly.* A class of states formed from territory acquired *by conquest.*

§ 474. Of the thirty-three states now constituting the Union, *thirteen* were of the first class, original states; *fourteen*, viz., Vermont, Maine, Kentucky, Tennessee, Alabama, Mississippi, Ohio, Indiana, Illinois, Michigan, Wisconsin, Iowa, Minnesota, and Oregon, were formed from the territory belonging to the original states; *four*, viz., Louisiana, Arkansas, Missouri, and Florida, were formed from *purchased territory*—the first three purchased of France, and the last of Spain; *one* state, Texas, was *annexed*, and *one* conquered, viz., California.

§475. At the election of General Washington in November, 1788, *eleven* states only voted (*vide* §463); but at the election of 1856, sixty-eight years afterward, *thirty-one* states voted. In the election of 1856, the relative proportion of electoral votes cast by the old and new states, were as follows:

The OLD states, including Maine (in 1788 voting with Massachusetts), cast electoral votes . . 159
The NEW states cast electoral votes 137

This fact may be cited to prove both the growth of the Union and the elasticity of its government, which thus develops a capacity to extend its numbers and territories to indefinite limits. The UNION and the REPUBLICAN, REPRESENTATIVE, and FEDERATIVE GOVERNMENT which it has established, is *capable*, so far as human judgment can now discern, of folding within its benign embrace an indefinite number of states and unnumbered millions of the human race.

CHAPTER IV.

THEORY OF THE STATE GOVERNMENTS.

§ 476. By article 4th, section 4th, of the United States Constitution, the United States *guarantees* to every state in the Union, *a republican form of government.* Most of the colonies had charters previous to the Revolution, especially the New England states, which conceded to them all the rights of self-government; but after the Declaration of Independence, and at the close of the war, nearly all of them formed constitutions for themselves. Connecticut continued to have her civil government administered by the charter of Charles II. till the year 1818; and Rhode Island likewise lived under the charter of Charles till 1842.

§ 477. The *order* of time in which the state constitutions were *formed*, is as follows, viz.:

1. The first constitution formed among the *states*, was that of New Jersey, which was ratified by the Provincial Congress, July 2d, 1776. This was two days before the Declaration of Independence; and it was provided, that if a reconciliation took place that instrument should be null and void.

2. The next constitution formed was that of Virginia, which was adopted, July 5th, 1776. In 1830, a

convention was called and the constitution changed and amended.

3. MARYLAND formed her constitution, August 14th, 1776, which was amended successively in 1795, 1799, and November, 1812.

4. NORTH CAROLINA formed her constitution, December 18th, 1776, which was amended in 1835.

5. MASSACHUSETTS formed her constitution, March 2d, 1780, which was altered and amended, November 3d, 1820.

6. DELAWARE formed her first constitution, September 20th, 1776, and a new constitution, June 12th, 1792.

7. NEW YORK formed her first constitution, April 20th, 1777, which was amended, October 27th, 1801, and further amended, November 10th, 1821. A new constitution was formed and adopted in 1846, which is at present in force.

8. PENNSYLVANIA formed a constitution, September 28th, 1776, another in September, 1790, and another in 1836.

9. SOUTH CAROLINA formed a constitution, March 26th, 1776, which was amended in March, 1778, and in June, 1790.

10. NEW HAMPSHIRE formed a constitution, January 5th, 1777, which was altered in 1784, and was further altered and amended in February, 1792.

11. GEORGIA formed a constitution, February 5th, 1777, a second in 1785, and a third in May, 1798.

§478. The above states were all that had regular

constitutions prior to the admission of new states. Connecticut and Rhode Island still remained under the charters of Charles II.

§479. The provision of the Constitution under which *new states* are admitted, is that of the 3d section of the 4th article, and also that of the 4th section of the same article. These clauses, taken together, impose three *laws*, or elements, which must enter into the admission of new states: 1st. The term of authority used is *may*—not shall. Hence, it is in the power of Congress to *deny* such admission, although the state applying for admission may be formed out of the territory and population of the United States. 2d. The United States, as a nation, *guarantees* to each of these new states, a *republican* form of government. This is a right, which belongs, not only to the state, but to the Union. The state has a right to demand, and the Union must enforce, a republican government. 3d. The Union shall protect each of the states against invasion and against domestic violence. These are the conditions attendant upon the admission of new states.

§480. Progress of the States.—The provision of the United States Constitution by which *new states* may be admitted, has proved elastic enough to add more than the original number, and indefinite in its power to extend the magnitude, numbers, and glory of the Union. The progress of the state constitutions, since 1790, has been as follows.

12. Vermont was formed from a part of the state of New York, by the consent of its legislature, by the act

of March 6th, 1790. Application was made by its commissioners for admission, February 9th, 1791, and it was admitted, March 4th, 1791. A constitution had been professedly formed in December, 1777; but its present constitution was adopted, July 9th, 1793.

13. Kentucky was formed from the territory of Virginia, with the consent of its legislature, by the act of December 18th, 1789.[1] The application of the convention of Kentucky was made, December 9th, 1790, and it was admitted, June 1st, 1792. The constitution of Kentucky was formed, August 17th, 1799, and again in 1849.

14. Tennessee was formed from territory ceded to the United States by the state of North Carolina. She formed a convention and adopted a constitution, February 6th, 1796. An act for its admission was passed and approved, June 1st, 1796.

15. Ohio was formed from the territory northwest of the river Ohio. This territory was ceded to the United States by the General Assembly of Virginia, in 1783, and accepted by the Congress of the United States, March 1st, 1784. On the 13th of July, 1787, Congress passed what is called the Ordinance of 1787, for the government of this territory. (See the Ordinance in full, page 283 of this work.) On April 30th, 1802, Congress passed an act to allow the eastern division of said territory to form a constitution and state government. On the 1st of November, 1802, a constitution was

---

[1] Bioren and Duane's edition of the Laws, vol. i., p. 678.

formed, and presented to Congress, January 7th, 1803. On February 19th, 1803, an act was passed and approved for the due execution of the laws within that state.

16. Louisiana was formed out of the territory ceded to the United States by France, by treaty of April 30th, 1803. The act to enable the President to take possession of this territory, was passed, October 31st, 1803. Louisiana was divided into two territories by the act of Congress, March 26th, 1804. One was called the Territory of Orleans, the other the District of Louisiana. March 2d, 1805, an act was passed, authorizing the people of Orleans Territory to form a constitution and state government, when their number should amount to sixty thousand. On the 20th of February, 1811, an act was passed, allowing them to form a state constitution and to have one Representative till the next census. January 22d, 1812, the people formed a constitution and state government, and gave the state the name of Louisiana. By the act of April 8th, 1812, these proceedings were approved, and the laws of the United States extended over the new state.

17. Indiana was formed out of the Northwestern Territory, ceded to the United States by Virginia. (See Ohio.) The territory was established by an act of May 7th, 1800. The territory was divided into two separate governments, and that of Michigan created by act of January 11th, 1805.

The territory was again divided into two separate governments, and that of Illinois created by act of February 3d, 1809.

The legislature of Indiana applied to be enabled to form a state constitution. (See Journal of the House of Representatives, 1815–16.)

An act to enable the people of Indiana to form a state government, was passed, April 19th, 1816.

The people of Indiana formed a constitution accordingly, June 29th, 1816.

Indiana was received into the Union, by joint resolution, December 11th, 1816.

18. Mississippi was formed out of territory ceded by the state of South Carolina, August 9th, 1787, and by the state of Georgia, April 24th, 1802.

The government of the territory was established by act of Congress, April 7th, 1798.

A joint resolution of Congress, "requesting the assent of the state of Georgia to the formation of two states of the Mississippi territory," was passed and approved, June 17th, 1812.

An act to enable the people of the western part of Mississippi territory to form a constitution and state government, was passed, March 1st, 1817.

The people of this territory formed a state constitution, August 17th, 1817.

Mississippi was admitted into the Union as a state, by act of Congress, approved, December 10th, 1817.

19. Illinois was formed from a part of the Northwestern Territory, ceded to the United States by Virginia. (See Ohio.)

An act (see Indiana) was passed, February 3d, 1809,

dividing Indiana into two separate governments, and organizing Illinois.

A memorial to the House of Representatives from the legislative council, to be allowed to form a state government, was presented, January 16th, 1818.

An act to enable the people of Illinois territory to form a constitution, was approved, April 18th, 1818.

The people of Illinois formed a state constitution, August 26th, 1818.

The state of Illinois was admitted into the Union by act of Congress, December 3d, 1818.

20. Connecticut, though one of the old thirteen states, lived under the charter of Charles II., April 23d, 1662, till the year 1818, September 15th, when a constitution was formed and adopted.

21. Alabama was formed out of a part of the territory ceded by South Carolina and Georgia. (See Mississippi.)

The eastern part of Mississippi territory was made into a separate territory, called "Alabama," by act of Congress, March 3d, 1817.

A petition from the legislative council of Alabama, praying that the people might be allowed to form a state constitution, was presented to the House of Representatives, December 17th, 1818.

An act to enable the people of Alabama to form a constitution and state government, was passed, March 2d, 1819.

The people formed a constitution, August 2d, 1819.

Alabama was admitted into the Union by act passed, December 14th, 1819.

22. Maine was formed out of a part of the territory of Massachusetts.

An act of the legislature of Massachusetts was passed on the 19th of June, 1819, permitting that part of the state known as Maine, to form a separate state.

A petition from a convention of the people of Maine, praying to be permitted to form a separate state, was presented to the House of Representatives, December 8th, 1819.

A constitution was adopted in convention, October 8th, 1819.

Maine was admitted into the Union on the 15th day of March, 1820.

23. Missouri was formed out of part of the territory ceded by France, by the treaty of April 30th, 1803. (See Louisiana.)

By act of March 26th, 1804, Louisiana was divided into two territories.

By act of March 3d, 1805, a separate government was formed, under the title of the Territory of Louisiana.

By the act of June 4th, 1812, it was provided that the territory before called Louisiana, should be called "Missouri."

A memorial of the legislative council and House of Representatives of Missouri, for admission into the Union as a state, was presented to the Senate, December 29th, 1819.

An act to authorize the people of the Missouri Territory to form a constitution and state government, was passed, March 6th, 1820.

By act of March 2d, 1821, Missouri was admitted into the Union on a certain "condition." That "condition" was accepted by the legislature of Missouri in a public act, June 26th, 1821.

By proclamation, dated August 10th, 1821, the President declared the admission of Missouri complete, according to law.

24. Arkansas was formed out of part of the territory ceded by France to the United States, by treaty of April 30th, 1803. (See Louisiana.)

An act establishing a separate territorial government in the southern part of the territory of Missouri, was passed, March 2d, 1819, by which it was named Arkansas.

A memorial of the inhabitants, by convention, praying that Arkansas may be admitted into the Union, accompanied by a constitution formed by said convention, was presented in the House of Representatives, March 1st, 1836.

The constitution of Arkansas was formed on the 30th of January, 1836.

An act for the admission of the state of Arkansas into the Union, was passed, June 15th, 1836.

25. Michigan was formed out of a part of the Northwestern Territory, ceded to the United States by the state of Virginia. (See Ohio.)

An act to divide Indiana territory into two separate

governments, and establish the territory of Michigan, was passed, January 11th, 1805.

A memorial for admission was presented in the House of Representatives, December 11th, 1833.

An act to establish the northern boundary of the state of Ohio, and to provide for the admission of the state of Michigan into the Union, was passed, June 15th, 1836.

An act to admit the state of Michigan into the Union, upon an equal footing with the original states, was passed, January 26th, 1837.

26. Rhode Island, though one of the original thirteen states, remained under the charter of Charles II., granted in 1662, till September, 1842, when this state formed a constitution for herself.

27. Florida was formed out of territory ceded by Spain to the United States by the treaty of February 22d, 1819.

An act to enable the President to take possession of East and West Florida, and establish a temporary government therein, was passed, March 3d, 1819.

An act to establish a territorial government in Florida was passed, March 30th, 1822.

A memorial of Florida, with a constitution formed, was presented to the House of Representatives, February 20th, 1839.

An act for the admission of the states of Iowa and Florida into the Union, was passed, March 3d, 1845.

28. Iowa was formed out of the original territory of the United States.

An act to divide the territory of Wisconsin, and to establish the territorial government of Iowa, was passed, June 12th, 1838.

February 12th, 1844, a memorial from the legislative assembly of Iowa, for admission into the Union, was presented in the Senate.

December 9th, 1844, a memorial of a convention, with a copy of a constitution adopted by the people of Iowa, was presented in the Senate, asking admission into the Union.

An act for the admission of the States of Iowa and Florida into the Union, was passed, March 3d, 1845.

29. Texas was an independent republic, formed out of Mexican territory, and annexed to the United States by a joint resolution of Congress, approved, March 1st, 1845.

In July, 1845, Texas formed and adopted a constitution.

On the 29th of December, 1845, a joint resolution was passed by Congress, declaring Texas a state of the Union, on equal terms with the original states.

30. Wisconsin was formed out of the Northwestern Territory, ceded to the United States by Virginia. (See Ohio.)

A memorial of the legislative council of Michigan was presented in the House of Representatives, March 1st, 1836, for the division of that territory, and that the territory of Michigan be established.

An act establishing the territorial government of Wisconsin, was passed and approved, April 20th, 1836.

On March 20th, 1845, a resolution of the legislative council of Wisconsin was presented in the Senate, asking that provision be made for holding a state convention for forming a constitution.

August 6th, 1846, a bill to enable the people of Wisconsin territory to form a constitution and state government, and for the admission of such state into the Union, was passed and approved.

December 16th, 1846, the people of Wisconsin formed and adopted a state constitution.

March 3d, 1847, an act for the admission of the state of Wisconsin into the Union was passed and approved.

Two members of Congress from that state, took their seats in the 30th Congress.

31. CALIFORNIA is part of the territory ceded to the United States by Mexico, at the treaty of Guadaloupe Hidalgo, Feb. 2d, 1848. The discovery of gold leading to a vast influx of American settlers, a convention was called, which, on the 13th October, 1849, adopted a constitution, ratified by the people, November 13th, 1849. Congress then, by act of September 7th, 1850, admitted California as a state.

32. MINNESOTA is a part of the Louisiana purchase, and was subsequently part of Iowa territory. It was organized under a territorial government in 1849, a constitution was adopted in November, 1857, and Minnesota admitted as a state, in May, 1858.

33. OREGON, also a portion of the Louisiana purchase, was organized as a territory in 1848, and

divided, in 1853, into Oregon and Washington territories. In 1855, Oregon applied for admission as a state, and having adopted a constitution in November, 1857, was admitted in May, 1858.

§481. Modes of admitting States, and the Formation of new States.—In section 473, it was stated that there were four modes in which states were *constituted* —from the original states, from territory belonging to them, from territory purchased, and by annexing an independent state. Thus, there were *thirteen* original states, *eleven* from territory which belonged to the original states, viz.: Vermont, Maine, Kentucky, Tennessee, Alabama, Mississippi, Ohio, Indiana, Illinois, Michigan, Wisconsin; *seven* from territory purchased, viz.: Louisiana, Missouri, Arkansas, Iowa, Minnesota, Oregon, and Florida; and *one* by annexation, viz.: Texas. But there are also different *legal* modes of admission. Thus, the thirteen original states came into the Union, as we have seen, by *ratifying*—that is, adopting—a constitution formed by a national convention. The moment they *ratified* that constitution, they became subject to its duties, rights, and liabilities. *Three* of the present states became members of the Union *from parts of other states*, by the *joint act* of Congress and those states, viz.: Vermont, Kentucky, and Maine. This was in conformity to section 3d of article 4th of the Constitution. *Fourteen* of the present states were admitted as states, after previously passing through the condition of a territory, by *act of Congress*. *One* state (Tennessee) was admitted from territory of the United States, by act of Congress, without having had a territorial government; and *one* state (Texas) was admitted by *joint resolution* of Congress, having been an independent state.

An analysis of these modes shows, that there are really three *legal methods* of receiving a state, established by the practice of the government under the constitution.

1st. A state may be formed *from part of a state*, by the joint act of the Congress of the United States and of the state from which it was formed.

2d. A state may be formed from *a territory* already organized, by a simple act of Congress.

3d. A state may be formed *by the annexation of an independent state*, with the consent of that state and a joint resolution of Congress.

In the latter case the theory is, that receiving an independent state into the Union is an act of national sovereignty, and that it is only necessary that the constituted authorities of each should consent. It is not forbidden by the constitution, and is, therefore, one of those national powers which may be exerted with the national consent.

There is one other *legal method* of admitting a state, which has not yet been practised. This is by the formation of a state *from parts of two states*. For example, East Tennessee and Western North Carolina *might* be formed into a state. In that case it may be received by the joint act of Congress and of *each of the states* from which it was formed.

§ 482. The *thirty-three states* which, in 1858, made up the American Union, have all regularly formed constitutions. These constitutions are all formed upon the *same principles* with each other and with the Constitution of the United States. They all observe the same division of the government into the three parts, of executive, legislative, and judicial. They all adopt the *representative principle*, and are all *republican.* One-half of them are accompanied with *declarations of right*—a measure of *superabundant caution*—for the *evils* which they are generally intended to operate against could not take place if the state constitutions had no existence, as the Constitution of the United States effectually prohibits them.

§ 483. As all the state constitutions are similar to each other, and nearly, in form, the same with the Constitution of the United States, it will be unnecessary, for the purpose of instruction, to consider more than one of them; and for this purpose we may take the constitution of New York, and point out, also, some *differences* between that and the constitutions of other states.

CONSTITUTION OF NEW YORK.

§ 484. The constitution of New York, adopted in 1846, contains fourteen articles.

ARTICLE 1st is a Bill of Rights.

ARTICLE 2d defines who shall be electors in state elections, and what shall be their rights.

ARTICLE 3d declares in whom the legislative power

shall reside, and gives rules for the election of the members and their mode of conducting proceedings.

ARTICLE 4th defines the power of the executive.

ARTICLES 5th and 10th regard other state officers, their election, removal, and duties.

ARTICLE 6th defines the organization and powers of the judiciary.

ARTICLE 7th forbids the sale of the canals and salt springs, and limits the power of the state to contract debts.

ARTICLE 8th requires corporations to be formed under general laws.

ARTICLE 9th provides for the accumulation and distribution of the School and Literature Funds.

ARTICLE 11th organizes the militia, making brigadier-generals and all inferior officers eligible by the corps to which they belong, major-generals by the governor.

ARTICLE 12th requires all officers to take an oath to support the constitution of the state and of the United States, and faithfully to discharge the duties of their office.

ARTICLE 13th declares that amendments to the constitution must pass two successive legislatures and then be submitted to the people, and directs that every twenty years the vote of the people shall be taken as to the propriety of calling a convention to amend the constitution.

§ 485. The Bill of Rights recites all those things which are considered as inherent elements of personal liberty, such as the right of citizenship, trial by jury, free exercise of religion, free and impartial trial, right of property, freedom of speech, of public meeting, and petition, with clauses restricting the legislative power in regard to public money or private property, and prohibiting feudal rights.

§ 486. Article 2d defines electors to be male citizens of the age of twenty-one years, a citizen for ten days, for thirty days a resident of the district, four months of the county, and one year of the state. But no man of color can vote till he has been for three years a citizen of the state, and for one year been seized of a freehold estate worth two hundred and fifty dollars, and paid taxes thereon.

§ 487. Article 3d declares that the legislative power shall be vested in a senate and assembly. The senate of thirty-two members, chosen for two years. The assembly of one hundred and twenty-eight members, annually elected and apportioned according to the population.

In the general assembly thus constituted, are vested all the legislative powers which are not inconsistent with the constitution of the state or of the United States, and which concern the affairs of the state, and the rules and regulations of their own bodies.

§ 488. Article 4th vests the executive power in the governor, to be elected at the time and place of choosing members of the assembly, and to hold his office for two years. His powers are to command the military and naval forces, to convene the legislature on extraordinary occasions, and take care that the laws are faithfully executed. He has also power to pardon after conviction all offences but treason, and power to veto any act passed by the legislature, which does not become a law unless it is subsequently passed by two-thirds of each house.

§ 489. Article 6th vests the judicial power in the court for the trial of impeachments, consisting of the senate, lieutenant-governor, and judges of the Court of Appeals; in a Court of Appeals, consisting of four judges elected by the people for eight years, and four selected from the judges of the Supreme Court; in a Supreme Court, having original jurisdiction, of thirty-two or more judges elected; in county judges, inferior local courts civil and criminal, and in justices of the peace. Judges are removable by the legislature, and, in some cases, by the senate, on the recommendation of the governor. Tribunals of conciliation are authorized, and steps taken to prepare a simple code of practice in courts of law.

§ 490. We observe that, in the *outlines* of the constitution of New York, it corresponds very well with that of the United States.

1st. Like that of the United States, *power* is divided into three departments—legislative, executive, and judicial.

2d. That the legislative department is likewise divided into two branches—the senate and the house.

3d. That, like Congress, they decide on the qualifications of their own members, and determine the rules of their own proceedings.

4th. The executive, like the President, is chief of such naval and military force as the state may employ.

5th. The judiciary is constituted on the same plan of Supreme and minor courts.

In fine, the general principles of the state constitutions and those of the United States are the same. The great *differences* consist in the *subject-matter* upon which they respectively act, and the *kind of power* which is granted.

§ 491. The principal differences between the national and state constitutions may be thus defined: The Constitution of the United States, being national, regards *national* objects, and is vested with powers *chiefly external*, while the state constitutions, being subordinate and local, act almost wholly upon *municipal* and *internal affairs.*

§ 492. What, then, is the object and extent of state legislation? The Constitution of the United States expressly defines all *power* into three distinct classes:[1] 1st. Those powers and rights delegated to the government of the *United States* in the national Constitution; 2d. Those delegated to the *states* in the state constitutions; 3d. Those reserved to the *people*. For the first class, we must refer to the Constitution of the United States; for the second, to the constitutions of the states; and the last are all those not included in the two former. The last class of rights are those generally called *inalienable*—such as the rights of personal

---

[1] See 10th Amendment to the United States Constitution.

liberty and of private worship, and the great right of amending or abrogating government—for, as every people have the right to make their government, they cannot be deprived of the right of abrogating it; though the last cannot be exercised by individuals, in opposition to existing laws. It must be the sovereignty of the people creating *revolution*.

The powers of the state governments, then, *are all that great body of authority* which the Constitution of the United States does not, directly or indirectly, *prohibit to the states, and the people have not themselves retained.*

§ 493. Without entering into details, we may briefly notice *some of the most important powers possessed by the states.*

1st. The Constitution of the United States, while directing that a *representative* body should be chosen, left the *regulation* of the *elective franchise* to the states; for it [1] directs that the "electors" shall have the same qualifications as *electors for the most numerous branch of the legislatures.* Each state, then, in regulating the elective franchise for itself, also regulates that of the government of the Union, and may make it as enlarged or as restricted as it pleases.

2d. Another power possessed by the states,[2] is that of partaking in the formation of the national Senate. Though this would seem to place the existence of the Senate in the power of the states, yet such is not the

---

[1] Art. 1, Sec. 2, U. S. Constitution. [2] Idem, Section 3.

fact; for the [1]Constitution, in another provision, gives Congress the power to *make and alter regulations as to times and manner* of choosing senators: if, then, Congress make such regulations, and the states do not choose their senators at that time and in that mode, they will act unconstitutionally, and place themselves in the wrong.

3d. Another power possessed by the states,[2] is contained in the mode of choosing the President. The *states* appoint, in such manner as the legislatures direct, the electors; but, in this case, as in that of senators, the power to act or not to act, is not left with the states. By another clause,[3] *Congress* appoints the *time* of choosing electors, and the day of giving their votes.

§ 494. But the greatest and most important authority of the state governments, is that of enacting the *whole body of local and municipal laws*, and enforcing them by the organization and process of judicial courts. This class of laws is that which most intimately concerns the happiness and prosperity of the people. An act of incorporation by the legislature, or the location of a canal, may double the value of property, or a series of unwise enactments destroy the peace or paralyze the industry of society, when the distant war, upon which the *nation* is engaged, is scarcely felt.

§ 495. The state governments are chiefly concerned with *four classes* of laws. 1st. Those which relate to *private property and private rights*—such as the laws

---

[1] Art. 1, Sec. 4, U. S. Constitution. [2] Idem, Art. 2, Sec. 2.
[3] Idem, Art. 2, Sec. 3.

of inheritance, of wills, of debtor and creditor, &c. 2d. Such as relate to *corporate and public bodies*—such as turnpike and bridge companies, chartering cities, charitable, and literary institutions. 3d. Those which relate to *public property*, *public works*, and *public institutions*—such as public buildings, state canals, public schools, and state institutions of benevolence. 4th. Those which relate to the *punishment of crime*—such as what constitutes crime, the extent of punishment, and the mode of conviction. But crimes committed on the high seas, or those against the laws of the United States, are not within the jurisdiction of the states.

In addition to these great powers of state legislation, there are some of a miscellaneous character—such as the organization of the militia, and the co-operation of the states in *amendments* to the national Constitution.[1]

DIFFERENCES IN THE STATE CONSTITUTIONS.

§ 496. Within the last few years, several of the states have made new constitutions, and many new states have been admitted to the Union. The result, in general, has been to reduce the state constitutions to very nearly the same general principles. Some *differences*, however, may be noted.

1st. One of the principal differences in the state gov-

---

[1] Article 5, United States Constitution.

ernments is in the power of the *executive.* In some instances, he has the same *veto power* as the President of the United States. His signature is required to a law; and if he refuse, it requires *two-thirds* of the legislature to pass it. Such is the case in Georgia, Mississippi, and New Hampshire.

In other states, such as Ohio, his signature is not required to laws at all, and it is never affixed.

In another class of states, such as Kentucky and Indiana, the governor's signature is required, and he may make objections; but if he does object, the two houses of the legislature may *reconsider* the law, and pass it, notwithstanding his objections, by a majority of all the members *elected* to each house.

In Vermont, the passage of a law may be *suspended* till the next legislature, by the governor and council.

2d. Another difference in the state constitutions consists in the *definition* of the right of suffrage. Of late years, however, and in the new constitutions, this difference has almost dwindled away—almost all the constitutions having provided for *universal suffrage* in the case of white males over twenty-one years of age.

The *variations* of the right of suffrage consist chiefly in the *time of residence.* Thus, in New Hampshire, the right of suffrage is vested "in *every male inhabitant* of twenty-one years of age, except paupers and persons excused from paying taxes by their own request." This seems to leave the right to depend on the definition of *inhabitancy,* without reference to *time.*

In Maine, *three months'* residence is required.

In Illinois, the requisition is *six months'* residence in the *state*.

In Tennessee, it is *six months* in the *county*.

In Connecticut, it is *six months'* residence and militia duty, or state tax, and moral character.

In Indiana, Vermont, North Carolina, Georgia, Alabama, Missouri, New Jersey, Maryland, Massachusetts, New York, Mississippi, Ohio, and Louisiana, *one year's residence* is required. In Georgia, Alabama, and Missouri, the voter must have resided three months within the county.

In Maryland, Massachusetts, and Mississippi, there must be six months' residence within the county.

Pennsylvania, Delaware, and South Carolina, require *two years'* residence and state tax.

Kentucky requires a residence of *two years in the state*, and of one within the county.

In North Carolina and Virginia there is a slight property qualification. But, generally, the qualifications required of a voter are so slight, that suffrage is said to be universal.

3d. Another difference between the various state governments consists in the organization of the judiciary. Thus, some states have separate chancery courts, and in some, the powers of chancery are vested in the common-law courts. In some states, there are separate probate courts, and in some, the duties of probate courts are performed by the courts of Common Pleas. So, also, criminal and civil courts are sometimes separate and sometimes conjoined.

These variations in fact, however, amount to nothing; for, in substance, the same general system of laws pervades all the states, and is, with some necessary changes, modelled on the laws and courts of England. In the state of Louisiana, indeed, there is an exception. The civil code, or Roman law, prevails there.

CHAPTER V.

THE NATURE AND GENERAL PRINCIPLES OF THE GENERAL AND STATE GOVERNMENTS.

§ 497. There are certain general principles which pervade the federative system of the United States government. We shall state these, with a citation of the several parts of the Constitution upon which they rest, without any further comment upon them:

§ 498. Proposition 1. *The government of the United States is a Republic.* Refer to the 7th definition (page 17), and then to article 1, section 1st and section 2d, of the United States Constitution.

§ 499. Proposition 2. *The government of the United States is a Federative Republic.* See article 1, section 2d and section 3d; article 4, sections 2d, 3d, and 4th.

§ 500. Proposition 3. *The government of the United States is a Democratic Federative Republic.* See definition 8th (page 17), also article 1, section 1st, and section 2d, and section 3d. Refer to the state constitutions for the right of suffrage, vesting the power of election in the whole body of the people.

§ 501. Proposition 4. *The democracy of the United States is a Representative Democracy.* Senators, representatives, and electors are *chosen.* See article 1, section 2d and section 3d; article 2, section 1st and section 2d.

§ 502. Proposition 5. *The foundation of the government is the consent of the people.* See the Declaration of Independence.

§ 503. Proposition 6. *The sanction of the government is responsibility to the people.* Refer to modes of election for representatives, article 1, section 2d, of the Constitution; for executive, article 2, section 1st; for impeachment, article 1, section 3d; for power of appointment, see article 2, section 2d. The judiciary is appointed by the President, who is responsible to the people.

§ 504. Proposition 7. The principle of the government is the virtue of the people. Upon what other foundation can republican government rest? Refer to the history of Greece, Rome, and France.

§ 505. Proposition 8. *The Constitution of the United States proceeds from the people, in their sovereign capacity.* Refer to article 7 of the Constitution, and to the terms of the original ratifications by the states.

§ 506. Proposition 9. *The Constitution of the United States acts upon both individuals and states.* For its action on the *states*, refer to article 1, section 3d, section 4th, and section 10th. For *individuals*, see article 1, section 8th.

§ 507. Proposition 10. *The constitutions of the states act upon individuals, but not upon the government of the United States, nor upon each other.*

That they act upon individuals, refer to the state constitutions. That they do not act on each other is evident, because they are independent and sovereign as to each other.

That they cannot exercise any power over the national government, is decided by the Supreme Court. See M'Cullough *vs.* The State of Maryland, 4th vol. Wheaton's Reports, 316.

§ 508. PROPOSITION 11. *The government of the United States is not a mere league.* The powers vested in the national government prove this. For a complete exposition of this point, see President Jackson's proclamation, 10th December, 1832.

§ 509. PROPOSITION 12. *The government of the United States is sovereign in its national capacity.* For a nation to be sovereign, it must govern itself. Now, the government of the United States does govern itself. It lays taxes, declares war, makes peace, enters into treaties, coins money, regulates commerce. See article 1, section 8th; article 2, section 2d; article 3, section 2d.

§ 510. PROPOSITION 13. *The governments of the states are sovereign in their municipal, and are not sovereign in a national capacity.* Refer to the state constitutions for the objects of state legislation. Refer to article 1, section 10th, for the *prohibitions* in the United States Constitution, on state power.

§ 511. The above propositions are sufficient to show the nature and general principles of the United States government. The American people are one nation, governing itself, by virtue of the original, natural, and inherent rights of man. The government thus constituted has no foundation but the common consent of the governed, and no sustaining principle but the virtue and capacity of the people to govern themselves. This government is twofold: one a national government and one the government of states united with one another. Both these forms of government are founded on the representative system. The whole constitutes a democratic, federative republic. It is a government which, proceeding from the people, exists only at their pleasure; but, within its constitutional limits, has absolute authority over individuals. The laws, both of national and state governments, constitutionally enacted, are of binding obligation upon all individuals within their jurisdiction. It is a government of laws, but of laws sustained by the whole community.

CHAPTER VI.

PRACTICAL OPERATION OF THE NATIONAL CONSTITUTION.

§ 512. When the Constitution had been *ratified* by the requisite number of states, it had acquired its *legal force*, but was inert till properly put into operation. The people had made it an instrument of great and beneficent powers; but their *action* under it was necessary to give it life. The *mode* of doing this had been provided by the convention. They had "resolved, that as soon as the conventions of nine states should have ratified the Constitution, Congress should fix a day on which electors should be appointed by the states which should have ratified the same, and a day on which electors should assemble to vote for President, and the *time* and *place of commencing proceedings under the Constitution*. That, after such publication, the electors should be appointed, and the senators and representatives elected," and such other regulations as were necessary, &c.; and that "after the President was elected, *he* and *Congress* should without delay, proceed to *execute the Constitution*."

§ 513. Accordingly, Congress, after the ratification of a sufficient number of states, in July, 1788, ordered,[1] that the several ratifications of the Constitution of the

---

[1] Elliott's Debates, 221.

United States be referred to a committee, to examine and report an act for *putting said Constitution into operation.* A committee was appointed, and the following resolution passed.[1] "Resolved, that the first Wednesday in January next, be the day for appointing the electors in the several states which, before said day, shall have ratified the Constitution; that the first day in February next, be the day for the electors to assemble in their respective states, and vote for a President; and that the first Wednesday in March next be the time, and the present seat of Congress the place, for commencing proceedings under said Constitution."

§ 514. In pursuance of this resolution, the elections in the several states were held at the time appointed; and on Wednesday, the *4th of March,* 1789, *the Constitution went into practical operation.* On the 30th April, George Washington, unanimously elected, was inaugurated President of the United States. Subsequently to this, North Carolina and Rhode Island, which had not then ratified, joined the Union. Soon after, a nnmber of amendments, the effect of which we have heretofore considered, were recommended to the states by two-thirds of Congress, and adopted.

§ 515. Thus the operation of the Federal Government was begun. The arrangement of the judiciary, the rules of proceedings, the organization of the departments, and the appointment of officers, were within the power of Congress and the executive, and formed the earliest objects of their consideration.

---

[1] Elliott's Debates, 222.

§ 516. In practice, as well as theory, the government is divided into three great departments, having distinct duties to perform,—the executive, the legislative, and the judicial. In this order we shall consider the practical operation of the government.

I. Of the Executive.

§ 517. By article 2, section 1st, of the Constitution, *the executive power is vested in the President.* By section 2d, *he is commander-in-chief* of the army, of the navy, and of the militia when called into actual service. He may require the opinion in writing of the principal officers of the executive departments, upon any subject relating to the duties of their offices, and has power to grant reprieves, pardons, &c., &c. He has the appointment, in conjunction with the Senate, of ambassadors, other public ministers, consuls, judges of the Supreme Court, and all other officers of the United States, except those inferior officers whose appointment the Congress may vest in the heads of departments, courts, &c. He receives ambassadors and other public officers, takes care that the laws are faithfully executed, and commissions officers.

§ 518. These are all the general duties annexed by the Constitution to the office of President. We have already seen that they could not be performed till *Congress* had first *erected* the *offices* which were to be filled, and *enacted* the *laws* which were to be executed. We shall now see how this was done.

§ 519. The *constitutional duties* above enumerated,

comprehend all *the executive* duties of the government; for the *President* is the *only* executive officer known to the Constitution, and the only one responsible to the people. The duties, however, are obviously too numerous and various for one man; hence, the Constitution contemplated the appointment of inferior officers, and the division of labor among subordinates. For this purpose, Congress has, at different times, created the Departments of State, Treasury, War, Navy, Post-Office, Attorney-General, and Home Department. The duties of each of these departments have been prescribed, and may be considered separately.

I. OF THE DEPARTMENT OF STATE.

§ 520. This department was created by the act of the 15th September, 1789. The presiding officer is called Secretary of State, and, like other officers, is commissioned with the advice and consent of the Senate. His duty is to conduct the foreign affairs of the United States, whether by correspondence, commissions, instructions, or memorials, with foreign powers or public ministers. He keeps the seal of the United States, and affixes it to all civil commissions, provided they have the signature of the President. He is intrusted with the publication and distribution of all acts and resolutions of Congress, and all treaties with foreign nations, and Indian tribes.[1] He preserves the original of all treaties, public documents, laws, and correspondence

---

[1] Act of April 20th, 1818.

with foreign powers; he preserves copies of the several statutes of the states, grants passports to citizens, and controls the Patent Office.

§ 521. These duties may be divided into classes. 1. Those which concern *foreign* intercourse; 2. Those which concern the preservation and distribution of the *laws;* 3. Which regard the *authenticity of commissions;* 4. Those which concern *copyrights and patents.*

1. *Of Foreign Intercourse.*—It is necessary that nations should hold intercourse together, for the purpose of regulating trade, avoiding injuries, and terminating differences. It is equally obvious that *they cannot treat together immediately*, as two individuals; they must, therefore, hold their conferences by means of *delegates*—that is, by *public ministers.*[1]

§ 522. A public minister properly signifies any one charged with public affairs, but is here understood as one who *is charged with the care of public affairs at a foreign court.* Of these, there are now *several orders.*

§ 523. The highest order is one which properly *represents* the government, or *sovereignty*, and is entitled to act for it upon all occasions. A person of this rank is called an *Ambassador.*[2]

§ 524. The next rank is that of *Envoy.* This term signifies one *who is sent*, and means a minister sent for a particular purpose—as to adjust a special commercial treaty, or arrange disputed boundaries. There are

---

[1] Vattel's Law of Nations, Book IV., chap. v., sect. 55, 56.

[2] Idem, chap. vi., sect. 71, 72.

envoys *ordinary* and *extraordinary;* of the same rank, also, are ministers *plenipotentiary*, who are sent with powers to make a particular treaty: thus, Messrs. Adams, Clay, &c., were Ministers *Plenipotentiary* to form the Treaty of Peace at Ghent.

§ 525. The *third order* is that of *Ministers Resident*, or *Chargé d'Affaires*—which means one who is *charged with the ordinary affairs of the nation at a foreign court.*

§ 526. These are all the orders of public ministers as commonly understood, resident at foreign courts. There are, however, several other classes of public officers, through whom intercourse is held with foreign nations.

§ 527. To each *foreign embassy* is attached a *Secretary of Legation.* This officer performs the duties of a secretary, or clerk, to the mission, and is frequently left in *charge of affairs* when a minister is recalled.

§ 528. *Consuls* are *commercial agents*, appointed to reside in the seaports of foreign countries, with a commission to watch over the commercial rights and privileges of the nation deputing them.[1]

Their duties are limited and defined in *treaties* of commerce, and by the statute regulations of the country they represent. No nation is bound to receive a consul, unless it has agreed to do so by treaty, and its refusal to do so is no violation of peace and amity. They are, however, almost universal among civilized

---

[1] 1 Kent's Comm., 40.

nations, and are important both to commercial interests and national affairs.

§ 529. The *duties* of consuls, prescribed by the laws of the United States, may be defined as follows: 1. To act as *administrators* upon the estates of such American citizens as die abroad, without leaving legal representatives abroad, and then account to the treasury. 2. When *vessels are stranded*, to take care of the property and deliver it to the owners. 3. To receive from American vessels abroad, their sea-letters, legal documents, &c., and return them on departure of the vessel. 4. When a crew is discharged abroad, to receive from each seaman a month's pay, as a fund for the relief of American seamen. 5. To provide for the support and passage to the United States of *destitute* American seamen, in a reasonable manner.

These consuls are appointed by the United States, in all the principal commercial ports of the world, and their great *object* is to ascertain the *legality* of the trade in American vessels, and give protection and relief to American seamen and citizens.

§ 530. *Credentials.* A *public minister is known by his credentials.* [1]Letters of Credence are the instruments which *authorize* and *establish* a minister in his *character* with the government to whom they are addressed: they are his general Letter of Attorney.

§ 531. *Instructions* are the secret letter of directions

---

[1] Vattel, Book IV., chap. vi., sect. 76, 77.

given by a government to its minister, to inform him how he is to act and what he is to perform.

§ 532. For the purpose of preserving the dignity of their respective governments, and performing their duties with safety, *public ministers* and *their servants* are, by the *laws of nations*,[1] allowed certain privileges, viz.:

§ 533. The *persons* of ministers are *sacred* and *inviolable* among all nations. This privilege extends to them from the time they first enter the country to which they are sent. So, also, they are allowed *personal safety* in all *countries* through which they pass.

§ 534. [2] A *public minister* has an entire independence of the jurisdiction and authority of the state where he resides. To these rules there is an *exception*,[3] in case of an ambassador's converting these privileges into *licentiousness*. If an ambassador abuses his privileges and commits wrong, he may be restrained: 1st. By application to his master, and if he fail to recall him, by *ordering him out of the country*. 2d. In case he take up arms, or commit open violence, he may be *quelled by force*. In case he intrigue, or form a conspiracy, he may be arrested, or otherwise disposed of according to the exigency of the case. A well-known instance of that kind occurred in this country, in the case of Genet, the French minister, during the administration of General Washington. The President *only*

---

[1] Vattel, Book IV., chap. vi., sect. 81, 83, 92, 93. [2] Idem.

[3] Pitkin's Civ. Hist., vol. ii.

requested the French government to recall M. Genet, which was done; no doubt harsher measures would have been justifiable.

§ 535. [1] A *consul* is *not* such a public minister as to be entitled to the privileges of that character, nor is he under the special protection of the laws of nations.

§ 536. The *credentials* of foreign ministers are received by the Secretary of State, and examined; all the business and correspondence is carried on by him; it is in writing and placed on record.

§ 537. The other duties of the Secretary of State are to grant *passports* to citizens visiting foreign countries; to *preserve* the originals of public documents, and to *publish* the laws, resolutions, and orders of Congress; to publish a *biennial catalogue* of public officers; to *authenticate commissions* with the seal of the United States; and, in general, to perform all the duties which appertain to the authentication of national proceedings and intercourse with foreign nations.

II. OF THE TREASURY DEPARTMENT.

§ 538. The object of this department is to manage *the moneyed concerns* of the government. The general duties of the Secretary of the Treasury are to *receive and disburse the public revenues;* to propose and digest *plans* for the improvement and management of the public revenue and the support of public credit;

---

[1] 1 Kent's Comm., 43.

and to make reports to Congress upon all matters referred to him.

To enable him to perform these duties—many of which, in relation to auditing public accounts and collecting the revenue, are of a complicated character—the business of the treasury department is subdivided among several subordinate officers. These are:

First Comptroller, who examines and certifies the accounts and balances of the 1st and 5th auditors.

Second Comptroller, who examines and certifies the accounts of the 2d, 3d, and 4th auditors, and keeps a record of requisitions.

First Auditor receives and examines the accounts in relation to the revenue and civil list; certifies balances, and transfers them, with vouchers, to the First Comptroller.

Second Auditor receives and settles accounts in relation to the pay, subsistence, forage, clothing, hospitals, armories, arsenals, ordnance, recruiting service, and contingencies of the army, and those accounts relative to the disbursements of the Indian service.

Third Auditor examines and settles the accounts relative to the quartermaster's department of the army, the military academy, fortifications, and roads.

Fourth Auditor examines the accounts of the navy department, and certifies them, with vouchers, to the Second Comptroller.

Fifth Auditor is charged with the revision and settlement of accounts in relation to the state department, the general post-office, and the Indian department.

The Treasurer receives and keeps the public moneys, and disburses the same upon warrants drawn by the Secretary and countersigned by the Comptroller.

The Register keeps all accounts of the receipts and expenditures of public moneys.

The Solicitor of the Treasury is a law officer, who superintends the *civil suits* commenced in the name of the United States, until they come into the Supreme Court of the United States, when they pass into the hands of the Attorney General.

III. OF THE WAR DEPARTMENT.

§ 539. This is one of the original departments, having been organized in August, 1789. The general duties of the Secretary of War are, a superintendence over all military affairs.

§ 540. In order to facilitate business, this department is divided into the following subdivisions, the nature of which may be understood by their titles:—

1. The War Office is the office of the Secretary and his correspondence.

2. The Requisition Bureau, in which the requisitions of the war department on the Treasury are made out.

3. The Bounty Land Office.

4. The General Staff Office.

5. Office of the Adjutant-General.

6. Engineer Bureau.

7. Topographical Bureau.

8. Ordnance Department.

9. Quartermaster's Department.
10. Purchasing Department.
11. Pay Department.
12. Subsistence Department.
13. Medical Department.

IV. OF THE NAVY DEPARTMENT.

§ 541. The Navy department was not created till ten years after the establishment of the government. The office of Secretary of the Navy was created by the act of the 30th of April, 1798. He is, by usage, a member of the cabinet, and holds his office at the will of the President. He has a general superintendence of the naval establishments, and appoints such clerks, navy agents, and other subordinate officers as are necessary to the duties of that department.

§ 542. A Board of Navy Commissioners was established in 1815. Their office is attached to that of the Secretary of the Navy, and he discharges all the ministerial duties of said office, relative to the construction, armament, equipment, naval stores, and materials of vessels of war. They have clerks, a draughtsman, messenger, &c., for their ordinary business.

V. THE POST-OFFICE DEPARTMENT.

§ 543. The practical operations of the Post-Office department have been in existence ever since the Revolution; but the organization of the department in its present form was made by the act of April 30th,

1810. The office is under the direction of a Postmaster-General, with three assistants, and such clerks and other officers as are necessary.

The business of the Post-Office department is to transmit the mail, and distribute its contents throughout the United States. For this purpose, the Postmaster-General has the arrangement of mail routes, the decision on mail contracts, the appointment of postmasters, and, in one word, the supervision of the whole mail arrangement of the country. The enumeration of the following subordinate offices of the department will show in what manner this business is divided:

First Assistant Postmaster-General.

Book-keeper's Office,
Solicitor's Office,
Pay Office,
Examiner's Office,
Register's Office,

Second Assistant Postmaster-General.

Office of Appointments and Instructions,
Dead-Letter Office,
Office of Mail Depredations.

Third Assistant Postmaster-General.

Office of Mail Contracts.

VI. HOME DEPARTMENT.

§ 544. This is a new department, created by the act of March 3d, 1849. The Secretary of the Home Department takes his place, as other Secretaries, in what is called the cabinet. The Secretary of the Home Department has a supervisory power over those bureaus, or offices, which have by law been transferred from other departments to constitute the new department. The subordinate bureaus attached to this office are these, viz.:

1. The Land Office,
2. The Patent Office,
3. The Indian Department,
4. The Bureau of Pensions,
5. The Coast Survey.

§ 545. THE COMMISSIONER OF THE GENERAL LAND OFFICE superintends the surveys, sales, and records of the public lands of the United States. In a country of such vast public domain as this, the business of the General Land Office is very extensive. To transact it, there are the following subordinate officers:

1. Surveyors-General,
2. Registers of the Land Office,
3. Receivers of the Land Office.

§ 546. The Surveyors-General (of whom there are now *seven*) survey the public lands accurately into squares of six hundred and forty acres each, called *sections*, and these again into smaller squares of three hundred and twenty, one hundred and sixty, eighty, and forty acres, in which tracts they are sold.

§ 547. The Registers record the sales, issue certificates, and procure patents.

§ 548. The Receivers receive the money arising from the sales, and account for it to the government.

§ 549. The Commissioner for Indian Affairs has charge of the Indian bureau. This office is charged with the making treaties, holding intercourse, and all business connected with the Indian tribes. This is chiefly conducted by officers called Indian Agents.

§ 550. The Commissioner of Patents has charge of the Patent Office and the statistics of agriculture. The laws of the United States, under the Constitution, authorize a patent to be issued to inventors and discoverers. They must first make a *specification* of what the invention is, and if a machine, furnish a *model*. A patent, however, cannot be issued when there is already one for the same machine. The Commissioner of Patents decides on all such matters, and takes charge of all the business connected with patents.

§ 551. The Commissioner of Pensions has charge of the payment of pensioners. These are a large class, and pension agencies are established in most of the large towns of the United States.

§ 552. The Superintendent of the Coast Survey is also under the supervision of the Home department. This office was established for the trigonometrical survey of the coast, for the greater accuracy of geography, and the security of commerce.

VII. THE ATTORNEY-GENERAL.

§ 553. The Attorney-General is also, by courtesy, a member of the cabinet. His office is not so much that of an executive department of the government as that of a counsellor to the executive. He is, in fact, the law officer of the government. In this respect, however, he is rather the superintendent of law affairs than the attorney in particular suits. He attends to the business when prepared in detail, and argues cases before the Supreme Court.

The business of the Treasury and other departments at Washington, is attended to by the Solicitor of the Treasury. The local business of the United States in the several states, is attended to by an official in each judicial district, called the United States District-Attorney.

VIII. THE MINT.

§ 554. This is not a separate department, but may be regarded as a separate bureau of the government. The Constitution has made gold and silver a legal tender,[1] so far as regards the laws of the states, and has forbidden the states to coin money. The duty, therefore, of coining money devolves upon the national government, and hence Congress has instituted the office of the mint for that purpose. The law for this purpose was enacted April 2d, 1792.

The office of the mint has a general *director*, who is the chief of the establishment; a *chief coiner*, who attends to the coining; an *assayer*, who tests the purity of the metal; an *engraver*, who prepares the dies for the coin; a *melter and refiner*, who melts the

---

[1] Article 2, section 10th.

metal and prepares it in bars and ingots for the rolling mill; and a *treasurer*, who receives and gives receipts for all metals legally brought to the mint.

§ 555. Every person is allowed to bring gold and silver bullion to the mint to be coined, and it is coined as soon as practicable after it is brought there. If it be of the standard value of the United States, it is coined free of expense. If not, it is coined at the expense of the owner.

II. Operation of the Legislature.

§ 556. The operation of the National Legislature consists in the exercise of the law-making power. Congress consists of two branches, the Senate and the House of Representatives. The organization of these bodies respects—1st, their officers; 2d, their committees; and 3d, their rules.

§ 557. Of their *officers:* there are in each a presiding officer. In the Senate, this is the Vice President, if present. If not, one of the senators elected *pro tem.* In the House, it is the Speaker, elected by the House. The duties of the *Speaker* (and those of the presiding officer of the Senate) are to preside and keep order in the assembly; to appoint committees, unless specially directed otherwise by the House; to sign all acts, addresses, and joint resolutions passed, and all writs, warrants, and subpœnas issued by the House. He puts all questions to the House, and, in case of ballot, is entitled to vote; in other cases he is not, unless the

House is equally divided, or his vote would make it equal.

§ 558. Each House has, also, a *Clerk*. His duty is to make a complete journal of the proceedings of the House; to procure the printing of such bills, reports, documents, &c., as are necessary to the business of the House; and transact all such business as pertains to the duties of a recording officer.

§ 559. Each House has, also, a Sergeant-at-Arms and a Door-keeper. The *sergeant-at-arms* is the ministerial officer of the House; and executes its commands, issues its processes, and performs functions similar to those of a sheriff. The office and duties of *door-keeper* are explained by the name.

§ 560. The chief business of legislation is done by *committees* in each Assembly. To these, matters of business are referred for examination and report. In the House, the committees are appointed by the Speaker; in the Senate, by ballot. In the House they consist of *seven* members each, and in the Senate of *five*.

§ 561. The committees are appointed in reference to the chief subjects of legislation. The principal committees are:

The committee on Foreign Relations.
The committee on Commerce.
The committee on the Judiciary.
The committee on Military Affairs.
The committee on Manufactures.
The committee on Agriculture.

The committee on Naval Affairs.

The committee on Ways and Means.

§ 562. The committee of *Ways and Means* is peculiar to the House of Representatives, because, by the 1st article, 7th section, of the Constitution, all "*bills for raising revenue*" must originate in the House of Representatives. Hence, the House appoint a committee of "Ways and Means," which has become, in the course of practice, one of the most important parts of the machinery of government, because in this committee are first digested the various plans of revenue.

§ 563. These committees are called *Standing Committees;* but there are also others, raised by the House for any particular purpose, called *Select Committees.* The House may refer to these committees any subject it pleases, and has always power to control its own action. There is one committee which seems, at first, singular. This is *the Committee of the Whole.* In fact, the whole House resolves itself into a committee, and puts a member in the chair, for the purpose of more free discussion, untrammelled by the rules of the House. This *committee of the whole* rises and reports its doings to the Speaker of the House, in the same manner as any other committee. The members when in the House may, on second thoughts, confirm their own doings or not.

§ 564. The regular order of business at the regular sessions of Congress, is as follows: 1st. The Speaker, Clerk, and officers are elected. The House is then said to be *organized.* 2d. A committee is then sent to the President, to inform him that the House is ready to receive a communication from him. 3d. The President's message is then usually sent in. 4th. The House refers the different subjects of the message to different committees. 5th. After these proceedings, the House proceeds in the ordinary business of legislation.

§ 565. The order of daily business is:

1. *Petitions* from each state and territory.
2. *Reports* from standing or select committees.
3. *Resolutions.*
4. *The order of the day*, which is the unfinished business, or business appointed for that particular day.

§ 566. To carry a bill through the House, a certain process is necessary. Thus, every bill must be *read three* times previous to its passage—usually on three different days—and each reading must receive the formal sanction of the House.

The *first reading* of a bill is for information; and if opposition be made, the Speaker puts the question, "Shall this bill be rejected?" If no opposition be made, or the majority on the question of rejection is in its favor, the bill goes to its second reading without opposition. The final vote is *usually* (not always) taken on the *third reading* of the bill; but sometimes, when the vote is close, the vote is also taken on *its passage.* Whenever a formal vote is taken on the third reading or passage, it is taken by *yeas* and *nays.* The members vote alphabetically, as their names are called, in the affirmative or negative.

§ 567. The rules and usages observed in the American Congress, are those usually called Parliamentary Rules, and are adopted from the usages of the British Parliament. They are all favorable to deliberate and prudent legislation, and to the just rights of the minority.

§ 568. When a bill has passed, either in the Senate or House, it is carefully *engrossed* by the clerk, and sent to the other House by a proper person. When a bill has passed *both* Houses, it is duly enrolled on parchment by the clerk of the House of Representatives or secretary of the Senate, before it is presented to the President. It is carefully examined by committees appointed in both Houses, who make a report, when it is signed by the Speaker of the House and the President of the Senate, and sent to the President for his signature.

§ 569. The signature of the President is affixed to all bills which meet his approbation, and this completes the last act of *practical legislation.*

III. Operation of the Judiciary.

§ 570. By article 3d, section 1st, of the Constitution, the judicial power of the United States is vested in a *Supreme Court*, and such *inferior courts* as Congress may appoint. Congress has also power to make all laws *necessary* and *proper* to carry these provisions into effect; and in 1789, Congress passed the Judiciary Act, which has since been frequently amended, organizing the Supreme and inferior courts, and prescribing the mode of action. The courts are: 1st. A *Supreme Court*, composed of a Chief-Justice and eight Associate Justices; 2d. *District Judges*, of which districts there are now thirty-eight in number; and 3d. A *Circuit Court*, consisting of one Judge of the Supreme Court and the District Judge, sitting together.

§ 571. The object of the United States Judiciary is the administration of justice according to the United States laws. The *jurisdiction* of these courts we have defined in another place. See the discussion of the JUDICIARY, from § 328 to § 402.

§ 572. *The officers* of the United States courts, by which they execute their orders, are of *four* kinds, viz.: Clerks, Marshals, Attorneys, and Reporters.

§ 573. The duty of a CLERK is to keep an exact record and journal of all the proceedings of the court, with a history of each suit, and an entry of all the orders, decrees, judgments, and acts of the court. This record is of such solemn import, that when a cause has once been decided it cannot be impeached, but is conclusive against all the parties to it, their heirs and successors, forever.

§ 574. The MARSHAL is the executive officer of the court. He ministers, *or acts, for the court*, in all its executive proceeding. If the court make an order or judgment, he enforces it. If resistance is made, he acts by force; and for this purpose has a right to appoint deputies, and call upon all bystanders for assistance.

The marshal attends upon the sittings of the court,

and executes its process. He sometimes has other duties assigned him; but his general and proper duty is to execute the process of the court.

§ 575. ATTORNEYS AT LAW are persons supposed to be learned in the law, and as such, are appointed by the courts to practise law and conduct suits within their jurisdiction.

Attorneys at Law are, properly, officers of the court, being appointed by the court and removable at the pleasure of the court.

In the United States courts, any one may practise who may practise in the courts of highest judicature within their respective states.

§ 576. A REPORTER is likewise an officer of the court. He is one licensed by the court to report its judicial decisions and opinions. Any one may, doubtless, report the proceedings of a court, but they would have no weight or authority, unless done under the sanction and inspection of the court.

§ 577. The *decisions* of a court are carried out by, 1st. *A judgment or decree*, in which the court pronounces its decision, and directs what must be done: 2d. *By the process*, by which the judgment is executed. This process may be to *imprison the body*, or to confiscate and *sell the property* of a defendant, if judgment be given against him. In the case of capital crimes, the judgment may direct the prisoner to be put to death by hanging. In the United States courts, this *process* is executed by the marshal, who is the executive and ministerial officer of the court.

CHAPTER VII.

PRACTICAL OPERATION OF THE STATE GOVERNMENTS.

§ 578. The essential difference between the National and State Governments—that one regards *national*, or exterior affairs, and the other only *municipal*, or interior affairs—includes also the chief difference between the practical operation of the state governments and that of the nation. The state governments, like the national governments, have the three great departmental divisions, viz.: the Executive, the Legislative, and the Judicial operations.

I. The Executive.

§ 579. The duties of the governors of the several states are, in general, analogous to those of the President of the United States; but, of course, confined to the limits of the state. Here we may remark, that the governor of a state has no political or official power out of a state; for the limits of the state are the limits of his jurisdiction.

§ 580. The principal duties of a governor are:

1. To command the militia and military array of the state.

2. To see the laws faithfully executed, so far as depends on the executive, and not the judiciary.

3. To require reports and opinions from the heads of departments.

4. To communicate information to the legislature on the state of public affairs.

5. To exercise the pardoning power when necessary.

6. In some of the states the governor is vested with much of the appointing power; but in Ohio, he has none except the appointment of a very few minor officers.

§ 581. The states generally have a Secretary of State, a Comptroller or Auditor, Treasurer, &c., in analogy with the national government.

II. The Legislature.

§ 582. The *mode* in which the state legislatures act in legislation, is almost exactly the same with that of the national legislature. The state legislatures, like the national legislature, have two branches, the *House* and the *Senate*. Each has its speaker, sergeant-at-arms, and door-keeper. Each is governed by the same system of parliamentary rules; and the *process* by which laws are passed is the same.

In some of the states the governor, like the President of the United States, has a veto power over legislation; but generally the governors have no such power.

III. The Judiciary.

§ 583. The chief difference between the national and state courts, relates to the *jurisdiction* and the *number* of courts. The state courts have jurisdiction over all those things of which the courts of the United States have not jurisdiction, and some of which they have. In fact, the jurisdiction of the state courts extends over the whole mass of municipal objects, both small and great. It extends over debts and obligations, both minute and large; over all contracts and over all crimes, except those exclusively against the laws of the United States, which must be tried in the United States District Courts.

§ 584. In regard to the *number* of courts, we have seen that the United States courts are—the Supreme, the Circuit, and the District. In the same manner, the states usually have a *Supreme Court*, or Court of Appeals, which makes the final decision of all litigated law points. So they have, generally, Circuit Courts of inferior jurisdiction, and also County Courts. So far, there is a perfect analogy between the arrangement of the state and national courts. But in the states there are two or three other classes of courts In nearly all the states there are special *Criminal Courts*, for the sole purpose of trying criminal prosecutions. So, also, there are in incorporated towns, usually, a Municipal Court, for the trial of causes within the incorporated jurisdiction. But the chief difference between state and national courts is, perhaps, the institution of Justices of the Peace. They are local judges, holding a court usually for the township only, and of small jurisdiction in regard to the magnitude of the property involved in suit. Narrow as their jurisdiction is, it may be affirmed that they transact the largest portion of the judicial business of society. There are generally several in each township; and their courts are held every day.

§ 585. The chief officer of the state courts is, the SHERIFF. His is the most *ancient* office we have, and probably originated in very remote antiquity. Among the Anglo-Saxons of England, the earls held the county courts, and the sheriff was the deputy of the earl. The sheriff is the *ministerial* or executive officer of all the courts held in the county. He must serve all process, execute all writs, and furnish all escorts and force to execute the judgments of the court. He is also a *conservator* of the peace, and is bound to arrest all who break or attempt to break the peace. He is also the *jailer* of the county, and must imprison and subsist, at the expense of the county, all persons sentenced to imprisonment by order of the court.

§ 586. The CONSTABLE is, also, another officer peculiar to state courts. He is, properly, the ministerial officer of the justices of the peace, and has the same duties within a township that a sheriff has for a county, except that of jailer.

§ 587. From this statement we see, that as national governments the states have very little to do. All powers of a general nature are vested in the general government.

* * * * * *

Our work is now ended. It contains little ingenuity and less novelty; but the student should recollect that these are not the characteristics of truth and learning in constitutions and jurisprudence. Let him seek rather the accuracy of the legal historian, and a correct delineation of our political institutions. From the study of these he must ever go forth increased in knowledge, in love of liberty, and the ardor of patriotism.

CONSTITUTIONAL LAW—ADDENDA.

§ 588. Since the first publication of this work, there have been several decisions by the Supreme Court of the United States, which have added new light in regard to the true construction to be put on several clauses of the Constitution. Some of these are here given for the benefit of the student.

POWERS OF THE NATIONAL GOVERNMENT.

§ 589. The government of the Union is a government of the people. It emanates from them. Its powers are granted by them, and are to be exercised directly and for their benefit.—Massachusetts *vs.* Rhode Island, 12 *Peters*, 657.

§ 590. The government of the Union is *supreme* within its sphere of action.—*Ib.*

EXECUTIVE POWER.

§ 591. The Circuit Court of the United States for the District of Columbia, has a right to issue a mandamus on the postmaster-general of the United States.—Kendall *vs.* Stokes et als., 12 *Peters*, 524.

PRIORITY OF UNITED STATES CLAIMS.

§ 592. The local laws of a state cannot contract the operations of the United States act giving *priority* in favor of other creditors.—9 *Peters*, 182.

CONSTRUCTION OF STATE STATUTES.

§ 593. It is the peculiar province and privilege of the state courts to construe their own statutes; and it is no part of the functions of the Supreme Court to review their decisions, or assume jurisdiction over them, on the pretence that their judgments have impaired the obligation of contracts. The Supreme Court can only restrict the *unconstitutional legislation* of the states.—5 *Howard*, 317; 16 *Peters*, 525.

PROHIBITIONS ON STATES.

§ 594. States are not prohibited from passing *retrospective* laws, even though they may affect prior rights; but only *ex post facto laws.*—Watson *vs.* Mercer, 8 *Peters*, 88.

REGULATIONS OF COMMERCE.

§ 595. The law of New York requiring the masters of vessels carrying passengers into New York to make a report of their names, ages, places of birth, &c., affixing a penalty to the violation of that law, and requiring the master to give bonds, was held to be *constitutional* in regard to the report of names, &c. The act is not a regulation of commerce, but a regulation of *police.*—City of New York *vs.* Milne, 11 *Peters*, 102.

§ 596. Persons are not the subjects of commerce, and a law regulating their introduction is not affected by the reasoning which is founded upon the power given to Congress to regulate commerce.—11 *Peters*, 102.

§ 597. The law prohibiting the introduction of slaves

into the state of Mississippi, as merchandise and for sale, is constitutional.—Groves *vs.* Slaughter, 15 *Peters*, 449.

§ 598. The state restrictions upon the sale of spirituous liquors in less than a given quantity, are constitutional.—5 *Howard*, 504.

RELIGIOUS LIBERTY.

§ 599. The Constitution of the United States makes no provision for protecting the citizens of the several states in the enjoyment of religious liberty. This is left to the constitutions and laws of the states.—3 *Howard*, 589.

WRIT OF HABEAS CORPUS.

§ 600. The Supreme Court of the United States has no original jurisdiction to award the writ of habeas corpus to bring up the body of an infant child, alleged to be unlawfully detained.—Ex parte Barry, 2 *Howard*, 65.

EXPATRIATION.

§ 601. Allegiance may be dissolved by the mutual consent of the government and its citizens.—3 *Peters*, 99.

§ 602. The general doctrine is, that no person can, by an *act of his own*, cut off his allegiance.—3 *Peters*, 242.

FUGITIVE SLAVES.

§ 603. The owner of a fugitive slave has the same right to seize and take him in a state to which he has escaped or fled, that he had in the state from which he escaped; and it is well known that this right to seizure, or recapture, is universally acknowledged in the slave-holding states.—Prigg *vs.* Pennsylvania, 16 *Peters*, 539.

CONSTITUTION OF THE UNITED STATES.

Preamble.

WE, the people of the United States, in order to form a more perfect union, establish justice, insure domestic tranquillity, provide for the common defence, promote the general welfare, and secure the blessings of liberty to ourselves and our posterity, do ordain and establish this Constitution for the United States of America.

ARTICLE I.

Of the Legislature.

SECTION I.

All legislative powers herein granted shall be vested in a Congress of the United States, which shall consist of a Senate and House of Representatives.

SECTION II.

1. The House of Representatives shall be composed of members chosen every second year by the people of the several states; and the electors in each state shall have the qualifications requisite for electors of the most numerous branch of the state legislature.

2. No person shall be a representative who shall not have attained to the age of twenty-five years, and been seven years a citizen of the United States, and who shall not, when elected, be an inhabitant of that state in which he shall be chosen.

3. Representatives and direct taxes shall be apportioned among the several states which may be included within this union, according to their respective numbers, which shall be determined by adding to the whole number of free persons, including those bound to service for a term of years, and excluding Indians not taxed,

three-fifths of all other persons. The actual enumeration shall be made within three years after the first meeting of the Congress of the United States, and within every subsequent term of ten years, in such manner as they shall by law direct. The number of representatives shall not exceed one for every thirty thousand; but each state shall have at least one representative; and until such enumeration shall be made, the state of New Hampshire shall be entitled to choose three; Massachusetts, eight; Rhode Island and Providence Plantations, one; Connecticut, five; New York, six; New Jersey, four; Pennsylvania, eight; Delaware, one; Maryland, six; Virginia, ten; North Carolina, five; South Carolina, five; and Georgia, three.

4. When vacancies happen in the representation from any state, the executive authority thereof shall issue writs of election to fill such vacancies.

5. The House of Representatives shall choose their speaker and other officers; and shall have the sole power of impeachment.

Section III.

1. The Senate of the United States shall be composed of two senators from each state, chosen by the legislature thereof, for six years; and each senator shall have one vote.

2. Immediately after they shall be assembled, in consequence of the first election, they shall be divided as equally as may be into three classes. The seats of the senators of the first class shall be vacated at the expiration of the second year, of the second class at the expiration of the fourth year, and of the third class at the expiration of the sixth year, so that one-third may be chosen every second year; and if vacancies happen by resignation or otherwise, during the recess of the legislature of any state, the executive thereof may make temporary appointments until the next meeting of the legislature, which shall then fill such vacancies.

3. No person shall be a senator who shall not have attained to the age of thirty years, and been nine years a citizen of the United States, and who shall not, when elected, be an inhabitant of the state for which he shall be chosen.

4. The Vice President of the United States shall be president of the Senate, but shall have no vote, unless they be equally divided.

5. The Senate shall choose their other officers, and also a president *pro tempore*, in the absence of the Vice President, or when he shall exercise the office of President of the United States.

6. The Senate shall have the sole power to try all impeachments; when sitting for that purpose, they shall be on oath or affirmation. When the President of the United States is tried, the chief-justice shall preside; and no person shall be convicted without the concurrence of two-thirds of the members present.

7. Judgment in cases of impeachment shall not extend further than to removal from office, and disqualification to hold and enjoy any office of honor, trust, or profit under the United States; but the party convicted shall nevertheless be liable and subject to indictment, trial, judgment, and punishment, according to law.

Section IV.

1. The times, places, and manner of holding elections for senators and representatives, shall be prescribed in each state by the legislature thereof; but the Congress may at any time, by law, make or alter such regulations, except as to the places of choosing senators.

2. The Congress shall assemble at least once in every year, and such meeting shall be on the first Monday in December, unless they shall by law appoint a different day.

Section V.

1. Each House shall be the judge of the elections, returns, and qualifications of its own members, and a majority of each shall constitute a quorum to do business; but a smaller number may adjourn from day to day, and may be authorized to compel the attendance of absent members, in such manner and under such penalties as each House may provide.

2. Each House may determine the rules of its proceedings, punish its members for disorderly behavior, and, with the concurrence of two-thirds, expel a member.

3. Each House shall keep a journal of its proceedings, and from time to time publish the same, excepting such parts as may, in their judgment, require secrecy; and the yeas and nays of the

members of either House, on any question, shall, at the desire of one-fifth of those present, be entered on the journal.

4. Neither House, during the session of Congress, shall, without the consent of the other, adjourn for more than three days, nor to any other place than that in which the two Houses shall be sitting.

Section VI.

1. The senators and representatives shall receive a compensation for their services, to be ascertained by law, and paid out of the treasury of the United States. They shall, in all cases, except treason, felony, and breach of the peace, be privileged from arrest during their attendance at the session of their respective Houses, and in going to and returning from the same; and for any speech or debate in either house, they shall not be questioned in any other place.

2. No senator or representative shall, during the time for which he was elected, be appointed to any civil office under the authority of the United States, which shall have been created, or the emoluments whereof shall have been increased during such time; and no person holding any office under the United States, shall be a member of either House during his continuance in office.

Section VII.

1. All bills for raising revenue shall originate in the House of Representatives; but the Senate may propose or concur with amendments as on other bills.

2. Every bill which shall have passed the House of Representatives and the Senate, shall, before it become a law, be presented to the President of the United States; if he approve, he shall sign it; but if not, he shall return it, with his objections, to that House in which it shall have originated, who shall enter the objections at large on their journal, and proceed to reconsider it. If, after such reconsideration, two-thirds of that House shall agree to pass the bill, it shall be sent, together with the objections, to the other House, by which it shall likewise be reconsidered, and if approved by two-thirds of that House, it shall become a law. But in all such cases the votes of both Houses shall be determined by yeas and nays; and the names of the persons voting for and against

the bill shall be entered on the journal of each House respectively. If any bill shall not be returned by the President within ten days (Sundays excepted) after it shall have been presented to him, the same shall be a law, in like manner as if he had signed it, unless the Congress, by their adjournment prevent its return, in which case it shall not be a law.

3. Every order, resolution, or vote, to which the concurrence of the Senate and House of Representatives may be necessary (except on a question of adjournment), shall be presented to the President of the United States; and before the same shall take effect, shall be approved by him, or being disapproved by him, shall be repassed by two-thirds of the Senate and House of Representatives, according to the rules and limitations prescribed in the case of a bill.

Section VIII.

The Congress shall have power—

1. To lay and collect taxes, duties, imposts, and excises, to pay the debts, and provide for the common defence and general welfare of the United States; but all duties, imposts, and excises shall be uniform throughout the United States:

2. To borrow money on the credit of the United States:

3. To regulate commerce with foreign nations, and among the several states, and with the Indian tribes:

4. To establish a uniform mode of naturalization, and uniform laws on the subject of bankruptcies throughout the United States:

5. To coin money, regulate the value thereof, and of foreign coin, and fix the standard of weights and measures:

6. To provide for the punishment of counterfeiting the securities and current coin of the United States:

7. To establish post-offices and post-roads:

8. To promote the progress of science and useful arts, by securing, for limited times, to authors and inventors, the exclusive right to their respective writings and discoveries:

9. To constitute tribunals inferior to the Supreme Court:

10. To define and punish piracies and felonies committed on the high seas, and offences against the law of nations:

11. To declare war, grant letters of marque and reprisal, and make rules concerning captures on land and water:

12. To raise and support armies; but no appropriation of money for that use shall be for a longer term than two years:

13. To provide and maintain a navy:

14. To make rules for the government and regulation of the land and naval forces:

15. To provide for calling forth the militia to execute the laws of the Union, suppress insurrections, and repel invasions:

16. To provide for organizing, arming, and disciplining the militia, and for governing such part of them as may be employed in the service of the United States, reserving to the states respectively the appointment of the officers, and the authority of training the militia according to the discipline prescribed by Congress:

17. To exercise exclusive legislation in all cases whatsoever, over such district (not exceeding ten miles square), as may, by cession of particular states, and the acceptance of Congress, become the seat of the government of the United States; and to exercise like authority over all places purchased by the consent of the legislature of the state in which the same shall be, for the erection of forts, magazines, arsenals, dockyards, and other needful buildings:—And,

18. To make all laws which shall be necessary and proper for carrying into execution the foregoing powers, and all other powers vested by this Constitution in the government of the United States, or in any department or officer thereof.

Section IX.

1. The migration or importation of such persons as any of the states now existing shall think proper to admit, shall not be prohibited by the Congress prior to the year one thousand eight hundred and eight; but a tax or duty may be imposed on such importation, not exceeding ten dollars for each person.

2. The privilege of the writ of *habeas corpus* shall not be suspended, unless when in cases of rebellion or invasion the public safety may require it.

3. No bill of attainder or *ex-post-facto* law shall be passed.

4. No capitation or other direct tax shall be laid, unless in proportion to the *census* or enumeration hereinbefore directed to be taken.

5. No tax or duty shall be laid on articles exported from any

state. No preference shall be given by any regulation of commerce or revenue to the ports of one state over those of another: nor shall vessels bound to, or from one state, be obliged to enter, clear, or pay duties in another.

6. No money shall be drawn from the treasury but in consequence of appropriations made by law; and a regular statement and account of the receipts and expenditures of all public money shall be published from time to time.

7. No title of nobility shall be granted by the United States: and no person holding any office of profit or trust under them, shall, without the consent of the Congress, accept of any present, emolument, office, or title of any kind whatever, from any king, prince, or foreign state.

Section X.

1. No state shall enter into any treaty, alliance, or confederation; grant letters of marque and reprisal; coin money; emit bills of credit; make any thing but gold and silver coin a tender in payment of debts: pass any bill of attainder, *ex-post-facto* law, or law impairing the obligation of contracts; or grant any title of nobility.

2. No state shall, without the consent of the Congress, lay any imposts or duties on imports or exports, except what may be absolutely necessary for executing its inspection laws; and the net produce of all duties and imposts, laid by any state on imports or exports, shall be for the use of the treasury of the United States; and all such laws shall be subject to the revision and control of the Congress. No state shall, without the consent of the Congress, lay any duty of tonnage, keep troops or ships of war in time of peace, enter into any agreement or compact with another state, or with a foreign power, or engage in war, unless actually invaded, or in such imminent danger as will not admit of delay.

ARTICLE II.

Of the Executive.

Section I.

1. The executive power shall be vested in a President of the United States of America. He shall hold his office during the

term of four years, and, together with the Vice President, chosen for the same term, be elected as follows:

2. Each state shall appoint, in such manner as the legislature thereof may direct, a number of electors, equal to the whole number of senators and representatives to which the state may be entitled in the Congress: but no senator or representative, or person holding an office of trust or profit under the United States, shall be appointed an elector.

[3. The electors shall meet in their respective states, and vote by ballot for two persons, of whom one at least shall not be an inhabitant of the same state with themselves. And they shall make a list of all the persons voted for, and of the number of votes for each, which list they shall sign and certify, and transmit sealed to the seat of government of the United States, directed to the president of the Senate. The president of the Senate shall, in the presence of the Senate and House of Representatives, open all the certificates, and the votes shall then be counted. The person having the greatest number of votes shall be the President, if such number be a majority of the whole number of electors appointed; and if there be more than one who have such a majority, and have an equal number of votes, then the House of Representatives shall immediately choose by ballot one of them for President; and if no person have a majority, then from the five highest on the list, the said House shall in like manner choose the President. But in choosing the President, the votes shall be taken by states, the representation from each state having one vote: A quorum for this purpose shall consist of a member or members from two-thirds of the states, and a majority of all the states shall be necessary to a choice. In every case, after the choice of the President, the person having the greatest number of votes of the electors shall be the Vice President. But if there should remain two or more who have equal votes, the Senate shall choose from them by ballot the Vice President.] [1]

3. The Congress may determine the time of choosing the electors, and the day on which they shall give their votes; which day shall be the same throughout the United States.

4. No person, except a natural-born citizen, or a citizen of the United States at the time of the adoption of this Constitution, shall be eligible to the office of President; neither shall any person be eligible to that office who shall not have attained to the age of thirty-five years, and been fourteen years a resident within the United States.

---

[1] This clause is annulled. See Amendments, Art. 12.

5. In case of the removal of the President from office, or of his death, resignation, or inability to discharge the powers and duties of the said office, the same shall devolve on the Vice President; and the Congress may by law provide for the case of removal, death, resignation, or inability, both of the President and Vice President, declaring what officer shall then act as President, and such officer shall act accordingly, until the disability be removed, or a President shall be elected.

6. The President shall, at stated times, receive for his services a compensation, which shall neither be increased nor diminished during the period for which he shall have been elected, and he shall not receive within that period any other emolument from the United States, or any of them.

7. Before he enters on the execution of his office, he shall take the following oath or affirmation:

"I do solemnly swear (or affirm), that I will faithfully execute the office of President of the United States, and will, to the best of my ability, preserve, protect, and defend the Constitution of the United States."

Section II.

1. The President shall be commander-in-chief of the army and navy of the United States, and of the militia of the several states when called into the actual service of the United States; he may require the opinion, in writing, of the principal officer in each of the executive departments, upon any subject relating to the duties of their respective offices, and he shall have power to grant reprieves and pardons for offences against the United States, except in cases of impeachment.

2. He shall have power, by and with the advice and consent of the Senate, to make treaties, provided two-thirds of the senators present concur; and he shall nominate, and by and with the advice and consent of the Senate, shall appoint ambassadors, other public ministers and consuls, judges of the Supreme Court, and all other officers of the United States whose appointments are not herein otherwise provided for, and which shall be established by law: but the Congress may by law vest the appointment of such inferior officers as they think proper in the President alone, and in the courts of law, or in the heads of departments.

3. The President shall have power to fill up all vacancies that may happen during the recess of the Senate, by granting commissions which shall expire at the end of their next session.

Section III.

He shall, from time to time, give to the Congress information of the state of the Union, and recommend to their consideration such measures as he shall judge necessary and expedient; he may, on extraordinary occasions, convene both Houses, or either of them, and in case of disagreement between them, with respect to the time of adjournment, he may adjourn them to such time as he shall think proper; he shall receive ambassadors and other public ministers; he shall take care that the laws be faithfully executed, and shall commission all the officers of the United States.

Section IV.

The President, Vice President, and all civil officers of the United States, shall be removed from office on impeachment for, and conviction of, treason, bribery, or other high crimes and misdemeanors.

ARTICLE III.

Of the Judiciary.

Section I.

The judicial power of the United States shall be vested in one Supreme Court, and in such inferior courts as the Congress may, from time to time, ordain and establish. The judges, both of the Supreme and inferior courts, shall hold their offices during good behavior, and shall, at stated times, receive for their services a compensation, which shall not be diminished during their continuance in office.

Section II.

1. The judicial power shall extend to all cases, in law and equity, arising under this Constitution, the laws of the United States, and treaties made, or which shall be made, under their authority;—to all cases affecting ambassadors, other public ministers, and consuls;—to all cases of admiralty and maritime jurisdiction;—to controversies to which the United States shall be a party;—to contro-

versies between two or more states;—between a state and citizens of another state;—between citizens of different states;—between citizens of the same state claiming lands under grants of different states, and between a state, or the citizens thereof, and foreign states, citizens, or subjects.

2. In all cases affecting ambassadors, other public ministers, and consuls, and those in which a state shall be party, the Supreme Court shall have original jurisdiction. In all the other cases before mentioned, the Supreme Court shall have appellate jurisdiction, both as to law and fact, with such exceptions, and under such regulations as the Congress shall make.

3. The trial of all crimes, except in cases of impeachment, shall be by jury; and such trial shall be held in the state where the said crimes shall have been committed; but when not committed within any state, the trial shall be at such place or places as the Congress may by law have directed.

Section III.

1. Treason against the United States shall consist only in levying war against them, or in adhering to their enemies, giving them aid and comfort. No person shall be convicted of treason unless on the testimony of two witnesses to the same overt act, or on confession in open court.

2. The Congress shall have power to declare the punishment of treason, but no attainder of treason shall work corruption of blood, or forfeiture, except during the life of the person attainted.

ARTICLE IV.

Miscellaneous.

Section I.

Full faith and credit shall be given in each state to the public acts, records, and judicial proceedings of every other state. And the Congress may, by general laws, prescribe the manner in which such acts, records, and proceedings shall be proved, and the effect thereof.

Section II.

1. The citizens of each state shall be entitled to all privileges and immunities of citizens in the several states.

2. A person charged in any state with treason, felony, or other crime, who shall flee from justice, and be found in another state, shall, on demand of the executive authority of the state from which he fled, be delivered up, to be removed to the state having jurisdiction of the crime.

3. No person held to service or labor in one state, under the laws thereof, escaping into another, shall, in consequence of any law or regulation therein, be discharged from such service or labor, but shall be delivered up on claim of the party to whom such service or labor may be due.

Section III.

1. New states may be admitted by the Congress into this Union; but no new state shall be formed or erected within the jurisdiction of any other state; nor any state be formed by the junction of two or more states, or parts of states, without the consent of the legislatures of the states concerned, as well as of the Congress.

2. The Congress shall have power to dispose of and make needful rules and regulations respecting the territory, or other property belonging to the United States; and nothing in this Constitution shall be so construed as to prejudice any claims of the United States, or of any particular state.

Section IV.

The United States shall guarantee to every state in this Union a republican form of government, and shall protect each of them against invasion; and, on application of the legislature, or of the executive (when the legislature cannot be convened), against domestic violence.

ARTICLE V.

Of Amendments.

The Congress, whenever two-thirds of both Houses shall deem it necessary, shall propose amendments to this Constitution, or, on the application of the legislatures of two-thirds of the several states, shall call a convention for proposing amendments, which, in either case, shall be valid to all intents and purposes, as part of this Constitution, when ratified by the legislatures of three-fourths of the several states, or by conventions in three-fourths thereof, as the one or the other mode of ratification may be proposed by the Congress; provided that no amendment, which may be made prior to the year one thousand eight hundred and eight, shall in any manner affect the first and fourth clauses in the ninth section of the first article; and that no state, without its consent, shall be deprived of its equal suffrage in the Senate.

ARTICLE VI.

Miscellaneous.

1. All debts contracted, and engagements entered into, before the adoption of this Constitution, shall be as valid against the United States under this Constitution as under the Confederation.

2. This Constitution, and the laws of the United States, which shall be made in pursuance thereof; and all treaties made, or which shall be made, under the authority of the United States, shall be the supreme law of the land; and the judges in every state shall be bound thereby, any thing in the constitution or laws of any state to the contrary notwithstanding.

3. The senators and representatives before mentioned, and the members of the several state legislatures, and all executive and judicial officers, both of the United States and of the several states, shall be bound by oath, or affirmation, to support this Constitution; but no religious test shall ever be required as a qualification to any office or public trust under the United States.

ARTICLE VII.

Of the Ratification.

The ratification of the conventions of nine states shall be sufficient for the establishment of this Constitution between the states so ratifying the same.

Done in convention, by the unanimous consent of the states present, the seventeenth day of September, in the year of our Lord one thousand seven hundred and eighty-seven, and of the Independence of the United States of America the twelfth. In witness whereof, we have hereunto subscribed our names,

GEORGE WASHINGTON,
President, and Deputy from Virginia.

New Hampshire—John Langdon, Nicholas Gilman. *Massachusetts*—Nathaniel Gorham, Rufus King. *Connecticut*—William S. Johnson, Roger Sherman. *New York*—Alexander Hamilton. *New Jersey*—William Livingston, David Brearley, William Paterson, Jonathan Dayton. *Pennsylvania*—Benjamin Franklin, Thomas Mifflin, Robert Morris, George Clymer, Thomas Fitzsimmons, Jared Ingersoll, James Wilson, Gouverneur Morris. *Delaware*—George Read, Gunning Bedford, jun., John Dickinson, Richard Bassett, Jacob Broom. *Maryland*—James M'Henry, Daniel of St. Thomas Jenifer, Daniel Carroll. *Virginia*—John Blair, James Madison, jun. *North Carolina*—William Blount, Richard Dobbs Spaight, Hugh Williamson. *South Carolina*—John Rutledge, Charles Cotesworth Pinckney, Charles Pinckney, Pierce Butler. *Georgia*—William Few, Abraham Baldwin.

Attest:
WILLIAM JACKSON, *Secretary.*

[*Congress at their first session under the Constitution, held in the city of New York, in* 1789, *proposed to the legislatures of the several States* twelve amendments, ten *of which only were adopted. They are the first ten of the following amendments; and they were ratified by three-fourths, the constitutional number, of the States, on the* 15*th of December*, 1791. *The* 11*th* amendment *was proposed at the first session of the third Congress, and was declared in a message from the President of the United States to both Houses of Congress, dated the* 8*th of January*, 1798, *to have been adopted by the constitutional number of States. The* 12*th* amendment, *which was proposed at the first session of the eighth Congress, was adopted by the constitutional number of States in the year* 1804, *according to a public notice by the Secretary of State, dated the* 25*th of September*, 1804.]

AMENDMENTS

To the Constitution of the United States, ratified according to the provisions of the Fifth Article of the foregoing Constitution.

ARTICLE I. Congress shall make no law respecting an establishment of religion, or prohibiting the free exercise thereof; or abridging the freedom of speech, or of the press; or the right of the people peaceably to assemble, and to petition the government for a redress of grievances.

ART. II. A well-regulated militia being necessary to the security of a free state, the right of the people to keep and bear arms shall not be infringed.

ART. III. No soldier shall, in time of peace, be quartered in any house without the consent of the owner, nor in time of war but in a manner to be prescribed by law.

ART. IV. The right of the people to be secure in their persons, houses, papers, and effects, against unreasonable searches and seizures, shall not be violated, and no warrant shall issue but upon probable cause, supported by oath or affirmation, and particularly describing the place to be searched, and the persons or things to be seized.

ART. V. No person shall be held to answer for a capital, or otherwise infamous crime, unless on a presentment or indictment of a grand jury, except in cases arising in the land or naval forces, or in the militia, when in actual service in time of war or public danger; nor shall any person be subject, for the same offence, to be twice put in jeopardy of life or limb; nor shall be compelled, in any criminal case, to be a witness against himself, nor be deprived of life, liberty, or property, without due process of law; nor shall private property be taken for public use without just compensation.

ART. VI. In all criminal prosecutions, the accused shall enjoy the right to a speedy and public trial, by an impartial jury of the state and district wherein the crime shall have been committed, which district shall have been previously ascertained by law, and to be informed of the nature and cause of the accusation; to be confronted with the witnesses against him; to have compulsory process for obtaining witnesses in his favor, and to have the assistance of counsel for his defence.

ART. VII. In suits at common law, where the value in controversy shall exceed twenty dollars, the right of trial by jury shall be preserved, and no fact tried by a jury shall be otherwise re-examined in any court of the United States, than according to the rules of the common law.

ART. VIII. Excessive bail shall not be required, nor excessive fines imposed, nor cruel and unusual punishments inflicted.

ART. IX. The enumeration in the Constitution of certain rights, shall not be construed to deny or disparage others retained by the people.

ART. X. The powers not delegated to the United States by the Constitution, nor prohibited by it to the states, are reserved to the states respectively, or to the people.

ART. XI. The judicial power of the United States shall not be construed to extend to any suit, in law or equity, commenced or prosecuted against one of the United States by citizens of another state, or by citizens or subjects of any foreign state.

ART. XII. The electors shall meet in their respective states, and vote by ballot for President and Vice President, one of whom, at least, shall not be an inhabitant of the same state with themselves; they shall name in their ballots the person voted for as President, and in distinct ballots the person voted for as Vice President, and they shall make distinct lists of all persons voted for as President, and of all persons voted for as Vice President, and of the number of votes for each, which lists they shall sign and certify, and transmit, sealed, to the seat of the government of the United States, directed to the President of the Senate. The President of the Senate shall, in the presence of the Senate and House of Representatives, open all the certificates, and the votes shall then be counted; the person having the greatest number of votes for President shall be the President, if such number be a majority of the whole number of electors appointed; and if no person have such majority, then from the persons having the highest numbers, not exceeding three, on the list of those voted for as President, the House of Representatives shall choose immediately, by ballot, the President. But in choosing the President, the votes shall be taken by states, the representation from each state having one vote; a quorum for this purpose shall consist of a member or members from two-thirds of the states, and a majority of all the states shall be necessary to a choice. And if the House of Representatives shall not choose a President, whenever the right of choice shall devolve upon them, before the fourth day of March next following, then the Vice President shall act as President, as in the case of the death or other constitutional disability of the President. The person having the greatest number of votes as Vice President shall be the Vice President, if such number be a majority of the whole number of electors appointed, and if no person have a majority, then from the two highest numbers on the list the Senate shall choose the Vice President; a quorum for the purpose shall consist of two-thirds of the whole number of senators, and a majority of the whole number shall be necessary to a choice. But no person constitutionally ineligible to the office of President, shall be eligible to that of Vice President of the United States.

[NOTE 1. Another amendment was proposed as article XIII. at the second session of the eleventh Congress, but not having been ratified by a sufficient number of the states, has not become valid, as a part of the Constitution of the United States. It is erroneously given as a part of the Constitution, in page 74, vol. i., Laws of the United States, published by Bioren & Duane, in 1815.]

[Note 2. The Constitution, as above printed, has been carefully compared with the copy in the Laws of the United States, published by authority, and also with one in the National Calendar for the year 1826, which was copied from the roll in the Department of State.]

[NOTE 3. The ratification of the Constitution by the state of New Hampshire, being the 9th in order, was laid before Congress on the 2d of July, 1788, and, with the ratification of the other states, was referred to a committee, to report an act for carrying the new system into operation. An act for this purpose was reported on the 14th of the same month, and was passed on the 13th of September following.]—*American Almanac*, 1831.

ORDINANCE OF 1787.

THE following Ordinance is the fundamental law of the States of Ohio, Indiana, Illinois, Michigan, and Wisconsin. It is *fundamental*, because passed *prior to the Constitution*,—and is a matter of compact between the several states *vesting rights*,—which the Constitution, by its terms, did not control. It was reported by Nathan Dane, celebrated, both as the author of this Ordinance, and of a Digest of American Law.

IN CONGRESS, JULY 13, 1787.

An Ordinance for the government of the territory of the United States, northwest of the river Ohio.

BE IT ORDAINED, by the United States in Congress assembled, that the said territory, for the purposes of temporary government, be one district; subject, however, to be divided into two districts, as future circumstances may, in the opinion of Congress, make it expedient.

Be it ordained, by the authority aforesaid, that the estates, both of resident and non-resident proprietors, in the said territory, dying intestate, shall descend to, and be distributed among their children, and the descendants of a deceased child, in equal parts; the descendants of a deceased child, or grandchild, to take the share of their deceased parent, in equal parts, among them; and where there shall be no children, or descendants, then in equal parts to the next of kin, in equal degree; and among collaterals, the children of a deceased brother or sister of the intestate shall have, in equal parts, among them, their deceased parent's share; and there shall in no case be a distinction between kindred of the whole and half blood; saving in all cases to the widow of the intestate, her third part of the real estate for life, and one third part of the personal estate; and this law relative to descents and dower, shall remain in full force until altered by the legislature of the district. And until the governor and judges shall adopt laws as hereinafter mentioned, estates in the said territory may be devised or bequeathed by wills in writing, signed and sealed by him or her, in whom the estate may be (being of full age), and attested by three witnesses; and real estates may be conveyed by lease and release, or bargain and sale, signed, sealed, and delivered by the person, being of full age, in whom the estate may be, and attested by two witnesses, provided such wills be duly proved, and such conveyances be acknowledged, or the execution thereof duly proved, and be recorded within one year after proper magistrates, courts, and registers shall be appointed for that purpose; and personal property may be transferred by delivery, saving, however, to the French and Canadian inhabitants, and other settlers of the Kaskaskias, Saint Vincents, and the neighboring villages, who have heretofore professed themselves citizens of Virginia, their laws and customs now in force among them, relative to descent and conveyance of property.

Be it ordained, by the authority aforesaid, that there shall be appointed from time to time, by Congress, a governor, whose commission shall continue in force for the term of three years, unless sooner revoked by Congress; he shall reside in the district, and have a freehold estate therein, in one thousand acres of land, while in the exercise of his office. There shall be appointed from time to time, by Congress, a secretary, whose commission shall continue in force for four years, unless sooner revoked; he shall reside in the district, and have a freehold estate therein, in five hundred acres of land, while in the exercise of his office; it shall be his duty to keep and preserve the acts and laws passed by the legislature, and the public records of the district, and the proceedings of the governor in his executive department; and transmit authentic copies of such acts and proceedings, every six months, to the secretary of Congress. There shall also be appointed a court to consist of three judges, any two of whom to form a court, who shall have a common-law jurisdiction, and reside in the district, and have each therein a freehold estate in five hundred acres of land, while in the exercise of their offices; and their commissions shall continue in force during good behavior.

The governor and judges, or a majority of them, shall adopt and publish in the district, such laws of the original states, criminal and civil, as may be necessary, and best suited to the circumstances of the district, and report them to Congress, from time to time, which laws shall be in force in the district until the organization of the general assembly therein, unless disapproved of by Congress; but afterwards, the legislature shall have authority to alter them as they shall think fit.

The governor, for the time being, shall be commander-in-chief of the militia, appoint and commission all officers in the same, below the rank of general officers. All general officers shall be appointed and commissioned by Congress.

Previous to the organization of the general assembly, the governor shall appoint such magistrates and other civil officers, in each county or township, as he shall find necessary for the preservation of the peace and good order in the same. After the general assembly shall be organized, the powers and duties of magistrates and other civil officers shall be regulated and defined by the said assembly; but all magistrates and other civil officers, not herein otherwise directed, shall, during the continuance of this temporary government, be appointed by the governor.

For the prevention of crimes and injuries, the laws to be adopted or made, shall have force in all parts of the district, and for the execution of process, criminal and civil, the governor shall make proper divisions thereof; and he shall proceed from time to time, as circumstances may require, to lay out the parts of the district in which the Indian titles shall have been extinguished, into counties and townships, subject, however, to such alterations as may thereafter be made by the legislature.

So soon as there shall be five thousand free male inhabitants, of full age, in the district, upon giving proof thereof to the governor, they shall receive authority, with time and place, to elect representatives from their counties or townships, to represent them in the general assembly: provided, that for every five hundred free male inhabitants there shall be one representative, and so on progressively with the number of free male inhabitants, shall the right of representation increase, until the number of representatives shall amount to twenty-five, after which the number and proportion of representatives shall be regulated by the legislature; *provided*, that no person be eligible or qualified to act as a representative, unless he shall have been a citizen of one of the United States three years, and be a resident in the district, or unless he shall have resided in the district three years, and in either case shall likewise hold in his own right, in fee simple, two hundred acres of land within the same; *provided also*, that a freehold in fifty acres of land in the district, having been a citizen of one of the states, and being resident in the district, or the like freehold and two years' residence in the district, shall be necessary to qualify a man as an elector of a representative.

The representative thus elected shall serve for the term of two years, and in case of the death of a representative, or removal from office, the governor shall issue a writ to the county or township for which he was a member, to elect another in his stead, to serve for the residue of the term.

The general assembly, or legislature, shall consist of the governor, legislative council, and a house of representatives. The legislative council shall consist of five members, to continue in office five years, unless sooner removed by Congress, any three of whom to be a quorum, and the members of the council shall be nominated and appointed in the following manner, to wit: as soon as representatives shall be elected, the governor shall appoint a time and place for them to meet together, and, when met, they shall nominate ten persons, residents in the district, and each possessed of a freehold in five hundred acres of land, and return their names to Congress; five of whom Congress shall appoint and commission to serve as aforesaid; and whenever a vacancy shall happen in the council, by death or removal from office, the house of representatives shall nominate two persons, qualified as aforesaid, for each vacancy, and return their names to Congress, one of whom Congress shall appoint and commission for the residue of the term; and every five years, four months at least before the expiration of the time of service of the members of council, the said house shall nominate ten persons, qualified as aforesaid, and return their names to Congress, five of whom Congress shall appoint and commission to serve as members of the council five years, unless sooner removed. And the governor, legislative council, and house of representatives, shall have authority to make laws in all cases for the good government of the district, not repugnant to the principles and articles in this ordinance established and declared. And all bills having passed by a majority in the house, and by a majority in the council, shall be referred to the governor for his assent; but no bill or legislative act whatever, shall be of any force without his assent. The governor shall have power to convene, prorogue, and dissolve the general assembly, when in his opinion it shall be expedient.

The governor, judges, legislative council, secretary, and such other officers as Congress shall appoint in the district, shall take an oath or affirmation of fidelity, and of office—the governor before the president of Congress, and all other officers before the governor. As soon as a legislature shall be formed in the district, the council and house, assembled in one room, shall have authority by joint ballot to elect a delegate to Congress, who shall have a seat in Congress, with the right of debating, but not of voting, during this temporary government.

And for extending the fundamental principles of civil and religious liberty, which form the basis whereon these republics, their laws and constitutions, are erected; to fix and establish those principles as the basis of all laws, constitutions, and governments, which forever hereafter shall be formed in the said territory; to provide also for the establishment of states, and permanent government therein, and for their admission to a share in the federal councils on an equal footing with the original states, at as early periods as may be consistent with the general interest:

It is hereby ordained and declared, by the authority aforesaid, that the following articles shall be considered as articles of compact between the original states and the people and states in the said territory, and forever remain unalterable, unless by common consent, to wit:

Art. I. No person, demeaning himself in a peaceable and orderly manner, shall ever be molested on account of his mode of worship or religious sentiments in the said territory.

Art. II. The inhabitants of the said territory shall always be entitled to the benefit of the writ of *habeas corpus*, and of the trial by jury; of a proportionate representation of the people in the legislature, and of judicial proceedings according to the course of the common law, all persons shall be bailable unless for capital offences, where the proof shall be evident, or the presumption great; all fines shall be moderate, and no cruel or unusual punishments shall be inflicted; no man shall be deprived of his liberty or property, but by the judgment of his peers, or the law of the land; and should the public exigencies make it necessary for the common preservation to take any person's property, or to demand his particular services, full compensation shall be made for the same; and in the just preservation of rights and property, it is understood and declared, that no law ought ever to be made, or have force in the said territory, that shall in any manner whatever, interfere with or affect private contracts or agreements, *bona fide*, and without fraud previously formed.

ART. III. Religion, morality, and knowledge, being necessary to good government and the happiness of mankind, schools and the means of education shall forever be encouraged. The utmost good faith shall always be observed towards the Indians; their lands and property shall never be taken from them without their consent; and in their property, rights, and liberty, they never shall be invaded or disturbed, unless in just and lawful wars authorized by Congress; but laws founded in justice and humanity, shall, from time to time, be made, for preventing wrongs being done to them, and for preserving peace and friendship with them.

ART. IV. The said territory, and the states which may be formed therein, shall forever remain a part of this confederacy of the United States of America, subject to the articles of confederation, and to such alteration therein as shall be constitutionally made; and to all the acts and ordinances of the United States in Congress assembled, conformable thereto. The inhabitants and settlers in the said territory, shall be subject to pay a part of the federal debts contracted, or to be contracted, and a proportional part of the expenses of government, to be apportioned on them by Congress, according to the same common rule and measure by which apportionments thereof shall be made on the other states; and the taxes for paying their proportion shall be laid and levied by the authority and direction of the legislatures of the district, or districts, or new states, as in the original states, within the time agreed upon by the United States in Congress assembled. The legislature of those districts, or new states, shall never interfere with the primary disposal of the soil by the United States in Congress assembled, nor with any regulations Congress may find necessary for securing the title in such soil to the *bona fide* purchasers. No tax shall be imposed on lands the property of the United States; and in no case shall non-resident proprietors be taxed higher than residents. The navigable waters leading into the Mississippi and St. Lawrence, and the carrying places between the same shall be common highways, and forever free, as well to the inhabitants of the said territory, as to the citizens of the United States, and those of any other states that may be admitted into the confederacy, without any tax, impost, or duty therefor.

Art. V. There shall be formed in the said territory, not less than three, nor more than five states; and the boundaries of the states, as soon as Virginia shall alter her act of cession and consent to the same, shall become fixed and established as follows, to wit: The western state in the said territory shall be bounded by the Mississippi, the Ohio, and Wabash rivers; a direct line drawn, from the Wabash and Post Vincents due north to the territorial line between the United States and Canada, and by the said territorial line to the Lake of the Woods and Mississippi. The middle state shall be bounded by the said direct line, the Wabash from Post Vincents to the Ohio, by the Ohio, by a direct line drawn due north from the mouth of the Great Miami to the said territorial line, and by said territorial line. The eastern state shall be bounded by the last-mentioned direct line, the Ohio, Pennsylvania, and the said territorial line; provided, however, and it is further understood and declared, that the boundaries of these three states shall be subject so far to be altered, that if Congress shall hereafter find it expedient, they shall have authority to form one or two states in that part of the said territory which lies north of an east and west line drawn through the southerly bend or extreme of Lake Michigan: and whenever any of the said states shall have sixty thousand free inhabitants therein, such state shall be admitted by its delegates into the Congress of the United States, on an equal footing with the original states, in all respects whatsoever; and shall be at liberty to form a permanent constitution and state government: *Provided*, the constitution and government so to be formed shall be republican, and in conformity to the principles contained in these articles: and so far as it can be consistent with the general interest of the confederacy, such admission shall be allowed at an earlier period, and when there may be a less number of free inhabitants in the state than sixty thousand.

Art. VI. There shall be neither slavery nor involuntary servitude in the said territory, otherwise than in punishment of crimes whereof the party shall have been duly convicted: *Provided*, always, that any person escaping into the same, from whom labor or service is lawfully claimed in any one of the original states, such fugitive may be lawfully reclaimed and conveyed to the person claiming his or her labor or service as aforesaid.

Be it ordained, by the authority aforesaid, that the resolutions of the 23d of April, 1784, relative to the subject of this ordinance be, and the same are hereby repealed and declared null and void.

WASHINGTON'S FAREWELL ADDRESS.

Friends and Fellow-citizens:

THE period for a new election of a citizen to administer the executive government of the United States being not far distant, and the time actually arrived when your thoughts must be employed in designating the person who is to be clothed with that important trust, it appears to me proper, especially as it may conduce to a more distinct expression of the public voice, that I should now apprise you of the resolution I have formed, to decline being considered among the number of those out of whom the choice is to be made.

I beg you, at the same time, to do me the justice to be assured, that this resolution has not been taken without a strict regard to all the considerations appertaining to the relation which binds a dutiful citizen to his country; and that in withdrawing the tender of service which silence in my situation might imply, I am influenced by no diminution of zeal for your future interest, no deficiency of grateful respect for your past kindness, but am supported by a full conviction that the step is compatible with both.

The acceptance of, and continuance hitherto in, the office to which your suffrages have twice called me, have been a uniform sacrifice of inclination to the opinion of duty, and to a deference for what appeared to be your desire. I constantly hoped that it would have been much earlier in my power, consistently with motives which I was not at liberty to disregard, to return to that retirement from which I had been reluctantly drawn. The strength of my inclination to do this, previous to the last election, had even led to the preparation of an address to declare it to you; but mature reflection on the then perplexed and critical posture of our affairs with foreign nations, and the unanimous advice of persons entitled to my confidence, impelled me to abandon the idea.

I rejoice that the state of your concerns, external as well as internal, no longer renders the pursuit of inclination incompatible with the sentiment of duty or propriety; and am persuaded, whatever partiality may be retained for my services, that in the present circumstances of our country, you will not disapprove of my determination to retire.

The impressions with which I first undertook the arduous trust, were explained on the proper occasion. In the discharge of this trust, I will only say, that I have, with good intentions, contributed towards the organization and administration of the government, the best exertions of which a very fallible judgment was capable. Not unconscious, in the outset, of the inferiority of my qualifications, experience, in my own eyes, perhaps still more in the eyes of others, has strengthened the motives to diffidence of myself; and every day the increasing weight of years admonishes me more and more, that the shade of retirement is as necessary to me as it will be welcome. Satisfied that if any circumstances have given peculiar value to my services, they were temporary, I have the consolation to believe, that while choice and prudence invite me to quit the political scene, patriotism does not forbid it.

In looking forward to the moment which is to terminate the career of my political life, my feelings do not permit me to suspend the deep acknowledgment of that debt of gratitude which I owe to my beloved country, for the many honors it has conferred upon me; still more, for the steadfast confidence with which it has supported me, and for the opportunities I have thence enjoyed of manifesting my inviolable attachment, by services faithful and persevering, though in usefulness unequal to my zeal. If benefits have resulted to our country from these services, let it always be remembered to your praise, and as an instructive example in our annals, that under circumstances in which the passions, agitated in every direction, were liable to mislead; amidst appearances sometimes dubious, vicissitudes of fortune often discouraging; in situations in which, not unfrequently, want of success has countenanced the spirit of criticism,—the constancy of your support was the essential prop of the efforts, and a guaranty of the plans by which they were effected. Profoundly penetrated with this idea, I shall carry it with me to my grave, as a strong incitement to unceasing wishes that Heaven may continue to you the choicest tokens of its beneficence, that your union and brotherly affection may be perpetual, that the free Constitution which is the work of your hands may be sacredly maintained, that its administration in every department may be stamped with wisdom and virtue, that, in fine, the happiness of the people of these states, under the auspices of liberty, may be made complete, by so careful a preservation and so prudent a use of this blessing as will acquire to them the glory of recommending it to the applause, the affection, and the adoption, of every nation which is yet a stranger to it.

Here, perhaps, I ought to stop. But a solicitude for your welfare, which cannot end but with my life, and the apprehension of danger natural to that solicitude, urge me, on an occasion like the present, to offer to your solemn contemplation, and to recommend to your frequent review, some sentiments which are the result of much reflection, of no inconsiderable observation, and which appear to me all-important to the permanency of your felicity as a people. These will be offered to you with the more freedom, as you can only see in them the disinterested warnings of a parting friend, who can possibly have no personal motive to bias his counsel. Nor can I forget, as an encouragement to it, your indulgent reception of my sentiments on a former and not dissimilar occasion.

Interwoven as is the love of liberty with every ligament of your hearts, no recommendation of mine is necessary to fortify or confirm the attachment.

The unity of government which constitutes you one people, is also now dear to you. It is justly so, for it is a main pillar in the edifice of your real independence, the support of your tranquillity at home, of your peace abroad, of your safety, of your prosperity, of that very liberty which you so highly prize. But as it is easy to foresee that, from different causes and from different quarters, much pains will be taken and many artifices employed to weaken in your minds the conviction of this truth; as this is the point in your political fortress against which the batteries of internal and external enemies will be most constantly and actively (though often covertly and insidiously) directed, it is of infinite moment that you should properly estimate the immense value of your national union to your collective and individual happiness; that you should cherish a cordial, habitual, and immovable attachment to it, accustoming yourselves to think and speak of it as the palladium of your political safety and prosperity, watching for its preservation with jealous anxiety, discountenancing whatever may suggest even a suspicion that it can in any event be abandoned, and indignantly frowning upon the first dawning of every attempt to alienate any portion of our country from the rest, or to enfeeble the sacred ties which now link together the various parts.

For this, you have every inducement of sympathy and interest. Citizens, by birth or choice, of a common country, that country has a right to concentrate your affections. The name of AMERICAN, which belongs to you in your national capacity, must always exalt the just pride of patriotism more than any appellation derived from local discriminations. With slight shades of difference, you have the same religion, manners, habits, and political principles. You have in a common cause fought and triumphed together; the independence and liberty you possess, are the work of joint councils and joint efforts, of common dangers, sufferings, and successes.

But these considerations, however powerfully they address themselves to your sensibility, are greatly outweighed by those which apply more immediately to your interest. Here every portion of our country finds the most commanding motives for carefully guarding and preserving the union of the whole.

The *north*, in an unrestrained intercourse with the *south*, protected by the equal laws of a common government, finds in the latter, great additional resources of maritime and commercial enterprise, and precious materials of manufacturing industry. The *south*, in the same intercourse, benefiting by the agency of the *north*, sees its agriculture grow and its commerce expand. Turning partly into its own channels the seamen of the *north*, it finds its particular navigation invigorated; and while it contributes in different ways to nourish and increase the general mass of the national navigation, it looks forward to the protection of a maritime strength, to which itself is unequally adapted. The *east*, in like intercourse with the *west*, already finds, and in the progressive improvement of interior communications, by land and water, will more and more find, a valuable vent for the commodities which it brings from abroad, or manufactures at home. The *west* derives from the *east* supplies requisite to its growth and comfort,—and, what is perhaps of still greater consequence, it must of necessity owe the secure enjoyment of indispensable outlets for its own productions to the weight, influence, and the future maritime strength of the Atlantic side of the Union, directed by an indissoluble community of interest as one nation. Any other tenure by which the *west* can hold this essential advantage, whether derived from its own separate strength or from an apostate and unnatural connection with any foreign power, must be intrinsically precarious.

While, then, every part of our country thus feels an immediate and particular interest in union, all the parts combined cannot fail to find in the united mass of means and efforts, greater strength, greater resource, proportionably greater security from external danger, a less frequent interruption of their peace by foreign nations; and, what is of inestimable value, they must derive from union an exemption from those broils and wars between themselves, which so frequently afflict neighboring countries, not tied together by the same government, which their own rivalships alone would be sufficient to produce; but which opposite foreign alliances, attachments, and intrigues would stimulate and embitter. Hence, likewise, they will avoid the necessity of those overgrown military establishments, which, under any form of government, are inauspicious to liberty, and which are to be regarded as particularly hostile to republican liberty. In this sense it is that your union ought to be considered as a main prop of your liberty, and that the love of the one ought to endear to you the preservation of the other.

These considerations speak a persuasive language to every reflecting and virtuous mind, and exhibit the continuance of the union as a primary object of patriotic desire. Is there a doubt whether a common government can embrace so large a sphere? Let experience solve it. To listen to mere speculation in such a case were criminal. We are authorized to hope that a proper organization of the whole, with the auxiliary agency of governments for the respective subdivisions, will afford a happy issue to the experiment. It is well worth a fair and full experiment. With such powerful and obvious motives to union, affecting all parts of our country, while experience shall not have demonstrated its impracticability, there will always be reason to distrust the patriotism of those who, in any quarter, may endeavor to weaken its bands.

In contemplating the causes which may disturb our union, it occurs as matter of serious concern, that any ground should have been furnished for characterizing parties by geographical discriminations—*Northern* and *Southern*—*Atlantic* and *Western*: whence designing men may endeavor to excite a belief that there is a real difference of local interests and views. One of the expedients of party to acquire influence, within particular districts, is to misrepresent the opinions and aims of other districts. You cannot shield yourselves too much against the jealousies and heart-burnings which spring from these misrepresentations: they tend to render alien to each other, those who ought to be bound together by fraternal affection. The inhabitants of our western country have lately had a useful lesson on this head. They have seen, in the negotiation by the executive, and in the unanimous ratification by the Senate, of the treaty with Spain, and in the universal satisfaction at that event throughout the United States, a decisive proof how unfounded were the suspicions propagated among them of a policy in the general government, and in the Atlantic States, unfriendly to their interests in regard to the Mississippi. They have been witnesses to the formation of two treaties, that with Great Britain and that with Spain, which secure to them every thing they could desire, in respect to our foreign relations, towards confirming their prosperity. Will it not be their wisdom to rely for the preservation of these advantages on the union by which they were procured? Will they not henceforth be deaf to those advisers, if such there are, who would sever them from their brethren, and connect them with aliens.

To the efficacy and permanency of your union, a government for the whole is indispensable. No alliances, however strict, between the parts can be an adequate substitute; they must inevitably experience the infractions and interruptions which all alliances in all times have experienced. Sensible of this momentous truth, you have improved upon your first essay, by the adoption of a constitution of government better calculated than your former, for an intimate union, and for the efficacious management of your common concerns. This government, the offspring of your own choice, uninfluenced and unawed; adopted upon full investigation and mature deliberation; completely free in its principles; in the distribution of its powers, uniting security with energy, and containing within itself a provision for its own amendments, has a just claim to your confidence and your support. Respect for its authority, compliance with its laws, acquiescence in its measures, are duties enjoined by the fundamental maxims of true liberty. The basis of our political systems is the right of the people to make and to alter their constitutions of government. But the constitution which at any time exists, until changed by an explicit and authentic act of the whole people, is sacredly obligatory upon all. The very idea of the power and the right of a people to establish a government, presupposes the duty of every individual to obey the established government.

All obstructions to the execution of the laws, all combinations and associations, under whatever plausible character, with the real design to direct, control, counteract, or awe the regular deliberations and actions of the constituted authorities, are destructive of this fundamental principle, and of fatal tendency. They serve to organize faction; to give it an artificial and extraordinary force; to put in the place of the delegated will of the nation, the will of a party, often a small, but artful and enterprising minority of the community; and according to the alternate triumphs of different parties, to make the public administration the mirror of the ill-concerted and incongruous projects of faction, rather than the organ of consistent and wholesome plans, digested by common councils, and modified by mutual interests.

However combinations or associations of the above description may now and then answer popular ends, they are likely, in the course of time and things, to become potent engines, by which cunning, ambitious, and unprincipled men, will be enabled to subvert the power of the people, and to usurp for themselves the reins of government; destroying afterwards the very engines which have lifted them to unjust dominion.

Towards the preservation of your government, and the permanency of your present happy state, it is requisite not only that you steadily discountenance irregular oppositions to its acknowledged authority, but also that you resist with care the spirit of innovation upon its principles, however specious the pretexts. One method of assault may be to effect, in the forms of the Constitution, alterations which will impair the energy of the system, and thus to undermine what cannot be directly overthrown. In all the changes to which you may be invited, remember that time and habit are at least as necessary to fix the true character of governments, as of other human institutions; that experience is the surest standard, by which to test the real tendency of the existing constitution of a country; that facility in changes upon the credit of mere hypothesis and opinion, exposes to perpetual change, from the endless variety of hypothesis and opinion; and remember, especially, that for the efficient management of your common interests, in a country so extensive as ours, a government of as much vigor as is consistent with the perfect security of liberty is indispensable. Liberty itself will find in such a government, with powers properly distributed and adjusted, its surest guardian. It is, indeed, little else than a name, where the government is too feeble to withstand the enterprises of faction, to confine each member of the society within the limits prescribed by the laws, and to maintain all in the secure and tranquil enjoyment of the rights of person and property.

I have already intimated to you the danger of parties in the state, with particular references to the founding of them on geographical discriminations. Let me now take a more comprehensive view, and warn you in the most solemn manner, against the baneful effects of the spirit of party, generally.

This spirit, unfortunately, is inseparable from our nature, having its root in the strongest passions of the human mind. It exists under different shapes in all governments, more or less stifled, controlled, or repressed; but in those of the popular form, it is seen in its greatest rankness, and is truly their worst enemy.

The alternate domination of one faction over another, sharpened by the spirit of revenge, natural to party dissension, which in different ages and countries has perpetrated the most horrid enormities, is itself a frightful despotism. But this leads at length to a more formal and permanent despotism. The disorders and miseries which result, gradually incline the minds of men to seek security and repose in the absolute power of an individual: and sooner or later the chief of some prevailing faction, more able or more fortunate than his competitors, turns this disposition to the purposes of his own elevation, on the ruins of public liberty.

Without looking forward to an extremity of this kind (which, nevertheless, ought not to be entirely out of sight), the common and continual mischiefs of the spirit of party, are sufficient to make it the interest and duty of a wise people to discourage and restrain it.

It serves always to distract the public councils, and enfeeble the public administration. It agitates the community with ill-founded jealousies and false alarms; kindles the animosity of one part against another; foments occasional riot and insurrection. It opens the door to foreign influence and corruption, which find a facilitated access to the government itself, through the channels of party passions. Thus the policy and the will of one country, are subject to the policy and the will of another.

There is an opinion that parties in free countries are useful checks upon the administration of the government, and serve to keep alive the spirit of liberty. This, within certain limits, is probably true: and in governments of a monarchical cast, patriotism may look with indulgence, if not with favor, upon the spirit of party. But in those of the popular character, in governments purely elective, it is a spirit not to be encouraged. From their natural tendency, it is certain there will always be enough of that spirit for every salutary purpose. And there being constant danger of excess, the effort ought to be, by force of public opinion, to mitigate and assuage it. A fire not to be quenched, it demands a uniform vigilance to prevent its bursting into a flame, lest, instead of warming, it should consume.

It is important, likewise, that the habits of thinking, in a free country, should inspire caution in those intrusted with its administration, to confine themselves within their respective constitutional spheres; avoiding, in the exercise of the powers of one department, to encroach upon another. The spirit of encroachment tends to consolidate the powers of all the departments in one, and thus to create, whatever the form of government, a real despotism. A just estimate of that love of power, and proneness to abuse it, which predominate in the human heart, is sufficient to satisfy us of the truth of this position. The necessity of reciprocal checks in the exercise of political power, by dividing and distributing it into different depositories, and constituting each the guardian of the public weal against invasions of the others, has been evinced by experiments ancient and modern: some of them in our country, and under our own eyes. To preserve them must be as necessary as to institute them. If, in the opinion of the people, the distribution or modification of the constitutional powers be in any particular wrong, let it be corrected by an amendment in the way which the Constitution designates. But let there be no change by usurpation; for though this, in one instance, may be the instrument of good, it is the customary weapon by which free governments are destroyed. The precedent must always greatly overbalance in permanent evil, any partial or transient benefit which the use can at any time yield.

Of all the dispositions and habits which lead to political prosperity, religion and morality are indispensable supports. In vain would that man claim the tribute of patriotism, who should labor to subvert these great pillars of human happiness—these firmest props of the duties of men and citizens. The mere politician, equally with the pious man, ought to respect and cherish them. A volume could not trace all their connections with private and public felicity. Let it simply be asked, where is the security for property, for reputation, for life, if the sense of religious obligation desert the oaths, which are the instruments of investigation in courts of justice? And let us with caution indulge the supposition, that morality can be maintained without religion. Whatever may be conceded to the influence of refined education on minds of peculiar structure, reason and experience both forbid us to expect that national morality can prevail in exclusion of religious principles.

It is substantially true, that virtue or morality is a necessary spring of popular government. The rule, indeed, extends with more or less force to every species of free government. Who that is a sincere friend to it can look with indifference upon attempts to shake the foundation of the fabric?

Promote, then, as an object of primary importance, institutions for the general diffusion of knowledge. In proportion as the structure of a government gives force to public opinion, it is essential that public opinion should be enlightened.

As a very important source of strength and security, cherish public credit. One method of preserving it is to use it as sparingly as possible, avoiding occasions of expense by cultivating peace; but remembering also, that timely disbursements to prepare for danger, frequently prevent much greater disbursements to repel it; avoiding likewise the accumulation of debt, not only by shunning occasions of expense, but by vigorous exertions in time of peace, to discharge the debts which unavoidable wars may have occasioned, not ungenerously throwing upon posterity the burden which we ourselves ought to bear. The execution of these maxims belongs to your representatives; but it is necessary that public opinion should co-operate. To facilitate to them the performance of their duty, it is essential that you should practically bear in mind, that towards the payment of debts there must be revenue; that to have revenue there must be taxes; that no taxes can be devised which are not more or less inconvenient and unpleasant; that the intrinsic embarrassment inseparable from the selection of the proper objects (which is always a choice of difficulties), ought to be a decisive motive for a candid construction of the conduct of the government in making it, and for a spirit of acquiescence in the measures for obtaining revenue which the public exigencies may at any time dictate.

Observe good faith and justice towards all nations; cultivate peace and harmony with all: religion and morality enjoin this conduct; and can it be that good policy does not equally enjoin it? It will be worthy of a free, enlightened, and, at no distant period, a great nation, to give to mankind the magnanimous and too novel example of a people always guided by an exalted justice and benevolence. Who can doubt that in the course of time and things, the fruits of such a plan would richly repay any temporary advantages which might be lost by a steady adherence to it. Can it be, that Providence has not connected the permanent felicity of a nation with its virtue? The experiment, at least, is recommended by every sentiment which ennobles human nature. Alas! is it rendered impossible by its vices?

In the execution of such a plan, nothing is more essential than that permanent inveterate antipathies against particular nations, and passionate attachments for others, should be excluded; and that in place of them, just and amicable feelings towards all should be cultivated. The nation which indulges towards another an habitual hatred, or an habitual fondness, is in some degree a slave. It is a slave to its animosity or to its affection, either of which is sufficient to lead it astray from its duty and its interest. Antipathy in one nation against another, disposes each more readily to offer insult and injury, to lay hold of slight causes of umbrage, and to be haughty and intractable, when accidental or trifling occasions of dispute occur.

Hence, frequent collisions, obstinate, envenomed, and bloody contests. The nation, prompted by ill-will and resentment, sometimes impels to war the government, contrary to the best calculations of policy. The government sometimes participates in the national propensity, and adopts, through passion, what reason would reject; at other times, it makes the animosity of the nation subservient to projects of hostility instigated by pride, ambition, and other sinister and pernicious motives. The peace often, sometimes perhaps the liberty of nations, has been the victim.

So, likewise, a passionate attachment of one nation for another, produces a variety of evils. Sympathy for the favorite nation, facilitating the illusion of an imaginary common interest, in cases where no real common interest exists, and infusing into one the enmities of the other, betrays the former into a participation in the quarrels and wars of the latter, without adequate inducements or justification. It leads also to concessions to the favorite nation, of privileges denied to others, which are apt doubly to injure the nation making the concessions, by unnecessarily parting with what ought to have been retained; and by exciting jealousy, ill-will, and a disposition to retaliate, in the parties from whom equal privileges are withheld; and it gives to ambitious, corrupted, or deluded citizens (who devote themselves to the favorite nation), facility to betray or sacrifice the interests of their own country, without odium, sometimes even with popularity; gilding with the appearances of a virtuous sense of obligation, a commendable deference for public opinion, or a laudable zeal for public good, the base or foolish compliances of ambition, corruption, or infatuation.

As avenues to foreign influence, in innumerable ways, such attachments are particularly alarming to the truly enlightened and independent patriot. How many opportunities do they afford to tamper with domestic factions, to practise the arts of seduction, to mislead public opinion, to influence or awe the public councils! Such an attachment of a small or weak, towards a great and powerful nation, dooms the former to be the satellite of the latter. Against the insidious wiles of foreign influence (I conjure you to believe me, fellow-citizens), the jealousy of a free people ought to be constantly awake; since history and experience prove that foreign influence is one of the most baneful foes of republican government. But that jealousy, to be useful, must be impartial; else it becomes the instrument of the very influence to be avoided, instead of a defence against it. Excessive partiality for one foreign nation, and excessive dislike of another, cause those whom they actuate to see danger only on one side, and serve to veil, and even second, the arts of influence on the other. Real patriots, who may resist the intrigues of the favorite, are liable to become suspected and odious, while its tools and dupes usurp the applause and confidence of the people, to surrender their interests.

The great rule of conduct for us, in regard to foreign nations, is, in extending our commercial relations, to have with them as little political connection as possible. So far as we have already formed engagements, let them be fulfilled with perfect good faith. Here let us stop.

Europe has a set of primary interests, which to us have none, or a very remote, relation. Hence she must be engaged in frequent controversies, the causes of which are essentially foreign to our concerns. Hence, therefore, it must be unwise in us to implicate ourselves by artificial ties, in the ordinary vicissitudes of her politics, or the ordinary combinations and collisions of her friendships or enmities.

Our detached and distant situation invites and enables us to pursue a different course. If we remain one people, under an efficient government, the period is not far off when we may defy material injury from external annoyance; when we may take such an attitude as will cause the neutrality we may at any time resolve upon, to be scrupulously respected; when belligerent nations, under the impossibility of making acquisitions upon us, will not lightly hazard the giving us provocation; when we may choose peace or war, as our interest, guided by justice, shall counsel.

Why forego the advantages of so peculiar a situation? Why quit our own to stand upon foreign ground? Why, by interweaving our destiny with that of any part of Europe, entangle our peace and prosperity in the toils of European ambition, rivalship, interest, humor, or caprice?

It is our true policy to steer clear of permanent alliances with any portion of the foreign world; so far, I mean, as we are now at liberty to do it; for let me not be understood as capable of patronizing infidelity to existing engagements. I hold the maxim no less applicable to public than to private affairs, that honesty is always the best policy. I repeat it, therefore, let those engagements be observed in their genuine sense. But in my opinion, it is unnecessary, and would be unwise to extend them.

Taking care always to keep ourselves, by suitable establishments, on a respectable defensive posture, we may safely trust to temporary alliances for extraordinary emergencies.

Harmony, and a liberal intercourse with all nations, are recommended by policy, humanity, and interest. But even our commercial policy should hold an equal and impartial hand; neither seeking nor granting exclusive favors or preferences; consulting the natural course of things; diffusing and diversifying by gentle means, the streams of commerce, but forcing nothing; establishing, with powers so disposed, — in order to give trade a stable course, to define the rights of our merchants, and to enable the government to support them,—conventional rules of intercourse, the best that present circumstances and mutual opinion will permit, but temporary and liable to be from time to time abandoned or varied, as experience and circumstances shall dictate: constantly keeping in view, that it is folly in one nation to look for disinterested favors from another; that it must pay with a portion of its independence for whatever it may accept under that character; that by such acceptance, it may place itself in the condition of having given equivalents for nominal favors, and yet of being reproached with ingratitude for not giving more. There can be no greater error than to expect or calculate upon real favors from nation to nation. It is an illusion which experience must cure, which a just pride ought to discard.

In offering to you, my countrymen, these counsels of an old and affectionate friend, I dare not hope they will make the strong and lasting impression I could wish—that they will control the usual current of the passions, or prevent our nation from running the course which has hitherto marked the destiny of nations. But if I may even flatter myself that they may be productive of some partial benefit, some occasional good; that they may now and then recur to moderate the fury of party spirit; to warn against the mischiefs of foreign intrigue; to guard against the impostures of pretended patriotism; this hope will be a full recompense for the solicitude for your welfare, by which they have been dictated.

How far, in the discharge of my official duties, I have been guided by the principles which have been delineated, the public records and other evidences of my conduct must witness to you and to the world. To myself, the assurance of my own conscience is, that I have at least believed myself to be guided by them.

In relation to the still subsisting war in Europe, my proclamation of the 22d of April, 1793, is the index to my plan. Sanctioned by your approving voice, and by that of your representatives in both houses of Congress, the spirit of that measure has continually governed me; uninfluenced by any attempts to deter or divert me from it.

After deliberate examination, with the aid of the best lights I could obtain, I was well satisfied that our country, under all the circumstances of the case, had a right to take, and was bound in duty and interest to take, a neutral position. Having taken it, I determined, as far as should depend upon me, to maintain it with moderation, perseverance, and firmness. The considerations which respect the right to hold this conduct, it is not necessary on this occasion to detail. I will only observe, that according to my understanding of the matter, that right, so far from being denied by any of the belligerent powers, has been virtually admitted by all.

The duty of holding a neutral conduct may be inferred, without any thing more, from the obligation which justice and humanity impose on every nation, in cases in which it is free to act, to maintain inviolate the relations of peace and amity towards other nations.

The inducements of interest for observing that conduct will best be referred to your own reflections and experience. With me, a predominant motive has been to endeavor to gain time to our country to settle and mature its yet recent institutions, and to progress, without interruption, to that degree of strength and consistency which is necessary to give it, humanly speaking, the command of its own fortunes.

Though in reviewing the incidents of my administration I am unconscious of intentional error, I am nevertheless too sensible of my defects not to think it probable that I have committed many errors. Whatever they may be, I fervently beseech the Almighty to avert or mitigate the evils to which they may tend. I shall also carry with me the hope that my country will never cease to view them with indulgence; and that after forty-five years of my life dedicated to its service with an upright zeal, the faults of incompetent abilities will be consigned to oblivion, as myself must soon be to the mansions of rest.

Relying on this, as in other things, and actuated by that fervent love towards it which is so natural to a man who views in it the native soil of himself and his progenitors for several generations, I anticipate with pleasing expectation that retreat, in which I promise myself to realize, without alloy, the sweet enjoyment of partaking in the midst of my fellow-citizens, the benign influence of good laws under a free government, the ever-favorite object of my heart, and the happy reward, as I trust, of our mutual cares, labors, and dangers.

UNITED STATES, *September* 17, 1796.

PARLIAMENTARY RULES

FOR THE GOVERNMENT OF PUBLIC ASSEMBLIES.

A KNOWLEDGE of the rules which regulate the formation and order of business in public assemblies, is essential to every well-informed citizen. Every citizen is obliged, at some time, to take part in the primary assemblies of the people. These are constantly held, not merely for political purposes, but for those of business—commercial, literary, benevolent, or religious. In addition to these primary assemblies, there are various and numerous organized associations, with some one or more of which almost every citizen is connected. The rules for the transaction of business in the assemblies, or associations, are substantially the same in all of them. They were originally derived from the usages of the British Parliament; hence they were adopted by the American legislative assemblies, and became common law, by the practice of Congress and the state legislatures.

In religious assemblies, they are subordinate to their respective constitutions, also the rule of proceeding. In fine, there is no other code of regulations known to public assemblies, than that of parliamentary usage.

The most important of these rules are substantially as follows:

1. When a *primary assembly* of the people, or of any part of them, is called together for any purpose, the first thing to be done is to choose a *presiding officer;* for without such an officer nothing can be done. No question could be put, and the assembly would be an anarchy.

2. This officer is called *Chairman;* and he is chosen thus. Some one rises, at a proper time, and moves that A. B. be appointed chairman of the meeting. This is seconded; and *the person making the motion* puts the question; and if the motion be carried, A. B. takes the chair as presiding officer.

3. After this, all questions are put to the assembly by the chairman.

4. Regularly, there must be a *Secretary* to every public meeting, whose duty it is to record its proceedings, for future reference.

5. The assembly may appoint such other officers as they may deem expedient; and on important occasions there are usually appointed several vice-presidents, and additional secretaries.

6. In constitutionally organized bodies, such as the Episcopal Church, the Presbyterian General Assembly, the Congress of the United States, and the Legislatures of the states, there are usually presiding officers named in the constitution, and a mode of appointment provided for. Thus, in the Presbyterian General Assembly, the presiding officer is called a moderator, who is chosen by each General Assembly; but the last moderator presides until the new one is chosen.[1] So, too, in the Episcopal Church, when present, the eldest bishop is the presiding officer. In the Congress of the United States, the Vice President in the Senate, and the Speaker of the House, are the chairmen of their respective houses.

7. When thus regularly appointed, the chairman, or presiding officer, is vested with power to preserve order,[2] and to decide questions arising between the respective members of the body.

8. But in all legislatures, as well as primary assemblies, there is *an appeal* from the Speaker, or presiding officer, to the assembly itself.[3]

9. In preserving order in a public assembly, the presiding officer may call upon the house to sustain him. In a popular assembly, if this is not done the assembly becomes immediately dissolved, because in a state of anarchy. In the Senate of the United States, the Vice President has the sole power of preserving order. In the House of Representatives, the Speaker may call members by name, and require them to preserve order. If they do not, the House will require them to withdraw, and, after hearing the charge and the excuse, will proceed to consider the degree of punishment they will inflict.[4] In the Presbyterian General Assembly, all power of this kind is vested in the moderator.[5]

---

[1] Form of Government of the Presbyterian Church in the United States.

[2] Idem; Jefferson's Manual, chapter 19, pages 30 to 50; Rules of the House of Representatives, rule 2.

[3] Jefferson's Manual, 53; [3] Ney's Debates, 819.

[4] Idem, 49. [5] Form of Government, Chap. 19.

10. Every public assembly has the power of determining the *qualifications* of its own members. This it must, of course, have, or it would be liable to intermixture with foreign bodies, without any means of redress. In an ordinary assembly of the people, there is commonly no need of an inquiry into qualifications;—yet, common history shows, that many assemblies break up in disorder, in consequence of persons claiming to take part in the proceedings of the meeting, who are not properly within the terms under which the meeting was called. In regularly constituted bodies, this power is usually expressly granted:—for example, in the Constitution of the United States, this power is granted to both Houses of Congress.[1] So also of the Presbyterian General Assembly.[2]

QUORUM.

11. In every constitutionally organized body, there must be some number fixed, which are sufficient to do business. This number is called a *quorum*. In Congress, a *majority* of each House constitutes a quorum.[3] In Ohio, two-thirds of either house of the General Assembly, make a quorum. So also in Indiana. In Kentucky, a majority.[4] In the Presbyterian General Assembly,[5] fourteen Commissioners constitute a quorum.

12.. In primary assemblies of the people, there is, of course, no number requisite to constitute a quorum, and it frequently happens, that a very small number of persons act for a large community. The *citizen* generally should make it his *duty* to attend public meetings called on important subjects, lest he should find afterwards, that others had assumed to put forth opinions for the community, which the majority do not sanction.

13. Where a certain quorum is necessary to do business, in general the chair should not be taken by the presiding officer till *that quorum* is present. And whenever, in the progress of business, it is observed, that a quorum is not present, any member may call

---

[1] Constitution U. S., Art. 1, Sect. 5.

[2] Form of Government, Chap. 12, Art. 7.

[3] American Constitution, 331.

[4] Idem.

[5] Form of Government, Chap. 12, Sect. 3.

for a count of the House; and a quorum being found wanting, business must be suspended.[1]

14. In a constitutional body, after the chairman has taken his seat, and a quorum being present, the first thing to be done, is to read the Journal of the preceding day, in order that mistakes, if there be any, may be corrected, and the Journal become a true history of the proceedings.[2]

15. In the Senate of the United States, the Vice President has no vote, but a casting vote, when the House is equally divided.[3] When the chairman is a Senator, he has no vote, but his own vote as a Senator. That he has. In the House of Representatives, or the General Assembly of Ohio, the *Speaker* has only his *own vote.* This vote is felt when, by giving it in the negative, he makes the vote a tie,[4] and thus defeats the motion, or bill, or, when by giving it he makes a majority. In general, the chairman of a public assembly, has his own vote, and no more, though in a primary assembly, should the house be equally divided, the chairman may give a casting vote.

ORDER.

16. By the United States Constitution[5] each House of Congress, has the power to determine its own rules of proceedings. In any general assembly, where there is not a constitution forbidding it, this power naturally, and necessarily, belongs to the assembly. Public assemblies of the people do not make such rules,—because to do it, would consume time unnecessarily. Universal custom has made the rules of order, adopted in the British Parliament, and the American Congress, the rules of all popular assemblies.

17. When a person rises to speak, he must rise from his seat, and address the chairman, who should call him by name, that the assembly may know who it is, and pay attention.[6]

18. The person speaking, must confine himself to the question under debate, and avoid personality.[7] And if he transgress the rules of order, the chairman may immediately call him to order.

---

[1] Jefferson's Manual, 28. [2] Idem.
[3] Constitution, Art. 1, Sect. 3. [4] Rules of the House Repr., 9.
[5] Constitution, Art. 1, Sect. 5.
[6] Jefferson's Manual, 38; Rules of the House, 19. [7] Rules 18 and 19.

If he questions the correctness of the chairman, he may appeal to the house, who will decide the question.

19. If two persons rise to speak together, the chairman determines which shall have precedence: it may, however, be referred to the house.[1]

20. The chairman of an assembly cannot regularly speak to any thing but a point of order, or a question of fact.[2]

21. A person speaking cannot regularly mention another member of the assembly *by name.* He must *describe* him, as "The gentleman who has just sat down," "the gentleman, on the other side of the question," &c.[3]

22. All decisions of the chairman may be controlled by the house.[4]

ORDER OF BUSINESS.

23. In *every public assembly*, there are two technical terms, expressing the mode of *doing business.* One of them is *a Motion;* the second, a *Resolution.* At these, in a *primary assembly* of the people, the power of the assembly stops;—because, not having any formal, or constitutional powers to pass laws, they can only organize themselves,—discuss public matters,—and record, in the form of resolutions, their deliberate opinions. In a free country, opinions thus expressed by those who are the majority, become in the end laws. These laws are enacted by the *legislatures*, who are constitutional bodies, vested by the people, under certain sanctions and forms, with the power of *making laws.* In these legislative bodies, there are not only motions, and resolutions, but *rules, orders, and laws.*

24. A *Motion* is simply a desire expressed, by a member, that an opinion be expressed, or an act be done, by the assembly, which is then put to the vote, and if sanctioned, is said to be *passed.* Thus, when the assembly meets, it *moves* that B. takes the chair,—which, if approved by the majority, is *passed*, and B. takes the chair.

25. A *Resolution* is simply the expression of an opinion,—and, like all other matters brought before the assembly, must be *moved* by some one, and *passed* by a vote of the assembly. It is com-

---

[1] Jefferson's Manual, 38. [2] Idem, 40. [3] Idem, 41. [4] Idem, 40.

monly and properly expressed thus:—"Resolved, that in the opinion of this meeting, the United States should immediately take measures for ascertaining the northern boundary of the United States to the Pacific Ocean, and take formal possession of the country near the mouth of the Columbia river."

26. *Rules* are regulations drawn up by legislative or incorporated bodies, holding more than one session, for the permanent government of their proceedings. Accordingly, the British Parliament, the American Congress, and all legislative bodies have *rules* of proceeding.

27. *Orders* are what they express,—orders made by a legislative body, directing something *to be done*, which is within the power of the House, and relates to the assembly itself. Thus, the *Orders of the Day*, are those things which the assembly, in the course of its business, have directed to be done *on that day*. Thus, the House of Representatives *orders* its Sergeant-at-Arms to do certain acts relative to its police, or to bring certain persons before it.

28. *Laws* are formal orders, commanding or forbidding certain things to be done, not merely by the legislature itself, but by the whole community which that legislature represents,—and which it is, by the constitution of the country, vested with power to enact.

29. A *Motion* must regularly have a *second*:—because if it have no second, it is most obvious, it cannot pass the assembly.[1]

30. All motions must regularly be reduced to *writing*, because otherwise, there cannot be made out a correct *history* of the proceedings, which is necessary, in order to correct any misunderstanding which the members might afterwards have, to provide exact evidence of the doings of the assembly.

31. In all legislative bodies, whether civil or ecclesiastical, all the details and preparation of business is done by *Committees*. There are three kinds of committees: 1st. Committees of the Whole; 2d. Standing Committees; 3d. Special Committees.

32. A *Committee of the Whole* is when a legislative body resolves *itself* into a committee;—the object of which is to get rid of the restraints of the *standing rules* of order; for, as a legisla-

---

[1] Jefferson's Manual, 50.

tive body, it has established certain *rules of business, and discussion*, which cannot be avoided; but, as a committee, it is not bound by them.

33. A *Standing Committee* is a committee appointed by a legislative body, during its session, and to which is referred a certain portion of its business, to be prepared for action, and reported upon.

34. A *Special Committee* is one which is appointed on a particular subject, and by whom a report on that subject is to be made. This is the only kind of committee which strictly belongs to a *primary assembly*,—for as it has no permanent rules of proceeding, its discussions are as free as those of a committee of the whole; and, as it is in session but a short time, it needs no standing committee. The *resolutions* of primary assemblies are, however, almost always prepared by *special committees* appointed for that purpose.

35. In the House of Representatives, in the National Congress, there are appointed seventeen *standing committees*, whose business is of a *general nature*. They are as follows, and their business is explained by their titles:

A Committee of Elections.
" " of Ways and Means.
" " of Claims.
" " of Commerce.
" " on Public Lands.
" " on Post-Office, and Post-Roads.
" " on the District of Columbia.
" " on the Judiciary.
" " on Pensions, and Revolutionary Claims.
" " on Public Expenditures.
" " on Private Land Claims.
" " on Manufactures.
" " on Agriculture.
" " on Indian Affairs.
" " on Military Affairs.
" " on Naval Affairs.
" " on Foreign Affairs.

36. To these committees in the House of Representatives, are regularly referred all the subjects expressed by their titles, and,

generally speaking, the topics connected with these subjects are brought before the House only by those committees. These committees examine in detail the mass of documents connected with the public business, and by them that business is prepared for the discussion and action of the House.

37. A committee in a legislative body may report by bill, by resolution, or by asking *leave* to be discharged.

38. A *Bill* is the *form of a law*, prepared to be passed; and every law before it is enacted, must be presented, in some regular form.

39. A committee may also report a *resolution* simply expressive of the opinion of the House; or may ask leave to be discharged, —which the House will grant or not, at its discretion.

40. A bill must regularly *be read*, in a *legislative body*, *three times* before it becomes a law.[1] And no bill shall be twice read on the *same day* without *special leave*.[2]

41. The *first reading* of a bill is for *information*, and if opposition be then made to it, the question put to the House is, "Shall this bill be rejected?"[3] If no opposition be made, or the question of rejection be negatived, the bill goes to a second reading without a question.

42. A bill cannot be amended at the first reading.[4]

43. Upon the second reading of a bill, the Speaker states that it is ready for *commitment* or *engrossment*. Commitment is sending it to some committee for report, and *Engrossment* is the preparation of the bill, by a careful examination, and writing out in a full fair hand that there may be no mistakes.[5]

44. The *second reading* must regularly be on another day.[6] If, on motion, it is decided that the bill shall be committed, it may be referred to either of the committees named before, a committee of the whole, a standing committee, or a special committee. If it be referred to a committee of the whole, the House appoints a day on which it will be considered in committee of the whole.

45. If the bill be referred to a special committee, for amendment, the committee is regularly appointed by the Speaker; but the House has entire control of the appointment, if it chooses to

---

[1] House of Representatives, Rule 66. [2] Idem. [3] Idem, Rule 67.
[4] Jefferson's Manual, 53. [5] Rule 71. [6] Jefferson's Manual, 54.

exercise it. Regularly, the person who has introduced the bill or subject before the House, and the member who proposes to amend it, must be appointed on the committee; and on the other hand, one who does not propose to amend, but is altogether opposed to the bill, should not be appointed on the committee—for a "child should not be put to a nurse that cares nothing for it."[1]

46. The clerk may deliver the bill to either member of the committee, but properly to the chairman, who is the one first named.

47. A committee may meet where they please, but they cannot act except when together; and nothing can be the report of the committee except what is agreed upon in committee.

48. A majority of a committee constitutes a quorum for business.[2]

49. The committee to whom a bill is referred have full power over it, except as to its title; that they cannot change.

50. The natural order in considering any paper before a legislative body is to begin at the beginning, and proceed through regularly; to which there is a single exception, in the case of a preamble, because in the course of discussion, a bill may be so altered as to require a new preamble.

51. When the bill, resolution, or paper is ready to be reported, the chairman, standing in his place, reports the same to the House, with or without amendment. The report being made, the committee (if a special committee) is dissolved, and can no more act without new authority.[3]

52. After report to the House, however, and at any time before the bill is passed, it may be *recommitted*, for the purpose of further alteration and amendment.[4]

53. The amendments are read by the clerk, and considered by the House in order; when these amendments are all through with, the speaker puts the question, "whether this bill shall be read the third time?"

54. When the bill has been committed, amendments reported, accepted, or rejected, and the question is on the third reading, the bill is supposed to be made as perfect as its friends can make it, and at this stage of the proceedings it is commonly, and most

---

[1] Jefferson's Manual, 55. [2] Idem, 56. [3] Idem, 61.
[4] Rules of the House, 70.

properly, attacked by its opponents; and the discussion commences on its merits.

55. There are still two stages of proceeding before the bill is passed—its *third reading*, and its *passage* for engrossment. The trying vote is generally taken on the *third reading*, before which it is not generally known, when there is a difference of opinion on the merits, whether the bill will pass.

56. When a bill is engrossed, the title is to be indorsed on the back, and not within the bill.[1]

AMENDMENTS.

57. If an amendment be prepared inconsistent with one already agreed to, it is ground for rejection by the House; but is not within the power of the Speaker to reject, because such power would give him the power of deciding what was or was not consistent.[2]

58. *An amendment to an amendment*, is in order: as, for example, when it is moved to insert a paragraph by way of amendment, it is proper for its friends to make it as perfect as possible by moving amendments, either in words or matter.[3] If it were proposed to amend, by striking out certain words, an amendment may be moved *to the amendment*, by striking out certain words *from the amendment*, of which the effect is to leave them *in* the original bill, or resolution.

59. A totally different bill may be engrossed on, or submitted for another, under the words, "Be it enacted." The United States House of Representatives once engrafted a bill to support the Military Academy, on a bill to Improve Harbors and Erect Lighthouses.

60. It is in order to move an amendment to strike out certain words, and insert others;—this being rejected, it is in order to move to strike out, and insert a different set of words; this being rejected, it is in order to move to strike out the same words, and insert nothing: because each of these is a distinct proposition differing from the others. But it must be recollected, that it is *not in order*, if the motion to strike out and insert A. *is carried*, to

[1] Jefferson's Manual, 68. [2] Idem. [3] Idem, 86, 87.

move an amendment to *strike out* A. and *insert* B. To aviod this dilemma, the mover of B. must *give notice*, pending the motion to insert A., that he intends to move the insertion of B., in which case, he will gain the votes of all who prefer the amendment B. to the amendment A., in opposition to A.[1] But, after A. *is inserted*, it is in order to move an amendment by striking out the whole, or part of the *original paragraph, including* A.; for this is essentially *a different proposition* from that to strike out A. merely.

61. The *third reading* of a Bill is the proper period to *fill up blanks*.

62. After a *bill is passed*, there can be no further alteration of it on any point.

COEXISTING AND EQUIVALENT QUESTION.

63. Can the House be in possession of two questions at the same moment of time? A question may be interrupted by a vote of *Adjournment*, in which case it does not stand before the House in the same stage, at the next meeting, but must come before it in the usual way. So, also, when interrupted by the *orders of the day*, which are *privileged questions*. But by a motion to *amend, withdraw, or questions of orders*, the business is only *suspended, not removed;* and when these are decided, it stands before the House as before. None but the class of privileged questions can be brought forward while another is before the House.[2]

64. When questions are perfectly *equivalent*, or that the negative of one amounts to an affirmative of the other, and leaves no other alternative, the decision of the one necessarily includes the other. Thus, the negative of striking out amounts to the affirmative of agreeing, and, therefore, to put the question on agreeing, would, in effect, be to put the question twice over.[3]

65. The *question* is to be put by the Speaker, first on the *affirmative*, and then on the *negative* side. *After* the *affirmative* is put, a member may still rise to speak, because it is not a *full question* till both sides are put.[4]

66. If a question contain more parts than one, it may be divided

---

[1] Jefferson's Manual, 83. [2] Idem, 95. [3] Idem, 96. [4] Idem, 98.

into two or more questions, but not as the right of an individual member, but with the *consent of the House*;—for, who is to decide whether a question is complicated or not?[1]

67. When a question is divided, after the question on the first member, the second is open to debate and amendment, because, it is a known rule, that a person may rise and speak at any time before the question is completely decided; but the question is not completely put, when the vote has been taken on the first member only.

68. When a motion has once been made, and carried in the affirmative or negative, it shall be in order for *any member of the majority* to move for a *reconsideration* thereof, on the same, or succeeding day.[2]

69. A bill, or resolution, *reconsidered*, is restored to its former state, and is open for amendment and discussion on the third reading.[3] It is not settled how far this question of *reconsideration*, and the consequent continuation of the same discussion, may be continued.

PRIORITY OF MOTIONS, AND PRIVILEGED QUESTIONS.

70. By the 29th Rule of the House of Representatives, it is said, that when a question is under debate, no motion shall be received but—

1st. To adjourn.
2d. To lie on the table.
3d. For the previous question.
4th. To postpone to a day certain.
5th. To commit, or amend.
6th. To postpone indefinitely.

Which several motions shall have precedence in the order in which they are arranged; and no motion to postpone to a day certain, to commit, or to postpone indefinitely, being decided, shall be again allowed on the same day, and of the same stage of the proposition.

71. It is a general rule, that the question first moved and sec-

---

[1] Jefferson's Manual, 91.
[2] Rules of the House, 38.
[3] Jefferson's Manual, 109, 110.

onded shall be first put, but this rule gives way to what may be called *privileged questions*, which are those above stated.

72. The *Orders of the Day* are of course privileged; that is, the special order of the day takes place of all general business, and of all motions, except for an adjournment. When a member, therefore, moves the order of the day, the question is not on a particular one, but "whether the House will now proceed to the orders of the day," and on this motion all debate must cease.[1]

73. A motion to *adjourn* takes place of all others, because otherwise the House might be kept sitting against its will; yet, this motion cannot be received after another question is actually put, and the House is engaged in voting.

74. When the House is willing to consider a question, but has other business it prefers, or wants time for information, the motion or bill is ordered to *lie on the table*, whence it can be ordered up, when it suits the convenience of the House.

75. When a proposition is moved, which it is useless or inexpedient now to express or discuss, the *previous question* has been introduced for suppressing, for that time, the motion and its discussion.[2]

76. When any question is before the House, any member may move the *previous question*, which is: "Shall the main question be now put;" if it pass, then the main question is to be put immediately, without debate; but if lost, then the main question is not put, and the discussion goes on. If the previous question is carried, it cuts off all amendments, not yet acted on, and forces the question on the main proposition without amendment.

77. A postponement to *a day certain*, is used when a proposition is made which it is proper to act on—but information is wanted, or something more pressing claims present attention, and the question is adjourned to some day within the session. Sometimes this motion is made to a day beyond the session; when it is the same as indefinite postponement.

78. The previous question gets rid of a proposition only for a single day, and the same proposition may be renewed; if, therefore, they wish to get rid of it entirely, it is moved to *postpone it indefinitely*. This quashes it for the session.

79. By the rules of the House of Representatives, the question

---

[1] Jefferson's Manual, 71.

[2] Idem, 72.

of *committing* and *amending* has priority to that of indefinite postponement. The reason of which is, that if a question be indefinitely postponed, there is no room for amendment, by which perhaps that very proposition might have been made acceptable. On the other hand, if a proposition be amended in a way to make it most acceptable, it may still, if the majority choose, be indefinitely postponed.

80. As a general rule, the first question moved must be first put; but this is not universal. Suppose a motion is made to *amend*, and then a motion *to commit*. Here the question on *commitment*, though last moved, must be first put, because, really, it is friendly to the amendment.[1]

81. Competition may arise among the *privileged questions*, as in the instance last given. Some examples of this are as follows:

82. First, suppose it is moved the *previous question*, to *postpone*, to *commit and amend:* these questions have precedence, by the rule of the House of Representatives, in the order they are here put; and, consequently, the vote must be on the previous question. In this case, it is said the moving of the previous question defeats the question, in whatever way it may be decided. For if affirmatively, the *main question* must be *now* put. But if negatively, then the *main question* is removed from before the House.

83. If on motion for *postponement*, it be decided in the affirmative, there is nothing for the House to act upon: but if in the negative, the main question may then be put, and defeated by the *previous question*, or it may be committed and amended.

84. So, also, if a motion is made to commit and amend, and fails, the previous question or postponement may then be made, and the main question defeated without discussion.

85. By the rules of the House,[2] the motion to *amend* is cut off by the motion for the previous question, which forces on the main question.

86. The questions heretofore mentioned are supposed to be put on the original main proposition; but let us suppose them moved, not on the primary question but the secondary one. If it be moved to postpone, commit, or amend the primary proposition, and it be moved to suppress that motion by putting the *previous*

---

[1] Jefferson's Manual, 76.

[2] Rule 29.

question, it is not allowed; because it would embarrass questions too much, to allow them to be piled up several stories high.

87. Suppose a motion for the *previous question*, or a motion to commit and amend, and it be then moved to postpone the motion for the previous question, or the motion for commitment and amendment,—this motion is not allowed; because it would be absurd to postpone the collateral question and leave the principal one still to act upon.[1]

88. There are several questions which in their nature being *incidental to all* questions, will take place of every one, privileged or not. For example, a question of *order* may arise, at any moment, and must be decided before the regular business can proceed. A matter of *privilege*, arising out of a question, or from the quarrel of two members, or disorderly conduct, supersedes the original question, and must be first disposed of.[2] So, also, *leave* to withdraw a motion. Because when a motion is put and seconded, it is *in the possession of the House*, not the mover, and cannot be withdrawn without leave. This implies that *leave* may be given; and, consequently, as that is necessarily prior to any question or motion, the vote on it must be taken first.

89. Can the House be in possession of two questions at once? No question but a privileged one can be brought forward while there is another before the House; the rule being, that when a motion has been made and seconded, no other can be received, except it be a privileged one. Suppose, however, a question is intercepted by some of the privileged questions, in what way will it stand before the House? If it be intercepted by a question of adjournment, it is *removed* from before the House, and at its next meeting must come before it in the usual way. So, also, the *orders of the day*, and the *previous question*, *postponement*, or *commitment*, *remove* the question from before the House. But if the motion be one to amend, withdraw, read papers, or of order and privilege, then the question before the House is only *suspended*, and, when these are decided, stands again before the House.[3]

90. If on a question of rejection the bill is retained, it passes of course to its next reading; and a question of a second reading determined negatively, is a rejection without further question.

---

[1] Jefferson's Manual. [2] Idem, 81. [3] Idem, 85.

91. So in all questions which are perfectly *equivalent*, the negative of one is the affirmative of the other, and concludes, necessarily, the other. Thus, the negative of striking out is the affirmative of agreeing; and therefore the latter question is not put, because wholly useless.

MISCELLANEOUS RULES.

92. The *question* is first put on the *affirmative*, and then on the *negative* side; till which, it is not a full question; but in the case of small matters, such as receiving reports, petitions, reading papers, &c., the Speaker or Chairman will *presume* the consent of the House, unless some objection be formally made; which saves the time of taking votes on matters of mere routine.

93. When an essential provision has been omitted in a bill, rather than erase the bill, it is usual to *add a clause*, on a separate paper, engrossed, and called *a rider*, which is read and put to the question three times. Every one is at liberty to bring in a rider, without asking leave.

94. *Amendments* must be read as often as the original bill. If introduced at the second reading, twice; if at the third, three times. They are admitted at the third reading with great reluctance.

95. When a bill has been *read* a third time, and is on its final passage, the Speaker, holding the bill in his hand, puts the question on its passage, saying, "Gentlemen, all you who are of opinion that this bill shall pass, say *ay;*" and after the answer of the ayes, "All those of the contrary opinion, say *no.*"

96. After a bill has *passed*, there can be no further alteration in any point.

97. In putting a question to the House, the Speaker declares whether the *yeas* or *nays* have it by the *sound*, if he be himself satisfied; or if he be not satisfied, or, before any new member comes in or a new motion be made, a member rises and says he is dissatisfied, the Speaker is to divide the House. On a division in the British Parliament, one party goes forth, and the other stays in. One being gone forth, the Speaker appoints two tellers from the affirmative, and two from the negative side, who first count those sitting in the House, and then count those who went forth,

as they come in, and report the number to the Speaker. In the United States Congress, the process is shorter. The ayes first rise, and are counted standing in their places, by the Speaker. Then they sit; and the noes rise, and are counted in the same manner.

98. If any difficulty arise on a point of order during the division, the Speaker is to decide peremptorily, subject to the future censure of the House if irregular.

99. The voice of a majority decides; but if the House be equally divided, the question is lost. The former state of things, whatever it is, is not to be changed, except by a majority. In the Senate, the Vice President has a casting voice.

100. When, from counting the House, on a division, it appears there is not a quorum, the matter continues in exactly the state in which it was before the division, and must be resumed at that point at a future day.

101. On a question, whether a member having voted ay may change his opinion, there is precedent that he may.

102. A mistake in the report of the tellers may be rectified after the report is made.

103. After the bill has passed, and not before, the *title* to the bill may be amended, and is to be fixed by question.

104. When either House of a legislative body send a bill to the other, the latter may pass it with amendments. The bill is then sent back to the House in which it originated, where the House may either assent or dissent to the amendments: the regular progression is for the first House to *disagree* to the amendments. The House which made the amendments *insists* on them. The other then *insist on their disagreement.* The first then *adheres.* The time for *insisting* and *adhering* may be prolonged, at pleasure, in order to keep the subject open.[1]

105. To settle a difference of this kind, it is usual to appoint *committees of conference*, by each house. When such committees are appointed, they shall, at a convenient hour to be appointed by the chairman, meet in the conference chamber, and state to each other, either verbally, or in writing, as they choose, the reasons for and against the amendment, and confer freely thereon.[2]

106. Either House may *recede* from its amendment, and agree

---

[1] Jefferson's Manual, 113. [2] Joint Rules, and Orders of Congress.

to the bill, or *recede from their disagreement* to the amendment, and thus pass the bill either absolutely or with an amendment.

107. But the House cannot recede from or insist on its own amendment with an amendment, for the same reason that it cannot send to the other House an *amendment to its own act*, after it has passed that act. They may *amend an amendment from the other House*, because they have never assented to it; but they cannot amend their own amendment, because they have passed on the question in that form.

108. A motion to amend an amendment from the other House, takes precedence of a motion to agree or disagree.

109. It is not the custom for one House to inform the other by what members a bill has passed. Nor when a bill from the other House is rejected, to give notice of it; but it is rejected without notice, to prevent unbecoming altercations.

110. When bills are on their passage between the two Houses of a legislative body, they should be on paper, and under the signature of the secretary or clerk of each House respectively. So, also, in all public meetings of any kind, all resolutions, acts, and motions should be *in writing* when offered, and recorded verbatim, that the true intent of the body, and its accurate history should be preserved.

111. In the Houses of Congress, there is a joint committee of both Houses, called the committee on enrolled bills, whose duty it is to compare the *enrollment* with the *engrossed bills*, and correcting any errors which they may discover, make their report to their respective Houses.[1]

112. After a bill has passed both Houses, it shall be duly enrolled on parchment by the clerk of the House in which it was passed, before it is sent, in the United States, to the President for his signature, or where there is no signature of the executive required, as in Ohio, to the secretary of state, or other recording officer.[2]

113. By the Constitution of the United States,[3] each House of Congress is required to "keep a *journal* of its proceedings," and from time to time publish the same. The same is usual with all legislative bodies.

114. If a question be interrupted, by a vote to adjourn or to

---

[1] Joint Rules, 7. [2] Idem, 6. [3] Const., Art. 1., Sect. 5.

proceed to the orders of the day, the original question is not to be printed in the journal, it never having been a vote, nor introductory to a vote; but if it be suppressed by the previous question, the first question must be stated, in order to introduce and render intelligible the second. So, also, when a question is postponed, adjourned, or laid on the table, the original motion, though not yet a vote, must be expressed in the journals; because it makes part of the vote of postponement, and adjournment, or lying on the table. When amendments are made to a question, those amendments are not to be printed separated from the principal question; but only the question *as finally agreed to* by the House. There may be many questions proposed, which it would be improper to publish to the world, in the form in which they are made.[1]

115. On information of a mis-entry, or omission of an entry in the journal, a committee may be appointed to examine and rectify it, and report to the House.

116. A motion to *adjourn* simply cannot be amended, by adding to "a particular day." To obtain this, there should be a previous resolution, that "*when* the House adjourn, it adjourn to a particular day." On an adjournment simply, it is to the next sitting-day. If a question be put for adjournment, it is no adjournment till the Speaker pronounces it.

117. By *adjournment* the condition of things is not changed; and when the body meet again, every thing is renewed at the point where it was left. The whole session of a legislative body is considered in law but one day, and has relation to the first day thereof. *Congress* may separate in two ways: first, by adjournment; next, by dissolution at the termination of their legal existence; for they cannot constitutionally sit beyond the period for which they are elected.

118. The Speaker or Chairman has a right to name any person to perform the duties of the chair;[2] but this substitution cannot extend beyond an adjournment.

119. All committees shall be appointed by the Chairman or Speaker, unless otherwise directed; in which case they must be appointed by ballot, and a majority should be necessary to an election.[3]

---

[1] Jefferson's Manual, 126. [2] Rules of the House, 6. [3] Idem, 7.

120. In filling up blanks left in a bill or resolution, the vote must first be taken on the largest sum and longest time.

The rules above given are, for the most part, those of the British Parliament and the American Congress, and have been adopted generally in the state legislatures, and in all corporate bodies who assemble in a legislative capacity. They are applicable, also, with the exception of some obvious peculiarities, to the conduct of business in Ecclesiastical bodies, and in all assemblies which profess to transact their business with decorum, order, punctuality, and dispatch.

THE END.